come out the wilderness

The Cross-Cultural Memoir Series introduces original, significant memoirs from women whose compelling histories map the sources of our differences: generations, national boundaries, race, ethnicity, class, and sexual orientation. The series features stories of contemporary women's lives, providing a record of social transformation, growth in consciousness, and the passionate commitment of individuals who make far-reaching change possible.

THE CROSS-CULTURAL MEMOIR SERIES

Come Out the Wilderness: Memoir of a Black Woman Artist
Estella Conwill Májozo

A Lifetime of Labor
Alice H. Cook

Juggling: A Memoir of Work, Family, and Feminism
Jane S. Gould

Among the White Moon Faces: An Asian-American Memoir of Homelands
Shirley Geok-lin Lim

Fault Lines
Meena Alexander

The Seasons: Death and Transfiguration
Jo Sinclair

Lion Woman's Legacy: An Armenian-American Memoir
Arlene Voski Avakian

I Dwell in Possibility
Toni McNaron

come out the wilderness

MEMOIR OF A BLACK WOMAN ARTIST

ESTELLA CONWILL MÁJOZO

The Feminist Press
at The City University of New York
New York

Published by The Feminist Press at The City University of New York
Wingate Hall/City College, Convent Avenue at 138th Street, New York, NY 10031
http://www.feministpress.org

First edition, 1999

Library of Congress Cataloging-in-Publication Data

Májozo, Estella Conwill.
    Come out the wilderness : memoir of a Black woman artist / by Estella Conwill Májozo. — 1st ed.
        p.   cm.
    ISBN 1-55861-206-8 (alk. paper)
    1. Májozo, Estella Conwill. 2. Women poets, American—20th century—Biography. 3. Afro-American arts—New York (State). 4. Harlem (New York, N.Y.)—Intellectual life. 5. English teachers—United States—Biography. 6. Women teachers—United States—Biography. 7. Afro-American women poets—Biography. 8. Performance art—United States.   I. Title.
    PS3563.A29827Z465 1999
    811'.54—dc21
    [B]
                                                                        98-44371
                                                                        CIP

The author and publisher wish to acknowledge use of the following quoted material: Excerpt on page 55 from "A Poem to Complement Other Poems" in *Don't Cry, Scream* by Don L. Lee (Haki R. Madhubuti) (Chicago: Third World Press, 1969), © 1969 by Haki R. Madhubuti. Reprinted by permission of the author and the publisher. Excerpt on page 58 from "Black Art" in *Black Magic: Collected Poetry 1961–1967* by LeRoi Jones (Amiri Baraka) (San Francisco: City Lights, 1969), © 1969 by Amiri Baraka. Reprinted by permission of Sterling Lord Literistic, Inc. Excerpt on page 120 from "Ego-Tripping" in *Ego-Tripping and Other Poems for Young People* by Nikki Giovanni (Chicago: Lawrence Hill Books, 1995), © 1995 by Nikki Giovanni. Reprinted by permission of the publisher.

The Feminist Press is grateful to Florence Howe, Joanne Markell, Caroline Urvater, and Genevieve Vaughan for their generosity in supporting this publication.

Printed on acid-free paper by RR Donnelley & Sons
Manufactured in the United States of America

05 04 03 02 01 00 99   5 4 3 2 1

To the beautiful ones coming

CONTENTS

photographs appear on pages 129-138

I wish to acknowledge with deepest gratitude

Lucy Freibert—my cloud by day,

Gertrude Herndon—my fire by night,

Mary Luella Conwill—my sweet honey in the rock,

Our Blessed Mother Mary—my underground stream,

and above all,

Jesus Christ—my Most Sacred Manna.

Once upon a time, long before I was born, my grandmother had a dream about six water lilies floating on a dark green pond. The water lilies unfolded one by one and from inside each blossom a little naked baby came slipping turning squirming through the wet petals. Sometime later, when Momma came crying to Grandma that the doctor had said she couldn't conceive children, Grandma smiled at her. She had already received and was able to give the necessary assurance. "Child, don't you hardly believe it. That doctor knows an ounce of fact—but I have flashed in on the truth."

Ten months after my parents were married, Momma gave birth to a son. Eleven months later she gave birth to another son. Twenty months after that, she had another son. Twenty months after the third son, she gave birth to me—and then another son and yet another.

Grandma merely said we were meant to be.

In this memoir, I have attempted to go beyond the ounce of fact in search of some of the truth of my life, and of what my "being in the world" has come to mean to me. For as long as I have known of my grandmother's prophecy, not once do I remember disputing her word or attributing it to the imagination of a superstitious old woman. In those same years, I have come to give a sense of importance, if not prophecy, to my own dreams. I was taught how to nurture and to rely on the spirit's forelistening.

I am a Black woman artist. I am the child of my mother, Mary

Luella Herndon, and of my father, Adolph Conwill, but I have insisted most of my life that I am also one of the children from the water lilies of my grandmother's dream. And so I have come to see myself as a spiritual being and to see my life as a movement—sometimes slow and unassuming, other times at breakneck speeds—always, it seems, toward a deeper understanding of the mystery of my "self," that elusive construct that I, by virtue of my use of language and ideas, have tried in this memoir to set adrift.

I am rooted in contradictions, so many that I find it no small wonder that I am often undone by them. As a poet, I have long tried to discover some state of grace beyond the wilderness, beyond the physical, spiritual, and cultural contradictions in my life, in my experience, in just being. However, it was not until I came to write this memoir that I reconciled myself to the possibility that the act of writing the self is also an achievement of the state of grace, or at least an attempt at achieving that state—and that it is the will to believe that keeps me afloat.

The real reconciliation—indeed, the real state of grace—is couched in the symbol of the water lily, that fleshy open-petaled flower that appears to be floating freely on top of water but has a long-stemmed tubular root firmly fixed to the fertile life-giving ground below. The water lily—free and attached, open and closed, fragile and firm, floating and fixed. Somewhere in the balances, between reality and dream, at the burst of the blossom, find me.

1

I had climbed the walnut tree and swung my legs over the thick branch so I could see both gangs clearly. The Kirbys came unarmed into the jungle, the large weeded area that lay behind the sprawling yard that joined Momma's and Grandma's houses. The Conwills—my five brothers, Adolph, William, Houston, Spivey, and Joe—gathered into a crude semicircle, and the Kirby gang—Emerson, Mike, and Marcus Manning, Bony and Raven—positioned themselves likewise to make the circle complete. I could see that Squeaks was missing. He was deaf and may not have heard the call. The Kirbys had not missed him any more than my brothers had missed me. From where I sat, I could see Constance, whom the boys called Redbone, stretching to watch from her porch across the street. She was the only other girl who dared come to our yard that summer.

Adolph and Raven moved to the center, each staring hard at the other. William removed a pocket knife from his pants and opened it. Marcus Manning struck a wood-stem kitchen match and held it to the edge of the blade. Then, together, William and Marcus held the knife to the extended index finger of Adolph and then Raven. I did not see the blood, but I knew it was there because Bony swallowed hard and wiped his mouth with the back of his hand. I did not see the blood even when the two pressed their fingers together high above their heads.

As Adolph and Raven turned in a small circle, they chanted, "Blood brothers, blood brothers," and the rest of them joined in. I said nothing but felt something strange happening in my own body, something gathering like rain—clouds. It wasn't the blood that was now visible on both their fingers. And it wasn't even that fact that nobody would ever call me "blood brother" that caused my anxiety. It was, I know, that between those pressed fingers I saw myself, and the canary that had fueled the war in the first place.

Nobody remembered how the seven-week war got started that summer of 1958, when I was nine years old. But we all knew that when Adolph strangled the Mannings' canary, the war intensified. From then on, both gangs were fighting about the bird. Even I, throwing rocks, apples, clumps of dirt, or whatever was at hand, thought only of the bird.

There remains a sort of confusion about that time. It seems that after Daddy died, the impulse toward violence heightened in all of us. His death was an accident. He fell from a third-story fire escape while trying to help a friend who had locked his key inside his apartment. He fell through the air as helpless as a feather. I was with him when it happened. Actually, I was waiting at the front of the house for him, so I didn't see it exactly. A woman who lived in the building came out and ushered me inside to protect me from the horror. But that didn't stop me from hearing whispers and then sirens. It didn't stop me from running to look through her bedroom window and seeing the medics bring out a covered body to the ambulance. Daddy, my daddy, was under that blanket. Daddy, who could stand six foot six inches high and ride me on his shoulders into the sky, was there. Daddy, who called me "princess" and never came home without something in his pockets for me, who played Bessie Smith albums at night and laughed when I tried to sing along, who always let me have a taste of his brown beans drenched in hot sauce knowing I'd have to hide the tears, who always told my brothers "take care of your sister, now, because she is your sister," was under that dark green blanket.

I felt powerless. I didn't even scream then. But the canary's death was different. I saw the canary in Adolph's grip. I could have pleaded for its life, even at the risk of being called a traitor, but I didn't. I felt like an accomplice.

Now, as Adolph and Raven moved within that circle, the others joining the chant and marking time, I could not control the flashing lights and shadows before my eyes. I clung to the branch beneath me with the backs of my knees and reached above for the security of a smaller branch.

As I held on, I saw the bird in Adolph's hands again. He was vengeful, he said, because the Mannings had caught him outside the jungle, bloodied his nose, and smeared the purple clots into his eyes; because the Mannings had chased Houston, Spivey, and Joe, calling them "sissy-punk-Catholic-tiddy-teacher-sonsofabitch," through the park and all the way home; because they had come to make war on the Conwills after the gang of white boys stole the Kirbys' basketball and ran them out of Shawnee, the white folks' park, in the west end.

Shawnee had all the best things, bigger courts, newer swings, and an entrance to the Ohio River that was more shallow than the dropoff we had in Chickasaw Park. My brothers had stolen into Shawnee a week earlier to go swimming in the river and had been confronted by that same gang of white boys who appeared at the edge of the water, their BB guns cocked and daring. Spivey was so frightened he almost drowned. They had to save him first, they said, and then save themselves, fighting off the flying pellets that could sear the skin, blind an eye. They fought them, even without ammunition. Crawling through the mud, they came up on them, making their way through the barrage of nigger names, BBs, and sticks cracking against defiant bones, Adolph and William telling the little ones to run to the top of the hill. They fought them, the weaklings, and they won. Never mind that the white boys had brothers who were even bigger white boys and that they had cousins, uncles, and fathers who were part of a system that stretched from the Ku Klux Klan to the high courts of Kentucky and that could act as cannon against them. Never mind the possibility of their utter destruction. Never mind any of that. My brothers had triumphed over the attackers and had bonded with one another in a whole new way. They took a vow of secrecy to keep Momma and Grandma from ever finding out. Walking home that day, confidently, proudly, they refashioned the tale for themselves and, when they got home, they refashioned it again for me. By the time I had lent my voice to the telling, they were Igbos rising out of the water and marching, literally marching, across the idiotic unbelieving liquid faces of their foes. They had faced the enemy, but the Kirby gang had not. Instead, the Kirbys had used their rage against the white boys to come and take vengeance on the Conwills over some no-bouncing useless basketball, and had washed Chief Adolph's face in his own Conwill blood.

When Adolph got hold of the Mannings' canary, he said the bird in his hands had to be sacrificed because of those recent transgressions.

Sacrificed, he said—not killed, murdered, choked to death, or any other word that would have defined it more accurately, but sacrificed. He repeated it over and over again, the words coming at the end of a longer, almost chantlike explanation of his duty to carry out the act. There was not a crack in his voice, nothing that smacked of those unexpected, almost Tarzan-like breaks in tone that had marked him earlier that summer. His voice sounded strong. Those words stormed forth as if to control our reality.

The Mannings were holding my two older brothers, William and Houston, hostage for the bird. And Adolph was demanding that they be set free, never once letting up the pressure of his fingers on the bird's throat. I imagined the yellow puff of fear pulsating frantically in Adolph's hand, the little marble eyes bulging, begging for life. I bent down, my fingers clutching a fistful of weeds. Hearing Adolph repeat his vow to kill the bird, I knew that he meant for the bird to die. It didn't matter what the Kirby gang did—the bird would die. Their demand for the bird as ransom merely provided the occasion for Adolph to make the act a public one. Even William and Houston, the captives, demanded by their continued defiance that the bird die no matter what.

I wanted to summon a rush of energy and sweep the bird from Adolph's grip and set it free. But I didn't. I just sat there, saying nothing, feeling the power of Adolph's words and the tightening pressure in my own throat.

It was the same now, in the jungle. High above the ritual of blood brotherhood, I clung to the branches of the tree and could smell death, pitched back against the muscles of my throat, dripping hot and acrid into my lungs and stomach. I was dreaming of my father falling. I was the bird—alter ego and victim. The ritual of the blood brotherhood demanded my life. Below me, all my brothers danced and chanted and blended with the others. I could distinguish neither their forms nor their voices.

I found myself wishing that Grandma would call me in out of the jungle. Ever since the war between the Conwills and the Kirbys started, she had gotten into doing that more frequently. It was as if I was being banished from the activities out back. She and Momma believed, like my brothers, though surely for different reasons, that I should be seeking out my own separate territory that God had created for me. It didn't help that I grew breasts at age nine. "Mosquito bites," Spivey had called them. Spivey—who could not swim, who got everybody in even bigger trouble by having the nerve, after the water was coughed from his lungs, to mock the biggest white boy in the crowd with gorilla sounds that rivaled King Kong's—had begun riding me in offbeat moments by suddenly slapping himself across the chest as if swatting some worrisome insect. "Mosquito!" he'd yell, throwing up both his hands. No, it did not help that I grew breasts. Nor did it help that Squeaks, who could not talk, had begun just before the war to draw obscene pictures in the dust and scream wildly in a language only he understood whenever I showed up. Where I was concerned, my two oldest brothers became men overnight with no time or patience for girls. And even Houston, my third oldest brother and the one who always was on my side, took to offering me his slingshot or one of his june bugs to fly around instead of helping to defend me when Adolph or William said I had to go. Once it had gotten so bad that they had taken me by the arms and legs, screaming and kicking, back to the edge of the lawn, back to where it was mowed, trimmed, and whitewashed. It was only thirty yards away at most, but the very idea galled me. I begged Houston to come up front and play with me. We could play jacks, dodgeball, or racing like we always did. We could turn on the water and chase each other with the hose. We could play "close your eyes and read my mind." Anything at all. But the stakes had gotten too high for Houston, and despite what he said about why he couldn't come, I didn't want no slingshot and those green june bugs stunk when you kept them too long. That was their way of getting even. Who would want to have strings tied on their legs while they flew around in a circle? No, keep your june bugs and that little bug-eyed frog that looks just like all of you. "Mosquito bites!" I heard from somewhere deep in the weeds.

But, worse than all this, during the summer of the war Grandma and Momma conspired to just about do away with all the rest of the fun I had as a girl. Grandma would, out of the blue, call me into the house for piano lessons, to set the table, to crochet, or to have me sit down while she looked at me. Yes, simply looked at me. She said next to nothing directly. Rather, she told over and over the stories of her youth.

When she was three, her mother died. Her father, a preacher whose voice was thunder, died when she was a teenager and she had come to Louisville to live with Aunt Minnie. She worked two jobs for several years. Indeed, she would not work forever for folk who paid pennies for a day's labor, who demanded more bricks with no straw, who at five o'clock, just before the last bus was to leave, suddenly remembered one more thing that needed to be done. No, not forever for folk who thought you had nothing to celebrate or serve except their parties on Christmas Day and Easter, who demanded that you climb some rickety ladder, in your work dress, mind you, to wash the second-floor window "from the outside, girl! Junior, here, will be right underneath you helping to sturdy the ladder." Her father would have died again. No thank you, sir. I can do just fine. At twenty-one, not a day later, she opened her own storefront restaurant in the heart of the downtown Black community.

Her food was ambrosia. It could heal you. Make you fall in love. Make you remember parts you hadn't even learned yet. I'm talking about rolls that melted like manna in your mouth, mellow sauces that called you back long after dinner was over. She prayed and cooked and prayed again; then, in time, she converted to Catholicism, married my grandfather, and became Mrs. Estella Herndon.

Grandaddy was a loving, enterprising man, and together they worked out a scheme for selling pies. She baked them—apple, custard, lemon, and chocolate—and he distributed them every day to other restaurants and shops, and to folk throughout the city, especially those betting at Churchill Downs during Derby time. It worked, and over the years Grandma and, later, their four daughters—one of whom was Momma—baked, packaged, and had ready for delivery five hundred mini pies every morning before sunrise. They prospered and invested in real estate, renovating apartment houses and renting out the rooms. The houses that we helped paint each summer were gotten from that work. And from Grandaddy withstanding the scorching heat, Grandma said, for long hours hawking his wares with snatches of rhymes he created:

> Pieman, Pieman, heah comes the Pieman.
> Stuff's sweet as honey. Get out your money!
>
> Eat my pies for goodness sakes.
> They beat anything yo' momma can make!

The houses and land and even her own house that they had built together also came in part from his strategizing and straining over racing forms at night, studying the histories of the horses and then going to the stables early in the morning to talk to the horses themselves sometimes, so he could pass on tips to the big-time gamblers from around the country who sought him out—but who would have to buy one of his pies to get the tip.

> Why you always askin' credit?
> All you do with money's bet it!

Grandma told me that once in a while he'd have to dodge those who had taken one of his not so accurate tips. (It wasn't that the horses had taken to lying but that they had taken to double-talking, riffing on the truth, and you had to listen hard to catch it.)

Grandma's stories were filled with giving and loving and forgiving and selflessness, and the more I heard them, the more I was convinced that there must be some skills involved in being a girl. But my nine-year-old heart was not in it, especially when she'd call me in from the thick of whatever I was doing with my brothers.

Momma, who agreed with Grandma mostly all the time, had called me out of the jungle a few weeks before the war began to tell me, she said, something really special. Grandma got up from the porch to check on some rolls she had in the oven. Momma sat down in Grandma's chair and started telling me quite calmly about "periods" and woman's times. The only reason I was convinced that what she was saying was OK was because she kept smiling the whole time she was talking. No wonder Grandma got up to leave. She certainly wouldn't know anything about this. But Momma assured me that all women did it and every month, and that I would do it too when the time was right.

I wasn't sure what that meant. I was already feeling out of sync. Nobody in my class at school had breasts, not even my best friend, Betty Jo, and if my brothers ever knew that I had started my period they would probably try and banish me to the house. Momma assured me that it would be OK, that she would take care of my brothers. But, instead, she and Grandma started taking care of me.

The only time I remember being relieved to hear either of them call me was when Adolph was putting that final pressure on the canary's neck. Adolph had killed the canary at the count of ten, nine, eight . . . but in reality I had not seen it. Grandma had called me in. With her almost perfect sense of timing, she for whatever reason had called me in. I was about to commit treason that would likely have lost me honor among my brothers. I wanted to save the bird—just let it go free. Killing it was taking a life, and I had wanted to shout that out in my clearest voice when Grandma called me in.

I was not so blessed on the day of the truce. Grandma did not sense my need of her. She was busy in her flower garden, bent low against weed seedlings. I had to let loose of my grip on my own, drop down to the ground, and lose my brothers, the Kirby gang, the chanting, and the dancing to the labyrinth of paths leading toward the front of the two houses.

I could see her in the distance, the shrubbery and flowers all around blending into the floral print of her dress, could almost hear her prodding the ground beneath the roses, and working her thoughts in prayer. Her soul was being tended. "Love is patient"—she would sometimes whisper—"Love is kind"—touching one of the roses. "Love is not jealous, it does not put on airs . . . neither does it brood over injuries. . . ." I knew she was probably deep in meditation, but I wanted to tell her clearly that there was a war going on behind her. That it was all dressed up to look like peace but I, for one, didn't trust it. That they had knives out back and had sliced into each other's fingers and that it could well be their guts next round. That Adolph had said to William and Houston and me that there was such a thing as justice, and it's almost as great as the love you sing about, Grandma. That Joe was back there crying because Adolph told him that he was too little to get his finger cut open and Spivey was crying because he knew that he was next.

"Grandma," I said, meaning to go on and tell. But when she lifted her head, I could not go through with it. "Did you call me, Grandma?"

"No, girl, I didn't. What's the matter? Did Adolph put you out of that weed patch again?"

"No, Grandma," I said, trying to keep my voice from edging into a falsetto. And she turned on me that cut of her eye that signaled she already knew.

"Well, I told you and I told your momma that you ought not be back out in all them weeds. . . . You feeling all right, girl? You look a little flushed. What they done to you this time, Stella Marie?"

I told her as much as I could without blowing it for them, knowing full well that she'd set her watery black eyes on me, listen as though in some kind of trance, and say, "But you're a little girl." That nervous feeling in my stomach returned. And instead of being feverish, now I was chilled. I didn't like this feeling that seemed never able to make up its mind. I still wanted answers: Why did my brothers and the Kirby gang carry almost everything to the point of blood? And why should I have wanted to save the canary even in the briar patch ritual? Grandma did not answer me right away. Instead, she turned her back and stooped to scoop soil up around the base of the tulip bed.

"In that back yard that your brothers are calling the jungle, they supposed to be coming up with something more to do than kill canaries," Grandma said. It had not occurred to me then that the jungle was something more than a male territory, a space that my brothers could claim for themselves. Neither I nor my brothers saw it as a space to recognize order or our own potential creativity. It was only later that I consciously realized that Grandma's own garden had come out of that jungle. My brothers, likewise failing to see this order, were imitating the disorder or wildness that they thought they saw.

"Adolph and William know how they supposed to act back there, and I done told them the consequences if they don't."

"He ain't said nothing about no consequences, Grandma."

"That's OK; he sure enough knows."

I wanted to ask about the consequences, but she had already put it behind her. Her turning at that moment has become a fixture in my mind and in my many dreams of her since. In her turning, I saw a smiling woman child in plaits and a floursack dress leaving Tennessee to come to Louisville. I had heard the story many times, but I saw it then for the first time. Then I focused in on her, wanting to see her face.

"I pruned the dogwoods today, see?" she said over her shoulder. "You remember, you helped me plant them. They about finished growing now." It was Grandma's voice, not a little girl's at all. But I knew the two were the same. The same plum-colored skin. The same dark mirror eyes. "See here," she said, looking at me. I sat next to her and could smell the earth. It was the same scent you pick up right before it rains, when only one or two drops have fallen but the earth is already rejoicing. It soothed me, calmed my stomach. And the lilacs, late roses, and petunias all lent their sweetness to the song.

"There was a time, though," Grandma continued, "when dogwood trees like these would have grown tall and would have spread their limbs near about the whole yard." The three dogwoods separated the lawn from the jungle. There were two white ones and a red one in the middle. They were small trees, their blossoms like butterflies. "Now, they won't grow

9

much bigger than this. You know why?" she asked me, and before I could say anything she went on to answer herself. "Because it's the kind of tree they made the cross out of. This is the kind of tree Jesus was crucified on and its growth has been stunted ever since," she said. "Been stunted ever since."

I had known the answer. Grandma's whole yard was a garden, and she had stories about each of the varieties of plants—the roses, the tulips, the chrysanthemums; the catalpa, evergreen, and apple trees. The garden was a testament to her truths. To hear her stories, you'd believe that she let the briar patch grow for the contrast.

"I know," I said quietly. "The red one represents Jesus and the white ones are the two thieves." Grandma had impressed the catechism of her garden and I rendered the text. Each cluster of plants represented either the Ten Commandments, the Seven Sacraments, or the Eight Beatitudes. I knew them well and I recited them with the enunciation I knew would please her. The rose bush at the back entrance of the house I knew was the Blessed Mother. I had personally designated it so. She never appeared to me like Our Lady of Guadalupe did to Juan Diego in Mexico or the Immaculate Conception did to Bernadette in Lourdes, but I knew when I stood there that she was always with me. And I loved her as much as any child would a mother so tender.

"Who taught you so well about the dogwoods—Adolph?" Grandma asked proudly.

"No, Houston," I said.

"That's good," she told me, "that's good. And Adolph, he teaches them all." I tried to forget about what was going on behind us.

"And these right here, what are they?" she asked, pointing to some beautiful purple flowers surrounded by dark sturdy leaves.

"Oh, Grandma," I whispered, kneeling closer. "Where, I mean how did you get these?"

She laughed. "They're yours, Stella Marie. They're African violets. I planted them for you."

"African violets," I said, repeating after her, already feeling the other question rising up in me. "But what are they for us?" I asked.

"They're gifts of the Spirit, child," she said. "Gifts that the Lord gives to people called to do something really special."

"Like me, Grandma?"

"Of course, baby. I told you that a hundred times. Now looka here.

There're seven in all, see. This one here is wisdom, and there's understanding, and fortitude, and knowledge, and counsel and piety, and
fear of the Lord. They're all there. Gifts of the Spirit. Now, wisdom," she
said, "means having real good sense about things—like knowing how
to judge the earth. And understanding is what we're doing here, standing up underneath a thing and seeking its meaning. And fortitude, why
that means being strong—having inside strength," she said lifting her head.
"It ain't got nothing much to do with muscles or being able to wrestle somebody if they gang up on you or try to throw you out of a place."
I know I must have begun folding my arms defensively and tilting into
myself. "And counsel," she continued, "that means that you can give advice
lovingly, that you can look at people who might look to you like
snakes, rats, or even bug-eyed frogs, Stella Marie, and still tell them the
best way for unbugging, if that's what we're talking. That you can find
a way to tell them true. The gift of counsel can help change a person
into something really special, if you've got it. It does more good for a
person than a kiss can for any frog."

"But Grandma," I said, meaning to defend myself for the name-call-
ing she referred to—but she shushed me.

"But Grandma," I insisted, and she covered my mouth.

"And piety," she said slowly, deliberately, "piety means being holy. And
that's really all that you were sent here to be." She smiled. "Now what
did you want to say?"

"Grandma, I'm not trying to be smart aleck, but what if that frog you
talking about doesn't want to be kissed? Suppose he's just begging to
be told how ugly he is?" A chuckle rose out of her and on into me.

"Listen, little girl," she said, "this last flower here, it's fear of the Lord.
That means God don't take no mess so behave yourself, you hear?"

"Yes, Grandma, I will. But can I ask you something?"

She nodded.

"How come you don't ever answer whatever I ask you?"

Her face said, "Oh, child, please." But her words said, "Would it hurt
your feelings if I told you I honestly don't know? Some things you don't
say because you know the moment after you say them the meaning is
already changed in your head, changed sometimes even before you say
anything. You take that bird, now—you all talked about that canary bird
so much you had your momma crying about that thing. I said at the time
that it was a shame she let you all go on about it so. And the way you

talking about the bird, honey, you better let it go out your mind or it's gonna mess with you every chance it gets. Now everybody else done stopped talking about that bird. You told me yourself that the boys done made up over the thing 'cause it don't have one ounce of meaning between them anymore."

"But it ought to, Grandma."

"Well they're making peace now, girl."

"But they didn't have to choke it to death!"

"But the bird is dead, girl, dead. And you oughta leave it alone. You hear me?"

It was precisely at moments like this that I wanted Momma. I wished right then that she could just come home from work. The blunt edge of Grandma's authority had nailed me into the soil among the dogwoods. And suddenly I felt weighted with the memory of my father and was suspicious that Grandma herself had conjured his image into my mind. She did that sort of thing after I had worn down her tolerance. I was with my Daddy riding his shoulders again. He was a moving oak. Tall, graceful, strong. We were laughing and he was pulling something, maybe a bracelet, out of his pocket for me.

"Your daddy wouldn't have wanted to see you carry on like this," she said.

"I'll leave it alone, Grandma," I said, and turned to the path that my brothers and I had worn between her house and ours. Walking the path, I remembered Daddy and I was stepping, deliberately stepping, just like him. Working that hump-a-dip bluesman's walk that marked him the moment he set foot outside the house, whether on his way to the waiter job at the Brown Hotel or to the corner drugstore for a smoke. It was his "jitter juju," and I was doing it, the thing that transformed him into the aroma of strength and cool and readiness. But it wasn't working for me, not really. It just made me miss him more. So I went on to the front of our house and waited for Momma. If I could sit down next to her, put my head on her lap, maybe I would feel better. I pinched a little peppermint from the patch that grew at the bottom of the steps and chewed its leaves.

No sooner had I gotten the flavor juicy in my mouth when I heard the blood brotherhood coming out of the jungle. They were ready to play now, siding up for a game of baseball. A spot near the curb was first base, the rock in the center of the yard was second, third was a spot on the opposite side, and home plate was some magic spot one ran to and declared oneself safe.

I could see Constance across the street but kept my eyes staring at the spaces where the blood brothers swung their bats, popped their fists into empty palms, and rooted for their teams. Constance was everything Grandma seemed to want me to be. She dressed like a lady, sat out her summer days on the front porch in the green and white porch swing, sucker in hand or thumb in mouth. I knew I would go to her before the day was out, but I didn't want to talk just now. Constance knew things, and when we did talk, she told me things that Momma and Grandma wrapped in parables, axioms, and life stories. She said to me one day, out of the blue, "Stella, I do believe your grandmother wants to turn all your brothers into priests." Perhaps she was just fishing for information. Perhaps she knew about the Mass we held in the basement.

At the start of that summer, in an attempt to be strengthened or maybe just to play church, Adolph had gathered Momma's white linen table-cloth, her long white candles, and even a couple of her white summer dresses for robes, and we all had gone to the basement to hold Mass, the ceremony that we had come to accept as the blood rite of blood rites, as he called it. Adolph acted as priest and William and Houston concelebrated with him. Spivey and Joe were altar boys. We all had Communion made from regular slices of bread that I had pressed and clipped into wafers. We set up the basement like a church with an altar, candles, crucifix, chalice, Bible, and chairs.

Our house was already somewhat of a sanctuary. Momma had consciously designed it so. The crucifix and the statue of our Blessed Mother had their own special places in the front room. And we had the family ritual of coming together in the evening to say the rosary. Ella Fitzgerald, Nat "King" Cole, and whoever was on the radio would be silenced. The playing, laughing, and fighting would be stilled. During the holy seasons of Advent and Lent, our rituals intensified. The preparing, or "making ready the way," was serious, and sometimes the sacrifices or mortifications were considered for weeks in advance. Whatever you decided upon you announced before the first day. If you were giving up candy for forty days, refraining from bad language or thoughts, or from slapping somebody "upside the head," the commitment was made aloud. If the commitment was carried through, it would strengthen the others who witnessed it, and if it wasn't, then that person would endure a certain amount of hassle from the others. At church the sacrifices were written down and burned as offerings. They were considered to be between you and God. But at home, we made new offerings, and they were considered to be between you, God, and the family. Most of these sacrifices had to do with relationships, no doubt encouraged by Momma's insistence that if you can't recognize God in one another, then you're not going to be able to recognize God in Spirit.

That the focus was on relationships was especially important that year. Perhaps as part of the process of mourning my father, my brothers often came to knock-down drag-out battles in the house. In an attempt to keep the jungle from infringing upon her order, Momma made the across-the-board rule that no fighting would be allowed in the house. She would not necessarily stop the fights. She would simply say, "Take that chaos out of this house!" On the other hand, if you were taking a pretty bad beating in the jungle, you could always retreat to the house. But to avoid the shame of it, you would generally chance dying on the battlefield rather than retreating.

When we decided to have our Mass in the basement, we had put curtains on the window to keep the snoopers away, especially the Kirby gang. It was nobody's business what went on there. Constance wasn't even supposed to know about the Mass. It was private. With our heads bowed, we struggled through the Latin responses to Adolph's prayers. He started with the sign of the cross. "In Nomine Patris, et Filii, et Spiritus Sancti. Amen." We joined in and made up new responses if the real words failed us. "Hanna-hanna de hanna hanna," we mumbled the rhythm of the parts we didn't know.

When the consecration time came and all three of my older brothers extended their right hands over the bread, I joined in saying the sacred words with them. "Hoc Est Enim Corpus Meum": This Is My Body. You would have thought a sacrilege had been committed, that I had cursed heaven or strangled some precious belief so fiercely it left them all wasted. Houston's mouth fell agape. Adolph all but stopped the ceremony. William turned around as if to say, "Girl, you know you ain't supposed to be saying those words. You ain't hardly no man!" I bowed my head, retreated behind tear-filled eyelids, stayed there alone in the dark.

I had no problem knowing what I was supposed to do in a real church, but in the realm of play, especially play that was serious, something inside had been jolted. There they were, all five of my brothers at the altar playing priest, the representatives of God, each with a participant's role, and there I was on the other side, separated by a jump rope that they had strung to show the distinction, playing the congregation. All I understood then was that I was a girl and was being excluded from the ritual. Now I realize that what started happening there that summer had been happening in different ways all over the world for years. And that when we decide to stop playing church, we have a lot of coming out of the jungle to do.

As for Grandma, when she closed her eyes, I don't know if she saw what the future held for us at all, but heaven knows, we were anything but the royal priesthood she felt all people were called to be.

As for Constance, she probably didn't know everything about the Mass that day. She was probably following up on some tip. On the day of the truce, when I saw her get off her swing and start coming across the street, I got up to join her. I got up because Squeaks, who had no idea about the truce, come charging into the brotherhood. He leaped into the huddle and began clawing at my brothers. Everybody tried to stop him. I moved faster toward Constance because I knew that once they cleared it with Squeaks that the war was over, Adolph would want me to come join the Conwills in the game to make the teams even. I did not want to play. I almost made it across the diamond, but Squeaks saw me and let out a piercing holler, "Ah-ah-oh!" He rushed onto me, shimmying his haphazard hoodlum body across my backside. "Wa-a-ah!" he screamed. "Ah-o-o-oh!" he yelled again. I shoved him off and, at my back, heard my brothers yell in concert.

"Raven, you better tell that fool to be cool or I'll put a brick in his deaf skull!" Adolph shouted.

"Yeah," somebody else said, "you better get that no-talking devil before he start the whole damn war again."

Constance was on her feet, her hands balled into fists, the stem of a sucker twitching between her teeth. "Stella," she hissed in a voice that seemed sharp and guarded, "you get up here, girl. That dog'd attack his own mother. You hear that fool, honey. He's down there cussing. Tell me how a person who can't even hear learns to cuss. He can't even say two clear words of proper language and he's down there cussing blood up from the ground. Get him, Adolph, get him. Don't just stand there." Her voice carried only as far as the end of the porch, but I read her terror. My brothers had positioned themselves near Adolph, who stood with the bat cocked.

In front at the curb, Marcus held Squeaks in a full nelson, his fingers squeezed to knuckles at the back of Squeaks's head.

"He don't understand you, man. He don't know no better. He do what he see, man," Marcus said.

"Then somebody better teach the sucker some sense," William said, "or one day he gonna go picking his brains up off the sidewalk."

Then Constance started in. "If Adolph hauls off and hits him one, I bet he'll understand." I was almost crying. I knew the understanding she was talking about had nothing to do with anything except somebody getting hurt. Or maybe even killed like the bird. Or like my daddy, who said, "Wait right here, I'll be right back, this won't take but a minute, sweets." And Mr. Johnson taking me home and knocking at the door to face Momma's shock: "Where's my husband? Where is he? Boys, Adolph Junior, come and get your sister."

"Tell him the war is over," Adolph said. "Tell him we blood brothers now. Tell him no touch-feely on this street, least not my little sister. Or Adolph Conwill will pick his teeth with this baseball bat."

"Something terrible happened," I had said that day as Momma grabbed her coat to leave. My brothers stopped jumping from bed to bed long enough to look at me and ask, "What?" The stammering took too long, the search for how to say what never ended. "What is so terrible?" they asked. The discerning of things from their form. Knowing what was beneath the blanket by the contours of his face. Never finding the words to carry all that weight.

"Tell him the war is over," Adolph said. "Tell him and make him understand!" Marcus was restraining Squeaks, whose two arms were suspended like broken wings above the back of his head. One of his own gang, a voice I don't remember to name, declared that Squeaks wasn't even a member of the new brotherhood, having missed out on the ritual, and that he should be taught a lesson. I could not see Squeaks's face—but his body writhed under Marcus's hold.

"They oughta teach him a thing or two," Constance piped in, her voice edged with excitement.

"No," I said. "It won't do no good to hurt him. They should just let him go. Let him go on back home. Somebody can tell him that. Go home before he starts another war."

"He may be deaf and dumb, but he can't go around acting a fool all his life. I say he ought to have a lesson. That'll straighten him up," Constance insisted.

Squeaks was crying now. I could hear the chirping sounds from where I stood. Streaks of blood from the brotherhood's wounded fingers were all up and down his T-shirt. He began kicking, too, at first straight out at the air and then at my brothers and the members of his own gang. Bony caught one of his legs midair and held it. "Kick now, fool," he said. "Kick the other foot and gravity will have your ass."

Everybody was laughing; even Constance—and Squeaks's cries became louder. My own voice rose above his screams. "If y'all don't let him go, I'll call Grandma!" I yelled, knowing that it was treason and I'd suffer for it.

Contrary to the teasing I got for months afterward, I did not "like" Squeaks. I had just decided that I would not stand by and let them tease him to death. The new blood brotherhood had found a common victim, and I could see that they wouldn't stop until they had wrung out his last breath of air. Poor Squeaks would have hopped around on that one leg dragging Bony around with him until he dropped from exhaustion. Laughing all the while, the brotherhood would have then pounced upon him until there was blood.

The instant I said it, Bony dropped Squeaks's leg and Jimmy let go of his hold. Squeaks fell to the ground, drawing his knees up to his chest. It seemed that all eyes contorted toward me, and I felt unbelievably powerful. "Help him out of the street," I said to Adolph and Raven. And without hesitation, they did it, helped him to his feet, then stood there as if beaten. What was happening? Could mere words be that powerful? Could their very pronouncement command this kind of utter respect? Yes, indeed they could, if your very angry grandma suddenly appears at the screen door behind you exuding an almost stupefying rage.

"This. This don't make no sense," she seethed. "And you sure got pain to pay."

After staring for what seemed like hours at Adolph, William, Houston, and all of them and draining all the color from the summer sky, she turned like a sudden storm to sit down on the rocker.

"Grandma," Adolph tried to plead, but there was no need. We all knew that something vital had happened. That another war had been waged—though, for everybody except Adolph, it had not been named. And none of the rest of us dared to ask her what the consequences would be.

What I remember is that all of us, the Conwills, the Kirbys, and even Squeaks, were stretching to assume postures of normalcy. They were straightening out their clothes, then trying to pretend that there was no need at all to do so. They were stepping away (though surely not too far away) in pairs and bunches, whispering under stolen breaths about being sure enough in trouble this time. When William leaned in to ask Adolph what Grandma was going to do, Adolph shook his head as if in mourning.

"Get lost, Estella!" Adolph growled.

"Jerk!" William added.

"I can't believe she did that," Houston said.

"I wasn't trying to tell Grandma," I pleaded. "I was trying to tell you."

"Wasn't trying to tell Grandma, your butt," Spivey said.

"You done ruined everything now. How come you always gotta go tattling?" Adolph yelled.

"Me?" I said. "Me? How came you all always gotta carry things to the point of blood?" I yelled back.

"'Cause we ain't stupid like you!" he said, as if that made any sense. I walked away. There was no need to even try to explain. When Momma came home, Grandma's version could be all there was anyway.

Once I got back to the steps, it was Constance who answered the question: "Old folk say boys carry on to blood like that because they can't bleed like a woman." Wait a minute, Constance knew about women bleeding? Constance knew that? This opened a whole new terrain.

She looked hard at me. "You do know about women doing that, don't you?"

"Of course I know," I told her fast, knowing that she was probably already doing it—that she knew how it felt and what "when the time is right" meant.

"That's what they say," she said, ready to go on about men's blood rites. But I didn't want to talk about them anymore, not then anyway. I wanted to know everything she knew about women's times. Do you have to do anything to make it happen? Is it something you eat that'll help make it start? If it doesn't have anything to do with age, like Momma says, then does it have something to do with the size of your breasts? I looked at Constance's breasts, and even though she was three years older, mine were almost as big.

"I'm starting mine real soon," I said softly. She looked at me and tried to keep from laughing. "I am, Constance. I even dreamed it. It's true."

She reached over, plaited one of the ends of my hair. "I used to dream

I'd get mine, too. That's why you got to stop going out back with them," she said, stretching to see what was in the street. "It's a good thing you didn't let them cut your finger, girl. Your period probably would never come." My eyes widened. I wanted to know more.

"Constance," I asked, swallowing hard, "did you feel kind of funny when it happened?"

"Yeah, a little bit, but I was glad to get it."

"I mean, did you feel a little something down in here?" I asked, touching just below my navel. She looked at me curiously and began shaking her head in denial.

"Naw, uh-uh. You don't feel nothing. Not no cramps, not nothing," she said. "It just comes."

"Not hot, I mean, or a little cold neither?" I asked.

"Nothing," she said with an air of finality.

"Nothing." I repeated behind her.

Then she leaned in a little closer. "And remember, it's like I was saying, they do it because they can't," and she nodded her head and swept her glance into the wind.

It sounded awfully strange, though even now, I cannot say it was not the answer my sense of things required. Had I not witnessed my brothers nurse a war wound like a badge of courage? Had they not pressed the edges to let the blood flow, as if the flow itself was the rite of passage? "It's because," Constance went on, "it's because they can't be like us." She tied her hair ribbon back into a tighter bow. "Just like we can't be like them."

Contrary to what Grandma said, I did not dislike Constance because she wore fine dresses and pretty colored ribbons; it was just that she always tied the knots too tight. So when William yelled, "Come on, let's play dodgeball," I didn't think twice about joining in. I went on out confident that Grandma would not call me back.

Dodgeball was my game, and though I could not play at full speed that day, I tried. But in all honesty, I was distracted. I guess everybody was. Constance's words were ringing in my ears and Adolph was still mad at me. My skin was wet, my shirt was clingy, and even my shorts felt strange. That earth smell that comes after rain was suddenly everywhere and there was not a cloud in the sky.

"Come on, Stella!" Houston yelled. "Pay attention or they gonna put you out!" Was that all the heck they knew?

"You already out when Grandma gets through with you, so pay your own attention!" I yelled back, dodging the ball as it whizzed by my legs.

"What she say?" Adolph asked butting in the conversation. "What's Grandma gonna do?"

"She gonna stare a hole in your behind from that porch!" I yelled. "She gonna stare at you like that forever!"

The ball almost caught Adolph right upside the head and he was getting an attitude. "I ain't playing, Stella. What's she saying!"

"I don't know," I answered. "She ain't saying nothing."

The ball handlers changed twice and I still hadn't been hit. The ball handler threw the ball at the easiest mark or to the one he wanted to absorb his frustrations. The two most likely targets were me and Squeaks. I had an advantage—I could hear the ball coming. And Squeaks, who had simmered down, also had an advantage. We all claimed he was good at the game because, not hearing, he could see better than any of us. No doubt now, Marcus was aiming strictly for the two of us. However, the ball struck Houston, and he rushed to the end to throw the ball before we had a chance to fully distance ourselves from his end.

Squeaks suddenly began taunting the ball handlers with screams, and I watched Bony wind up and go for him. "Ooo—eee-ah," Squeaks screamed out, dodging the ball. He screamed again and nobody had even thrown the ball. Squeaks wouldn't let up hollering, now pointing frantically at the seat of my pants. "Um mahee-fuhee!" he screamed. "Mahee—fuhee ha ha ha!" he laughed hilariously, grabbing members of his gang to join him.

"Ah, come on, man, cut it out!" Marcus said as he spit on the ground. Squeaks continued screaming.

"Come on, Houston! Throw the ball!" Adolph said. And that was when I felt it. A warm wetness between my thighs. I froze at first, then ran behind the house to check myself. And my whole body flushed from the recognition. I ran inside with my secret—a secret no one knew except for Squeaks and he, thank God, couldn't tell anybody.

"Man, cut it out," I heard Marcus say through the window. And Adolph added, "Man, we in enough trouble as it is."

I didn't know what else to do except wait for Momma. I looked at the clock, got a drink of water, then looked out the door at Grandma.

"You waiting for your momma?" she asked. I stood there half smiling. "She got plenty to know today."

She kept looking out toward the bus stop and I kept looking too.

Didn't I tell Constance I was going to start? Didn't I tell her I had dreamed it? And it was there just like it had appeared in the dream: the spread of a flower unfolding right there upon the cotton. As if someone had used watercolors to paint a little violet in that spot. I looked at Grandma and wondered if I looked any different or if I should put tissue in my pants. Then I worried that if I kept standing there, any moment now, there would be a labyrinth of trickles down my legs like the paths from the tree house throughout the jungle. I closed my eyes and tried not to think about it.

The screeching of Grandma's chair and the ticking of the clock on the mantel gave off a funny little rhythm. "Mary Luella gonna be tired when she gets home this evening, but she gonna want to know about this. And I ain't covering for them, either, not this time," she said. And while I waited for my momma, I could hear them playing outside. I could hear our dog Bronda barking in the back. I could hear birds nesting right on the magnolia tree in front, but I could not hear the bus coming with my momma standing at its back door. Suppose she missed it or decided to work overtime at that stupid post office? All year long she taught at Immaculate Heart of Mary, our school. Why did she have to work summers? When I grew up I would make all the money and she could stay home forever and nobody would have to be crying about where is she and what am I supposed to do and what if something horrible happened to her too on that stupid yellow canary bus. Then she was at the corner.

The playing outside quieted and Grandma's chair came to a halt. The breath I was holding inside raced out to the open air. I wiped my tears and waited, patiently.

My brothers greeted Momma, all but kissing her feet. "My finger didn't get cut," Joe said, and she lifted him up, unsuspecting, to kiss it. She moved past them and made her way to the porch and smiled into Grandma's eyes. "I'm exhausted. It's good to be home. Estella, come give Momma a kiss."

I was reluctant to come past Grandma so I stuck out my finger and curled it for her to come inside with me. "I'm beat, Estella," she said. "Come on and sit down with me a minute."

"She may be trying to plead their case before I tell you," Grandma said. "It ain't gonna do no good, Stella Marie," she called out over her shoulders.

I backed up farther into the house, and still within eyeshot of Momma I stretched both my arms out and pleaded with her to please come in.

Then I heard the back door open and I knew one of them was coming. "What they saying?" Houston said, running up on me. "I want to know."

"They ain't saying nothing yet. She just got home."

"Stella, I know you didn't mean to tell," he said, moving too close for comfort.

"Just go away. I'll tell you what she says," I said, trying to keep myself at an angle so that the back of me wouldn't show.

"Naw, you won't. You still mad about what happened."

"Naw, I ain't, I'm just standing here, that's all. I ain't gonna tell on you."

"Well, I'm gonna stand here too," he said. "I'm gonna stand right here and see."

"You don't have to. Look, I'll let you have my jai alai bat if you just go on back outside," I said.

"What, you suddenly bearing gifts?"

"I ain't bearing no gifts, Houston," I said, straining not to intone in his voice. "Look, I just want to be by myself, that's all."

"Then why you standing here?"

"Because I want to be by myself standing here," I said—the same thing they had said to me that day I left the jungle but slipped back and found William and Houston with their pants down, seeing who could pee the farthest. "Pitiful," I said under my breath, but they heard me.

"I won't ever bother you again when you ask me to go," I pleaded.

"The heck if I believe you!" he said, looking at my jai alai bat. "You don't know the meaning of privacy."

"Yes, I do, Houston. I cross my heart," I said. "If you want to be alone, I will just let you be."

"I didn't say all the time," he said.

"I didn't say all the time neither."

"Let me see the jai alai bat."

I handed him my watch, too.

"Promise?" he asked, looking at me straight.

"Promise," I said, relieved. Then I watched him walk to the back door.

I heard Momma yell, "What?" and Grandma say, "They done gone too far." And I knew that I had now even less of a chance of capturing her attention; my timing was terrible.

"Momma," I signaled within her range, but she didn't want to hear it. "Momma," I signaled again. And Grandma, who maybe really did have eyes underneath the loose strand of hair, said, "Better go on and see what she wants. She been waiting long enough."

When I told Momma, she hugged me and held me there for a long, long time. Then she helped me with my necessities. For a few moments, it seemed none of what was happening outside even mattered. I had become a lady. And that was serious. I was even going to get a new dress. Momma was going to make it. And I could wear it every time I had a period and feel really pretty. She would start on it tomorrow, she said. But today she had to deal with my brothers.

She changed clothes and went outside and called out to them. "Adolph, William, Houston—come on," she said. "We gonna clear this out back here. The rest of you boys, good evening."

"We can't clear out the jungle, Momma!"

"Naw. Momma, uh-uh."

Momma's insistence became firmer against their defiant cries that surely they would be the laughingstock of the neighborhood, that they would be cursed as sissies the rest of their lives, that her demand that they love their rivals was as cold a command as death.

"How are we to grow into men of this house if we can't even demand respect?" William asked, and before Momma could answer, Adolph insisted, "Everybody listened to Daddy—even people who were bigger than him. They knew who he was!"

Momma stared unflinchingly into the eyes of her older sons, letting go a handful of weeds. "How many times," she asked, "did you ever see your father beat someone till he bled?" For a moment everything quieted. Adolph retreated, not out of submission but to recharge.

"He could, though," Adolph insisted. "He could have done it, he just didn't have to."

"Why not?"

"He probably got it straight when he was growing up with all those dudes."

"He's not from here. You know your father was from Mississippi. When he came to this town, how'd he get all those people, those dudes, straight? Did he strangle all their canaries to get his bluff in?"

"I don't know," William said sternly, and Adolph backed him up: "He didn't tell us."

If Momma had been in mourning up to that point, she certainly wasn't crying now. She braced herself like a giant eagle having flipped her babes from the nest. "That's what you need to learn," she said "What you've got that you can use other than your fists." She handed the sickle to Adolph just as he began to speak. "Get to work," she told him. It was final. The rest of us chopped harder. I felt a mixture of horror and release. I knew Adolph was crying when he turned his back. We all cried a little that day. Bony rode by on his bike. "Hey, man, what y'all doing?" he asked, unable to believe what he was seeing. Nobody answered.

The Queen Anne's, ragweed, thistles, and twigs were all cut down and hauled to the back to burn—a public sacrifice. Of course the rabbits left, the robins scattered, and the fuzzy-tailed squirrels scurried away. But they did that, anyway, every time the "blood brotherhood" entered bringing their wildness into the jungle. Their presence was already disturbing and undermining its creative potential. Cutting down the jungle was an effort to help them to come out of the wilderness within.

Seeing the tiny snakes and salamanders and crickets and baby spiders scurry into the secret bosom of the earth was arresting. We stood there in the end in awed recognition of the order that had been there all along—of all that hidden life and possibility over which we had so recklessly trampled.

2

CROSSING OVER JORDAN

There are jungles and gardens everywhere. Each has its own potential and requires a particular bearing, and each remains a wilderness until we figure out the demeanor that will enable us to perform our creative capacity within that landscape. And at the moment of that recognition we are out of the wilderness.

Now, if you were a teenage girl living in the predominantly white south end of Louisville, where I attended high school, you might have believed, as many of my classmates did, that Little Africa, where I lived, was certainly some kind of jungle. This belief was clear on the day in 1964 when they exploded over Martin Luther King, Jr., coming to town to join his brother, A. D. King, in a march for open housing through their neighborhood.

"What do the Black people want?" one of my classmates demanded in the open discussion.

"What did we do to them?" another added.

"It's just stirring up trouble!"

Amid the voices, I thought I heard Hilary's. I strained forward trying to catch her eye, but caught Sister Dymphna's buzzard gaze instead.

"What can be gained by the marches?" Sister Dymphna asked again. It was obvious she was directing the question straight to me. There was no way I wanted any part of this, so I played her off while the others fought to answer. One thing was clear to me at that point: I was in her space, the wilderness of the garden, and like the canary in the wilderness of the jungle, I was to be sacrificed, no matter what. How I wished it was already lunchtime and I was with my Black friends, touching the reality that was ours, apart from all this.

"Why," I asked my fourteen-year-old culturally shocked self, "are these people always doing death acts and pretending that it's normal? Showing up heckling, cursing the demonstrators from the sidelines when all they want is some freedom to spread out. It's the same thing that they're doing to Faith down in the principal's office right this minute. Another kind of death act—calling her down there, talking about pregnancy, threatening to kick her Black self out of school with only a month to go before graduation like this is the first time anybody ever got pregnant in this school.

"Well," Lucia said, responding to Sister's question, "I have a best girlfriend who dates a boy outside the race, and she sees him all the time, I mean, at my house, and I think it's OK to move next door and act responsibly because parents would never let you grow up." Good heavens, Lucia never made any sense. Hilary was mumbling "Dingbat!" under her breath, pushing her falling hair out of her face. But she still avoided my looks. Sister Dymphna pointed to another raised hand but kept her eyes fixed on me. "My parents said that if the Negroes"—she made it sound like "niggras"—"were to move into our neighborhood, they would make it a ghetto just like theirs, I mean, some would."

Little Africa, or what she referred to as the ghetto, was home for a lot of people, a place where we lived and worked out our survival. Considering the segregation and limitations of the 1960s, it was a place of remarkable resilience. Lots of people in there had once lived in Old Louisville or in Smoketown around Eighth and Walnut and Shelby Street, an area that proved to be even more threatening to whites. Before "urban renewal" it was definitely a place where you could go and remember the drum. Grandma would go back often to take care of business, to greet old friends, and eventually to lament its passing.

Folks were always gathering there, before the bulldozers came, seeking some outside space that matched the inner realm that needed expression. Here, Black men who worked behind the night shift eight ball came to shoot a little pool of their own. Here, dark silent women dissolved their masks and gave air to their souls. Folk would slap their triumphs into each other's hands, and sometimes force their struggles

violently onto each other's pain. There were churches, Black businesses, and little family stores, and jack-in-the-box juke joints with laughter spilling out onto the street.

Ah, ain't it hard to stumble when you got nowhere to fall.
I say ain't it hard to stumble when you got nowhere to fall.
In this whole wide world, I ain't got no place at all.

The entire square was only about seven or eight blocks, just long enough,
if landscape were music, to be one good boogie-woogie lowdown
blues song. The vibrations there drew you through alternate whiffs of
funk and disinfectant, denial and dream, barbecue chicken and Tabu cologne.
There was sadness, but hope was always quickening at some turn. It felt
like it would never end. But in sure enough offbeat timing, it did.

Buildings were leveled. People were scattered. And the renewal was
long coming. The disruption disoriented everybody at first. It is too much
the reminder—a people again displaced from the land and denied the
right to root, even within segregated spaces, all in the name of progress.
Families were tossed pennies and sent scurrying for shelter. Where in
the world were people to go? In time, marchers came lock-armed
through the streets, demanding "open housing now."

Oh Freedom, oh Freedom, oh Freedom over me.
And before I'll be a slave I'll be buried in my grave
and go home to my Lord and be free.

The discussion in the classroom continued: "Do they think you can
order people's feelings into law?"

"They come through disturbing the peace. I can understand these people wanting to have better housing, but . . ."

A hot embarrassment from having my people put under scrutiny coupled with a rage at their presumptuous white arrogance flooded my body.
Ann Bradens they were not. Ann and her husband, a white couple, had
bought a house in a white neighborhood and "blockbusted" by turning it over to a Black couple. The house, of course, was bombed. There
was no way Blacks could live in the neighborhoods of our choice.

Segregation was so entrenched that most white people were sure that
what we needed was a good stomping reminder of our place in the world.

It was a shame because nobody was dealing with the injustice or the fact that the city merely wanted the old square's prime riverfront location. Their remedy was to build more projects, stack us in like rats, so they could have room with a view. The injustice struck me on a more personal level because of what it had meant to Grandma. Just when Grandma and people like her had gotten some of the buildings livable, in came "urban removal," as Black folk called it, and tore the whole thing down. Grandma worried, Lord, she worried, and worked herself up resisting it. But to no avail. That winter my Grandma passed, still hoping, still believing in Jesus, still talking about roses blooming in springtime and Black people entering the promised land.

We brought her home for the wake, and people came from everywhere, the church folk and folk who had known her in her restaurant days, and ones who knew her when she was interlocutor for the minstrel show, and who were in the secret society that cared for the uncared-for and buried the dead. Even people she had put out of her apartments came by. They all paid last respects to the lady who planted hope, and knew how important it was for anybody to have a place to grow and call home.

I just looked at her. I couldn't believe she wasn't moving. Even in her sleep, she had always moved. Even in her dreaming, somehow. A part of me was stilled, too, for a long time after that.

But in this classroom this day, among these people, my heart quickened again. I felt urged to take up my grandmother's battle, but didn't know how to do it. I did sense, though, that our people's need for housing and Faith's struggle to stay in school and graduate, despite her advancing pregnancy, were intricately connected.

"But what is it that they want?" Sister Dymphna asked. She probably was not aware of how she said "they" as if "they" could not have possibly wanted the same things other human beings wanted. I dared not look at her. She would surely expect an answer this time. There were so many times, in cases like this, that I wanted to say, "I have consulted the twenty million Black folks in this country—and it is their consensus opinion that they want you to stop asking me to speak for everybody—even if I am the only Black person in this class." What possibly could I say to her if forced to answer except something like "What do you mean?"

That was always a good question because, as far as I could see lately, white folks said one thing and meant another. Most of the time I liked this school, but now I hated it. Sister Dymphna rephrased her question: "What do you think about the marches?"

A heck of a question. Dr. King had joined his brother in leading a march for open housing. The site had been strategically chosen. The organizers had not only anticipated the harassment from these particular whites, they had counted on it. Many people in this area were blue-collar workers and had already demonstrated their desperation to feel superior to somebody, anybody—just don't let us be the bottom. They were not afforded the buffer enjoyed by rich whites whose wealth could buy, among other things, a false sense of separateness. And at the same time, they could not bring themselves to acknowledge the fact that they, like us, had been thrown into a jungle to work the factories, streets, and marketways for a piece of a house, a car in twenty years. They could not acknowledge this commonality or seize upon its potential power. And so, as if on cue, they came out, heckling the marchers. And the television cameras documented the racism, sweeping its horrors right from the streets and into the front rooms of Black and white, rich and poor alike. To make sure that Holy Rosary's students wouldn't fill the ranks of the hecklers, the school ruled that no one would be permitted to attend the marches. We were told that it was considered unchristian and unbecoming for a Rosary lady. Which "it" did they mean? The heckling? The protesting? All political activity? How was I supposed to answer her question?

When the discussion first opened up in the classroom, I listened quietly at first, realizing that I, as well as the other ten Black students in the school, had either been overlooked in the decision to bar attendance or purposely banned from demonstrating for our cause. When Sister asked me about the marches, I realized that it didn't matter to her what I thought. She was just going through the motions as she had done so many times before. I was supposed to be the "Blackologist" of the class. My visibility was, to say the least, time-released—destined to run out when the topic of Black folk did.

I said nothing, a strategy that was supposed to protect me from immediate attack. "Unchristian and unbecoming for a Rosary lady"—the words would not cease ringing. It wasn't just the heckling by the crowd that was being referred to, but the demonstration itself. I was sure of it. Why was it so unbecoming? I played with the reference, pulling one world of implication from the womb of the next. I had my own understanding of what was wrong with the condemnation of the march as "unchristian." But "unbecoming"—this I dissected curiously. Perhaps it was unbecoming because this was war and ladies don't indulge in war; ladies don't fight?

The ruling, of course, could be perceived as an attempt to "pull everyone out of the jungle," but I knew that analogy fell short. When Momma made her ruling at home that we come out of the jungle, she knew we still had to contend with the Kirby gang. We just had to find new ways of dealing with one another. The school's ruling on the march, on the other hand, seemed designed to perpetuate the spiritual amnesia that had reached epidemic proportions. The faculty merely suggested that Black people and white people find new ways of dealing with one another. They never told us to find how to overcome the injustices. They never suggested that we seek better understanding. They just said for us not to go to the marches, playing down the reasons why the marches existed in the first place. They secured the scales and gave blindness their blessing.

In my frustration, I had talked about it with Momma. She felt that much could be gained by the marches, and furthermore that something could be gained by my staying in the school. She reminded me that both white and Black people had come a long way. She reminded me that I was to be part of Holy Rosary's one hundredth graduating class. This meant the school had been in existence when she was a girl, but she could never have dreamed of going there. The only Black Catholic education available during her time was at Catholic Colored High, whose books were secondhand books destined to create second-class citizens. It was located around a so-called red light district. Imagine the things you would learn just on your way to school! You would pass not only the honky-tonk man or the hoochie coochie woman in front of the juke joint, but hear the rhythms of homeboy Lionel Hampton on the vibes and Big Mama Thornton singing, "You ain't nothing but a hound dog." And if you were lucky you could catch Bojangles' feet tapping out the beat, hey-bop-a-reebop. The environment, though creative and culturally rich, lacked the necessary educational tools for advancement. My grandparents sent Momma to Rock Castle in Virginia for a more fluent and conventional Black Catholic education with the Sisters of the Blessed Sacrament.

Now, Momma reminded me that a little more than a hundred years ago it had been against the law for Blacks even to be caught reading. She insisted that both Blacks and whites had a long way to go, but we had gotten somewhere, she said, because I was sitting in that classroom, having had the opportunity to take the same exam given the white girls. And despite what Sister's eyes said to me day after day, I was no dummy. When I made it through and Betty Jo made it through to graduation, we would make it a lot easier for those coming after us. Just like Faith, Sandy, Eunice, and Michelle had made it easier for us.

That day in the classroom, however, I resented that the questions were political. Granted, Martin Luther King had challenged the political and social order, but he had evoked moral codes to expose the injustice. A segment of Black people had made an ascension; we had risen above oppression and were granted a communion with our God—a communion that had consecrated us to a new consciousness. And at this point I had come to see the ruling as an attempt to deny me that opportunity. The attempt, of course, was futile, because spiritual reality is not subject to the same confines as physical reality, and because those who had ascended had by their communion become catalysts, inspiring others toward awakening.

In fact, white Louisville should have been glad that Malcolm X hadn't been called in with his theory of "by any means necessary." The awakening was not the same for everyone—at least it wasn't for me. This is what Sister must have misunderstood—otherwise, I would not have been asked to speak for twenty million other Black people. The movement became for me not merely a comforter but my "come-forther," inspiring me toward higher ground.

So when Sister repeated the question as if she were talking to Lazarus or somebody equally dead, I found myself, a secret lotus, opening under just the right slant of gray cool light. I found myself answering my own question, as well as Sister's, out loud, instead of just inside my head.

"I think that rule gives an easy out"—her eyes strained—"by ignoring what we claim to be about as Christians"—her nose scowled—"and I feel pretty badly about seeing only Baptists and Methodists on the front line." I don't think I blinked even once.

"Then you've been going to the marches, Miss Conwill?" Sister asked, clearing her throat.

"Yes, Sister, I went down once," I said. And somebody—I wasn't sure, but I thought it was Hilary— said that the ruling wasn't meant for me; that it wasn't made for the Black students at all. Hilary had made me sick with her wishy-washy, sporadic support of the Black cause. She had gone from "What do the Black people want?" to this?

"Why only once, Miss Conwill?" Sister asked.

"Because," I said, "after the rally, when we were getting ready to go, the leader kept saying, 'If you can't take what's out there waiting or you, don't go—for the sake of the cause.'"

"And?" she prodded.

It took a few seconds before I could answer. "Sister," I said, "I don't think I could stand all that screaming and war." Of course I went on about not understanding why people insisted on acting so cruelly to people groping so fiercely for life. The seriousness began quilting in the faces of my classmates. Had "war" been too heavy a word? Was everyone there going to find me strange, the way some of my Black friends had when I left the marches?

All of this mattered, but not enough to keep me from saying the rest. "And what's worse, I don't like the idea of looking out and seeing all those so-called friends right out there along with the rest of them, selling 'guaranteed rotten eggs' and splintered sticks."

"We don't go to heckle!" my classmates screamed.

"We just come to see!"

Amid the clamor of voices, I heard Hilary's. I was sure of it. I looked at her and she was straining back at me. I felt betrayed.

"Spectating is heckling," I said, directing it mostly to Hilary. Didn't she know that if she was not on line with the marchers, her merely being there among the whites put her on line with the hecklers?

"And now you stay home?" Sister Dymphna asked.

"Sister," I said as honestly as I could, "it isn't because of the ruling, and it really isn't because of just the fear, it's mainly because the man said, 'If you can't take what's out there waiting for you, then go home—for the sake of the cause.'"

"And you couldn't turn the other cheek?"

"I wouldn't turn the other cheek," I said.

Hilary followed me to the lunch table.

"You are such a contradiction," she said. I didn't want to see her.

"Maybe if you march, the so-called war would end quicker," she insisted. "Why don't you march, Estella? Why do you make it all sound like the Civil War recycled? I guess you know you forfeited your A."

This was the first time I wished I had the power to make someone disappear. It wasn't exactly that I wished her dead. I just wanted her to disappear—maybe become like the air. Then she would know what it felt like to be me. I would be able to breathe her in—and then there'd be no need for her stupid questions.

"Just leave me alone." I was not as much frustrated with her as with my own inability to create my world for her in mere words—especially since there were so many spaces in my life that words had not yet lighted.

In many ways, this period was one of those moments filled with possibilities for directing human destiny. Not only had ecumenism been initiated in the Church, but the Civil Rights Movement had evolved full scale, and the women's movement had gained new strength. Iconoclastically and creatively, the movements shifted the very essence of society. I was experiencing my own rites of passage in the midst of intense forces, sometimes unconscious of their dynamic influences and at other times too engrossed and overwhelmed to know that life was anything other than confluences and changes.

Hilary resented my contradictions. At the time I did, too. While it seemed that most people's level of commitment had drawn them into one camp or another, I stood somewhere outside them all. While many followed Martin Luther King's strategy, there were others who passively accepted segregation and still others who simply prayed for the best. I found myself in a sort of no-man's-land, forced into a much more individualized stance than I probably ever intended. I was again outside of a vital knife-cutting yet brutally aware of it. What, I wondered, was my role in relation to all this? What was I being called to do?

Perhaps at that particular stage I was too close to childhood and groping too intently toward womanhood to have much understanding or respect for taking what I considered to be the position of a child. Besides, we had all seen the dogs in Selma attacking the demonstrators. We had seen how merciless the policemen were. We had read about the four little girls in Birmingham getting bombed. I could not understand this. Was there no way to overcome other than by handing over my body to be burned? No sooner had the thought come than I remembered the garden again and felt the power of those words challenging me: "If I give everything I have to feed the poor and hand over my body to be burned, but have not love, I gain nothing." Grandma again. Indeed, at that moment, to care about Hilary when I surely wanted to kick her behind was harder than going out on line with the marchers.

She had come to the Black girls' lunch table with me before, but this time I wanted her to leave. I didn't want her around me.

"You know what really gets me, " I said to Betty Jo, my best friend since first grade. "You know how some words have a silent 'E' at the end of them?"

"Oh, come on, Estella," Theresa interrupted, but I continued.

"Well, these houses out in the south end have a silent white in front of them."

"If you feel that way, why don't you march like the others do?" Hilary insisted.

"Because," I said "when I go and look out in the crowd, I don't just see blobs of whiteness, Miss Hilary. I see faces. I see you!"

"All the more reason," Hilary said. "If people saw some people they knew marching, maybe they would—"

"What?" I said back to her. "Just come to see? You couldn't even look at me in there."

"Estella, you didn't even march. What's the big deal?"

"Life," I said. "That's the big deal."

Betty Jo, the only other Black sophomore in the school—and she was in another class—sat there, her glance volleying back and forth between Hilary and me, wondering why I was talking in-house talk and exposing my inside self in the presence of this white girl. Suddenly, aware of my nakedness, I stopped talking and wondered, too.

I was sorry I knew Hilary. The lunches and parties meant nothing because there she was playing "Miss White Lady." I looked at Betty Jo, then at Sandy and the others.

"Where's Faith?" I asked.

Nancy nodded toward the office. "I was thinking about transferring to Central High," she said sarcastically. "There you can be Black in peace."

"She was called down to the office because she's pregnant, for heaven's sakes," Eunice said. "It has nothing to do with her being Black."

Everybody at the table made puking noises.

"OK, OK," Eunice said jokingly. "I was just checking. But check or no check, we all gonna be having to prove ourselves after this."

What was happening to us, to all of us? Hadn't we studied and proved ourselves enough? Hadn't Sister Martha Joseph, and Mrs. Boone, and our other teachers back at Immaculate Heart of Mary done overtime to prepare us? Hadn't they cared for us like we were the promised ones coming to help transfigure the world? And even when things went wrong, hadn't our parents made everything all right? Some of us were the first students to attend Immaculate Heart when it opened. The parishioners had been holding Mass in the barn until the new building was complete. The Blackmans, Christians, Elerys, and Conwills were among the first families there. In the eight years before my coming to Rosary, hundreds of families joined. There were spelling bees and math quizzes, and many of us simply took turns taking first place; James Reed one week, me the next, Charles London, then Betty Jo. When my brother Adolph graduated, he left home for the Verona Fathers Seminary in Cincinnati, and later graduated valedictorian of his otherwise all-white class. When William finished Immaculate Heart and took the entrance exam for high school, he had placed the highest in the state, Black or white. Academically, socially, spiritually, there had been plenty to prepare us. And there were volleyball and basketball tournaments, and we were always in the finals, even when white parents from the opposing team murmured racist names when it was our time to serve, making our server fumble the ball. Sometimes it made us sick. But we acted like champions anyway. Sister Martha Joseph said it was the thing to do. I shook their hands because maybe Jesus would have wanted it that way, but we had cried all the way home, Betty Jo loudest of all. We couldn't curse them so we cried, and Father Simon took us for doughnuts like he always did and began the script for yet another dramatic play—one that would give us perspective on the situation. We would act out the characters, memorizing whole soliloquies, not always conscious then that the plot was a variation on our own lives. And the transcendence could be ours as well. Father Simon was Italian and would come to me, even as early as my sixth grade, asking for synonyms, "How do you say 'cheating'? How do you say 'bravado'?" And I would wrestle the raging wind inside myself, feeling the words work their way up. I would pronounce them, bear their sound to the wind, see which ones would fly. And he would smile, scribble a thing or two, then go on creating. In a little while, half the class would be on stage and the other half handing out period costumes made by the mothers, and Roman gear and gumption. All moving toward that moment of death, that point of resurrection when Jesus would walk straight up center stage, not staggering anymore, not humbly talking about being thirsty or forgotten, but standing there smiling, Jesus triumphant, yeah: "Oh, Death, where is thy sting?"

Now, the clamor of forks against plates clashed against the silence. Everybody at the table was uneasy about Hilary and me. Then, mostly out of nervousness, Sandy snickered. "Why don't you ask her how come she doesn't march?" she whispered.

I was about to laugh when I saw Hilary's confusion and hurt welling up inside of her. I pushed against my impulses.

"Look, Hilary," I said. "It's not just you and it's not just me—it's a whole system of stuff. It's Sister thinking she's a Black expert just because she talks at me, and it's everybody talking together in there and nobody responding alone." Hilary said that she suspected a sense of prejudice setting in on my part. Betty Jo said that was ridiculous, and she got up to get more milk.

How could I tell her that white people's prejudice had been legitimized—that it had been backed up by a whole political system; while my prejudice was simply my own, with the power to destroy only me. I didn't know how to go about it, but I tried explaining it, anyway.

"What do you mean?" Hilary kept asking. I kept trying to find the words to explain myself. We went around in circles. Strangely, she tried to follow me, just as her feet had done earlier when she had tried to learn Black dances in time for the school's spring dance. She would slow me up on Stevie Wonder's "Butterfingers" and want me to count the beats and measure the steps. I wanted to tell her what Professor Grand had told us that day at the studio: "It's not just the count and it's not just the feeling." Finally I told her, "Look, even though I don't march, I just don't believe that the people who do should have to be heckled, that's all. Now do you see?" Some understanding crept over her face and the both of us smiled.

"Now do you see?" The phenomenon of seeing is deep. I am convinced that our struggle is most often like the struggle of the ghost who yearns to take presence among the living. Because we are in some sense "invisible," our sense of wholeness comes not merely in efforts to spiritualize but to materialize—in our efforts to strain beyond mere visibility so our half-blind brothers and sisters can see.

"Now that that's over," Eunice said, "maybe somebody can tell me what's happening with Faith." The fact is that between classes, games, and rap sessions at the table, we participated in the sport of "watching the nuns watch us." They would be looking to see if anybody was pregnant. Sister Phillip Celine would check us out all year, but spring was her celebrated hunting season. It was then that the heat would force us to shed our dark blue uniform blazers and our tight-waisted skirts would show.

Everybody knew Faith's breasts had begun to protrude and that her waist had rounded and the flesh beneath her eyes was swollen. And like a lot of women during their pregnancies, Faith had a spitting problem. In the middle of a conversation, at the height of a laugh, Faith would have to spit. And spit. Sister Phillip called her down to the office and asked her outright if she was pregnant.

"No, Sister."

"She's not the first girl in the school to get pregnant, quiet as it's kept," Hilary said in response to Eunice. I was glad to hear her say that. We both knew that a few of the older girls had started taking the pill. We also knew that a few married and had babies six months after graduation. It was even rumored that one had been pregnant one weekend and not pregnant the next. It comes down, as my Aunt Gert used to say, to a matter of deciding whether "to have the baby on your lap or on your soul."

Now, a couple of weeks later, Sister had called Faith back and told her that she wasn't satisfied with her answer. Faith was filling up her clothes too quickly. Again Faith denied being pregnant.

Although she was a bit "uppity" about associating with underclasswomen, or the Black table for that matter, we all backed her in her struggle to remain in school and graduate. Sandy sang,

> Three more weeks before graduation
> got no time for no ruination.

I jumped in singing,

> Worked too hard to let it go now;
> gonna get that piece of paper anyhow!

Betty Jo, the saner voice among us, sang,

> She might get out of here; who knows—maybe,
> but honey, my momma would kill me and the baby!

We all laughed, but of course, we had all been given a similar lecture. Faith didn't come back to the table that day. That night I prayed that she could make it to graduation and that her baby could make it to life. I prayed for her as much as I did for the marchers, because regardless of what they were saying about us, we needed some kind of resurrection. And Faith's baby would do just fine.

It wasn't until after school the next day that we found out what had happened to Faith. She had come in midway through the day, and her boyfriend picked her up after school. Sandy had gotten the news and run breathlessly onto the bus.

"What is it?" we demanded.

"Is she staying?"

"Open your mouth, girl! Talk!"

Sandy played it for all it was worth. "Faith's got," she huffed, "a doctor's statement," she puffed, "saying she's got . . . a stomach ailment!"

What? She blew the house down! Laughter broke loose in bolts and bombs. You would've thought old Walnut Street was swinging again. We stomped. We laughed. We screamed till tears rolled out like some kind of baptism, like one of our band had broken loose of the shackles and made it over the River Jordan. We kept talking over one another, but the words getting squashed in the laughter. When the calm finally came, it started all over again until we ended up mimicking, reading the doctor's note in Sister Phillip's high-pitched shocked expression: "Stomach *ailment*!?"

Meanwhile, Faith got gradually bigger. She walked down the school corridors with a pregnant woman's wide-legged gait, and when she'd pass me I'd smile, knowing that we were winning one battle in an age-old struggle to survive.

By late spring, not only did Louisville, Kentucky, pass its Open Housing Bill, but Faith Grovesnor graduated.

3

GOLDEN SLIPPERS I'M GWINE TO WEAR

I learned not to expect merely safety in gardens or to anticipate only danger in jungles. I was sent to Holy Rosary because of the kind of safety it was supposed to provide for me as a young teenage girl. I found that my particular consciousness as a Black student made me vulnerable to a different kind of threat—of having my positions maligned, my ideas trivialized. What I wanted now was Black Consciousness and a deeper awareness of the cultural renaissance that was happening outside of Holy Rosary. When I learned that the local Black newspaper was holding its annual Miss Exposition contest as part of the Black Expo, I knew this was my chance to win a scholarship to one of three historically Black colleges, and go on to indulge in what I had duly termed "the culture."

In my teenage mind the culture was all things Black and beautiful. Black teachers and studies, and Blacker than Black fun. It was freedom to be your natural Black self without apology. It was the unadulterated joy at being nappy headed in the rain, ashy legged in the cold, proud in the butt as well as the back, loud in your laughter if you were gifted that way, and silent in those exalted spaces where words would be humbled. The culture was ancestral memory endowed with hope informing life today. Unlike my three older brothers, who had all left home one after the other and joined the seminary in Cincinnati, Ohio, I wasn't sure what God was calling me to do, but whatever it was, I knew it had to do with making the world better for Black people starting with me. So I set out forthrightly to win that title.

I put on hold any reluctance I might have had about securing an education by having to win a beauty contest when I was obviously an intelligent, creative, ambitious young woman. I justified my entry by pointing to the format, which in four nights provided opportunity for exposition of beauty in talent, intelligence, attitude, style, and physicality. The more immediate question was finding what I could present as my talent. Although I had taken piano lessons, there was no way I could claim music as my talent. There would also be women there who could break from the sheet and improvise those spots the audience grooved to best until they were all up rocking to a brand new song that even the player hadn't heard before. No, music wasn't my forte, and though I could jam pretty well on the dance floor, I couldn't claim that talent either.

To declare oneself a dancer took a lot of soul. A real dancer could twist and make the audience dizzy. She could transform into an eagle or a bad funky chicken. One of those Tina Turners would surely be there, jamming, justifying, funking her way to the crown.

My talent was poetry, and although I'd never written a piece long or good enough to present to a public audience, I believed I could. After all, I had the inspiration of Grandma's tales in the garden, and Father Simon's plays at church, and the wind—I had the wondrous wind blowing off the Ohio into my awakening spirit, saying, "Name this, Word Weaver! Find the word for this!" And each time, I would see again for the first time whatever was before me—the sun pouring gold out of the sky, the dark, knowing eyes of old Black women radiating at the same time both beauty and horror. "Name it," the wind would say, and I would scribble, leaving trails of ink that marked my quest. I would do it again, only this time I would write a poem to display my talent.

I would be Eve in the garden and the serpent tempting her. I would dramatize the voices—make them live again. All I had to do in the meantime was convince Momma to let me compete.

"I don't want nobody messing over you, Estella."

I tried to assure her that at seventeen I was mature enough to take care of myself.

"Mess is mess," she said, signifying, I was sure, on the rowdiness of the crowd. I had heard that the Expo audience could be more merciless than the sandman at the Apollo. They could make or break the competitors. They could affirm you in ways unimaginable or scream out in disgust and bring you to tears. In their signifying, they could as easily be entranced or turned off by your looks or your talent. The judges were not really supposed to be swayed by them, but certainly the participants who worked and overcame the audience's judgment were most triumphant.

"It's all right, Momma. I can handle it."

"To tell you the truth, I don't even know how up-and-up this pageant is. I know you want to go away to college, but I don't know if this is the way to do it."

"Momma, it's the only way. They offer a scholarship, three hundred dollars, and money for books," I said, showing her the ad. "The change I make selling popcorn at the West End Theater is not going to pay tuition anywhere. I do not want to go to Western University in Bowling Green. Betty Jo and Deborah might, but I don't want to see any more white schools. Momma, please, just say yes."

She agreed only with the stipulation that she accompany me to the orientation. After the initial introduction, those who needed accompaniment stayed to work it out with the musicians. I stayed just to get a sense of the competition. The first girl—no, she wasn't a girl at all but a woman—stood up and began letting a tune grovel up from her feet through her being like it was coming from the earth itself. She was the bark of some mastic tree that was mystically stretching its limbs out through her sound, and having its blooming in all the wind around us. Her song, "The Shadow of Your Smile," would not fade.

I went home, and spent the next several days frantically thinking about my poem. At first the shadow of the tree intimidated me. Then I was frightened by the five-minute length of the performance. Then I couldn't find a spot quiet enough to write in. I went for long walks through the neighborhood, toward the park, and then back to what was left of the garden. Nothing. That Wednesday when I got home from school, I found that my brothers had sent letters responding to the newspaper clippings I had sent containing photographs of the contestants. Adolph sent his best but had to stop because another chore bell was ringing. William said he could understand Momma's concern and that I was already a queen no matter what. Houston told me to go upstairs and write in the boys' quarters for inspiration. So I gave that a try.

The boys' quarters was one large room covering the span of the house. The summer before he left for the monastery, Houston had painted life-sized murals of the fourteen stations of the cross across all the walls. Joe had been his assistant, and I had written poems for each station. It was a meditative journey through the Passion of Jesus. The first station, "Jesus is condemned to death" was beside the study tables. "Veronica wipes the face of Jesus" was beside Houston's bed. "Jesus falls for the third time" was next to Spivey's bed. "The Crucifixion" was painted center ceiling. To me, the facial features of the figures bore subtle resemblance's to Houston's own. He was Simon, the Roman soldiers, and Jesus, and they were all he. One of my poems had said just that. Remembering how charged the house had been that summer, I anticipated a similar energy this time, but all I could do was remember how incredibly good Joe was with the brush, almost as good as Houston, as he duplicated the image of Jesus' face on Veronica's cloth, and how proud he was for our uncle Gene to see it. I remembered Spivey selling tickets to the neighbors to see the works.

"Michael the Angelo ain't got nothing on y'all," he had said, counting up the money. I laughed aloud, then looked down at the paper. I had only doodled.

"Eve," I whispered, "what about you? What was it like in your garden? What do you have to say for yourself?" I closed my eyes and concentrated, but within minutes, I was back among the voices of my brothers, Adolph and William, who had come home at their first year's end speaking Latin, Italian, and Greek and quoting the philosophers: "Cogito, ergo sum!" "I think, therefore I am!" And I remembered Momma quizzing them and them being astonished at her command of the argument. She in turn did not pinch their nose as she had done in previous duels before they joined the seminary but bestowed an encouraging yet triumphant wink upon them and walked away. Then, for whatever reasons, I remembered the day Houston told me he wanted to join the seminary too. He had just finished his sophomore year at Flaget High.

"Momma might make you wait," I told him. "She tried to make William wait."

"That's because she thought he was influenced by Adolph," he said, as if he had escaped such influence. "Why you looking so strange?" he asked.

"I was just thinking about what Uncle Julius said . . ."

"That God was calling Adolph so loud that William overheard it and thought He was calling him?" We both laughed.

"Come on, Eve," I whispered. "Let's get out of here. We can hang out better downstairs." I sat on my own bed in my own room, and within a few amazing minutes the opening for my piece was written. I wrote and wrote, murmuring over the paper madly. Within an hour, I had moved past the birth of Jesus and was heading toward the Passion. I wanted this. I hadn't wanted anything so badly since I begged to be the one select- ed at Immaculate Heart to crown our Blessed Mother.

The next morning on the bus, I shared my draft with Betty Jo. Reading it aloud, I could hear that the rhythm was off, so I scratched out whole phrases and scribbled in new ones. She nodded in approval. "I think writ- ing must be—a little like being in labor," I said.

To this she responded, "Stella-girl, You know you're off! You don't know nothing about birthing no babies!"—a line we borrowed from Butterfly McQueen in Gone with the Wind. Beneath our laughter, though, was a profound and searing sorrow. My best friend and I were parting. Not just going to separate schools after twelve years together but taking sep- arate paths. We promised each other against it but it was already hap- pening. My restless spirit was bearing witness helplessly to that fact.

A few days later, my poem was ready. "Come on down, Spivey!" I yelled up the stairs. I handed him the script and started to recite it. Before I was halfway through the serpent's dialogue, Spivey had sprung to his feet,, his limber body curling like the serpent's own. "Come on, Stella! You sounding like Eve again. You the damn devil—act like it! You can try to be pretty on this part if you want to, but that ain't gonna win you this beauty contest." I knew the woman with the tree in her mouth wasn't worried about how she looked singing her blues. I did the dialogue again— in a drier, more clutching voice.

"No," Spivey said, stopping me again. "Something still ain't right. The hands are good but something's not working. Think of telling a story, or giving a sermon. Yeah," he said, "do Professor Grand!"

My mind raced back to the magic of Professor Grand, the jack-of- all-trades, music-teacher-turned-preacher, who was also a philosopher and a storefront grocer with a fully stocked counter under the sliding window of his studio. His place was a musical fun house with old sax- ophones, trumpets, lollipops, fruit-flavored snowball machines, chalk- boards and the biggest cookie jars we had ever seen. There was an invisible dog (obviously some contraption rigged fortuitously in the back) who howled hysterically when the notes we played went flat. As an incentive, he promised to cut a demo record for us when we got to be really good. (He had the recording equipment for that in the back as well.) It smelt and felt like the inside of a cocoon there. The walls were always freshly papered with pages from Ebony magazine, which somebody said kept the devil busy reading so he wouldn't be bothering us. On Sunday evenings, the studio transformed into a chapel and Professor Grand became Reverend Grand. Momma had let us stay once for the service and it was incredible. We rearranged the chairs, and in a short while the members began coming with their "Praise the Lord" and "Alleluia, God is good!" Momma had made it clear after Mass that morning that we couldn't shout "Amen, Brother! or "Amen, Sister!" mostly because Joe had been practicing his all morning.

While many of our Protestant friends visited each other's churches, they were reluctant to visit ours with all the genuflections and the kneeling and the not knowing when to sit or stand. And if they seldom visited our church, we never visited theirs. It just wasn't the thing to do. We were Catholic. That we were there at all was phenomenal.

Our different ways of praying were as contrasting as organs and strings are to drums and tambourines. Their worship had nothing of the Latin aura I was accustomed to. In our church, the congregation participated decorously, honoring with quiet reverence the presence of Christ. Even at high Mass, prayers were highly structured and ecclesiastical. I learned later that some middle-class Blacks were attracted to Catholicism precisely for that reason. They were leaving the "rowdy church" of the masses to accept the "civilized" worship of Catholicism.

I didn't know then of these confusions surrounding religion. There were times when I became so emptied of myself and so taken up in the Spirit that by communion time I hardly felt the need to go to the rail. And although Mass was group worship, I never saw it as fellowship— even though the ritual started symbolically from a dinner, the Last Supper.

On one level it was like going to a special spiritual meal, and then being reluctant to meet eyes with the other guests and testify to the sweetness. Considering the differences between our native tongue and the Latin we talked to God in in our church, it was like one lover saying to another something as intimate as "I love you" in a foreign tongue.

At Reverend Grand's church, the congregation was actively a part of the service. As he began giving praise, the churchgoers joined in with joyous affirmation. They lifted up sounds I'd never heard before in a church—although I'd heard them many times at home, but sung only halfway through. Grandma would sing the roots of the song while pruning or cooking, "Every time I feel the Spirit . . ." then moan the rest: "Um-m-m . . ."

I'd strain like one in a desert toward barely discernible water in the distance. "Why don't you sing the rest?" I asked. She merely said that since words mean so much more than just words, there's hardly any reason to sing them. I did not understand. Moaning may be the way of the wise, but when there are no words for the young, we either create our own or moan meaninglessly. I created my own: ". . . turn to a butterfly so you don't have to die like a poor inchworm."

"Whatever in the world are you singing?" Momma had asked. Mine was nothing like the traditional version. She lifted her head and started to show me. She got halfway through and stopped cold, didn't moan, just stood there, a river all dammed up and bulging. She closed her eyes and left me outside of her.

That day at Reverend Grand's, the spiritual cadences continued. I looked at Momma and she smiled back. These songs held the rhythms of our trials and transcendence. They were our freedom songs—love songs to our God.

At the end of the singing, our music teacher-turned-preacher had lifted his arms and spoken. And now, here with Spivey, I began to intone his voice. "Lord," I said, "I want to thank you for waking me up this morning."

"Uh-huh," Spivey said, backing me up.

"I could've been tossing and turning in my grave."

"Lord, have mercy," Spivey said.

"But you woke me. You put down your mighty ha-and and you shook me, Lord!"

"Yes, you did," Spivey chimed in and out of the delivery.

"I didn't see you, Jesus, but I felt you—say that—it was the same hand that wiped the bleeding sweat from my feverish brow—Amen—the same mighty strong hand that reached out to save me from the clutches of mine enemies—Halleluia!—the same quick saving hand—uh—that snatched me—Oh Lord—from the grasp of ol' Satan—Mercy!—when times was so hard—Lord, Lord, Lord—Father, you always been there with your mighty hand even those times, Lord, when I couldn't understand—yes—

you always been there making my design and touching holy life to this ol' clay of mine—uh—and today Lord—uh-huh—right here this evening—yes—we reaching up our meager mortal hands—oh yes—to try and touch some thanks back to you—yes, Lord—to try and touch some thanks back to you."

"Now we talking," Spivey said, dancing in circles around me. "Float like a butterfly—sting like a bee!" We slapped our hands together victoriously.

My poem wasn't a sermon, but I was no longer inhibited about letting my spirit flow through my presentation.

"Do some of that," Spivey said, "and you'll be bringing your trophy home and strutting it big-time at Holy Rosary!" This was something I had to stop and simply imagine.

"Yeah," I said, pretending to hold my Academy Award. "I want to thank my agent—"

"Yeah, yeah, and all the little people," Spivey laughed. "It'll be like when I won the four-forty dash for Flaget. I got all kinds of respect. And you helped me do it, too. I mean you was worse than Coach Crazy. This is the least I can do for you, so get to work!"

And I did. I perfected the piece and then scheduled a dress rehearsal in the basement. Betty Jo, Sandy, and Jeanette and Paulette came. Spivey invited Guy Eaton, our next-door neighbor, whose parents had built on the land between Grandma's and Momma's houses that Aunt Scottie sold them. Even though he teased too much, I agreed he should come. It would prepare me for the hecklers. Of course, Aunt Lyda was glad to be invited. She showed up with pad and pencil as if she were going for the crown. And as we started, Aunt Gert slipped in, too. I listened to all of their pointers, and by opening night I was ready.

I stepped onto the stage, number nineteen out of twenty contestants. That first night went smoothly. It was simply the introduction. The second night was maddening. We took turns charging the stage with our talents. Just as expected, Miss Tina Turner came, and so did Lady Day. Others performed acrobatics, dramatic works, and dance routines. Having to wait my turn gave me fits. Finally the emcee introduced me.

"Ladies and gentlemen, put your hands together for Miss Estella Conwill, who will be presenting an original poem entitled 'Paradise Revisited and Made Real'!"

Suddenly I was center stage, facing thousands of audience members.

The ones at the foot of the stage were obviously poised for their own performance.

"Come on with it, baby!"

"Make it real to me, momma!"

I gathered my energy from all the nights of rehearsal, focused in on my support team, and began.

"Well, all right," I heard, but I stayed concentrated, moving from the creation of Adam and Eve on to the temptation by the serpent.

"Yeah, bring ol' Jody out here," one brother said. "I want to kick his ass!"

"Look away for one hot minute and he's rapping to your lady, man!"

A wave of heat flushed my body.

"Go on, baby," some woman encouraged. I could see them giving each other high fives and laughing at my expense. I curled into character and let them see ol' Jody in action.

> Eve, Eve, why don't you eat of this tree?
> you are mistress here—
> or do you hesitate to eat of it
> simply out of fear?

"Sybil! Man," one of them bellowed, "I'm scared of this lady!"

"Why don't y'all shut up," somebody said.

Seconds later, I was Eve again.

> I fear nothing
> for I am mistress here—
> I am simply obeying the Lord God's command
> who to me has been so dear.

"My girl has a problem, man. They got to give her something for this!"

> Yes, Eve, you are mistress here,
> a mistress without power—a mistress in a cage
> forbidden to touch the very things that are hers—
> oh, what an outrage!

"OK, Eve, your turn," I heard. The audience was actually listening. Even the hecklers were waiting for me to go on. I stared out into space until the form of the tree was practically there before them:

> The very day you eat of this tree
> you will die—
> These are the words of the Lord, my God—
> but why?

> Because Eve, there is no death
> beyond that tree but godlikeness
> See for yourself—
> Discover the brightness . . .

Eve and the serpent finished their argument. I went on to present as powerfully as I could the birth, death, and glorious resurrection of Christ. Only after I had reached my place in line again could I appreciate the cheering behind me. The ones making the most noise throughout the performance were now yelling the loudest. And I could hear throughout the rumbling the old women singing out, "Speak the truth, baby!" "Well, all right." My act won third place behind Lady Mastic Tree and Miss Tina Turner, leaving me still in the running for the crown. That night all of us went home, charged over the prospects of going before that merciless crowd in our skimpy swimsuits.

Once home, everybody gave me pointers. Lyda even pulled out her tally chart showing me exactly where I was in the running.

The next night as we stepped onto the stage wearing our revealing swimsuits, the people in the buffoon section began screaming and stomping and grabbing their chests as if in cardiac arrest. Every time one of us moved down the platform, there was another wave of howls. The emcee threatened to put them out if they didn't control themselves. They did, but then the next girl strolled down the aisle, determined to make her mark. Just as she was pivoting at the edge of the platform, her fingers deliberately flipped the edge of her swimsuit, exposing the fleshy roundness of her cheeks to the crowd. At this, laughter, moans, disgust, and delirium exploded like an awesome bomb. She then swept her eyes across the rest of us and all but smirked.

"Beat that!"

"She knows she's got a snowball's chance in hell—all that cackling she was doing last night!" Bonnie said.

The emcee tried to restore order. Momma was shaking her head and I could practically hear Aunt Lyda sucking her teeth, even through all that hissing. Spivey was all reared back in his chair, laughing like a hyena. James, whom I considered myself to be going with at the time, was just as bad. And my uncle Gene, who had gotten off early from work, was having a mighty time signaling for me to keep my composure. Lyda then crossed her legs and stared back even more firmly as if to reiterate her most recently favorite proverb: "Like a golden ring in a swine's snout is a beautiful woman with a rebellious disposition!"

"I don't know what the criterion is in this contest," said Rosalee, "but I sure hope it ain't audience approval!"

"Surely the judges got more sense than that!"

"We don't even know who the judges are!"

"I mean, she didn't even shave her underarms. She came ready to throw down!"

"Girl, don't worry about that. Just do your best, OK?"

"The wench."

The next night, after Count Basie played and made everybody mellow, we assembled in our evening gowns. We took turns moving down the ramp, posing for pictures, waving to the audience.

"First," the emcee said, looking out at the crowd, "we have an award that is, in the scheme of things, as important as the Miss Exposition Award itself."

"Yeah, right!"

"The recipient of this award is chosen by the young ladies themselves. This award goes to the one who they think is the most congenial among them, the most helpful, the most kind."

"Yeah, yeah, yeah."

"Even under all the pressure of these last few nights . . ."

When they called my name, I was shocked. Did this mean I was out of the running? I accepted the trophy with a polite "Thank you" and got back in line. What was going on? In the Miss America Pageant, does Miss Congeniality ever win the title?

"When the heck did we vote on this?" I asked Bonnie.

"Just before coming on, remember?"

I looked down at the edge of my formal, at the grape soda splashed against the powdered blue. Before coming onstage, a contestant named Shawna had opened the carbonated drink at a ready aim against my dress. I had jumped back just in the nick of time, and all that had gotten me were the traces at the hem. My girl had sprayed me.

"I am so sorry," she said, but I knew it was a lie. Everybody did.

"That's OK, Shawna. These kind of crazy things happen."

"I don't know what I could've been thinking," she said, sounding like molasses with mold growing on it.

"Me either, Shawna."

"Now what's that supposed to mean?"

"It just means it doesn't matter in the end—not if we got to be going through all this."

"I see you got a attitude!"

"Naw, Shawna, I got grape soda on my gown. Just forget it," I said, walking away.

"I'd report her," Bonnie said.

"You ain't even in it!" Shawna snapped.

"Look, let's just leave it alone, OK? And Shawna, why don't you put that soda down—"

"Yeah, 'fore you accidentally spill it on yourself!" Bonnie said.

I must have missed voting on Miss Congeniality when I went to douse the stains. I held the trophy with more affection now and listened to the emcee.

He loosened the envelope and announced the second runner-up, the girl that I had pegged as the competition. He announced the first runner-up, somebody I didn't even think was in the running. There's no telling what these judges were thinking. The emcee smiled wickedly.

"Now for the moment we have all been waiting for. Now for the moment that we all find out which one of these lov-a-lee ladies will be our new Miss Exposition." He was deliberately taunting us. I must have stopped breathing, but I was getting enough oxygen to think how ridiculous he was to prolong this.

"Audience, are you ready?"

"Give it up, Monkey Man!"

"All right, all right. The new Miss Exposition is, none other than, Estella Conwill, Number Nineteen, Estella Conwill."

"Thank you, Jesus! Thank you, Lord. Four-year college scholarship, here I come! Black school. Money for books! Thank you!" I walked

50

center stage and felt the crown descend upon my head. The tears just kept on coming. "Thank you so much."

"Isn't she lovely, ladies and gentlemen. Feast your eyes on a queen!" Cameras were flashing everywhere. I couldn't find my people.

"I knew she was bad, man. I knew it!"

"Get down, Little Eva!"

Blue and white dots were forming and fading before me. The blindness was already setting in.

"Baby, take me to college with you!"

"Damn that, baby. Teach me!"

I finally focused on Momma. I waved her down. The emcee agreed. "The mother of Miss Exposition, ladies and gentlemen! And the fruit doesn't fall far from the tree." Momma moved royally to the edge of the ramp.

"Mom looks like she don't play," somebody said.

"You're beautiful," she said as I leaned to kiss her.

Just as quickly, she walked back to her seat, waving to the crowd. I turned to join the other contestants, and caught all those disappointed eyes staring dead into me. One of the girls, it's easy to imagine who, stormed right on off the stage.

"Don't worry about her," Bonnie said softly. "She lost."

"She didn't lose," I said, my voice trembling stupidly. "She just didn't win."

That moment in time sagged, pulling what light was left from their dim faces and wrenching from my own insides much of the joy of the moment's triumph. Tears welled up inside of me, then fell in confusion. "You were wonderful," I told them one after another once we had gotten backstage. "I really need to go to a Black school. If it wasn't for the scholarship, I swear, I wouldn't even be in it." They laughed and packed up their belongings to leave. "I'm serious," I told Bonnie, and she said, "Congratulations again, Estella."

Spivey waited behind stage. He was so proud that he didn't see anything else. He carried my trophies out and kept telling the contestants I was his sister. "As a matter of fact, I'm her coach!" Some of them laughed and flirted with him on the way out.

The next day my picture was on the front page, and the news spread around the school. That afternoon, the principal invited me to read at the assembly. I did, and it seemed this was my moment at Rosary too.

But in time one of the nuns suggested that, based on what she knew of my performance in class, I could not possibly have written the poem.

Only two teachers spoke up on my behalf, and they asked that the charge be kept from me. I found out anyway and was devastated at first.

> Yes, Eve, you are mistress here
> a mistress without power—a mistress in a cage
> forbidden to touch the very things that are hers—
> oh, what an outrage!

The members of the faculty decided that some simple research into the matter was needed to clear Holy Rosary's good name from the charge of plagiarism by one of its students, since the school was mentioned in the news article. Of course, there was nothing to be found.

Beyond the contest, the real test for me was to face the serpent inside who uncurled to mock and chide me, making it appear that I was powerless in situations like this to do anything but hate. I had to learn that these tests do more than tempt us to godlessness—that they can, if we want them to, inspire us toward godliness.

"Speak the truth, baby."

"Well, all right."

4

Men, Blood, and War. Houston had left St. Meinrad's Monastery and was stationed at Andrews Air Force Base now, living with the knowledge that at any time he might receive orders to serve in Vietnam. We had all hated that he was drafted. Houston himself didn't open the summons right away, but stood in the drizzling rain gripping it, the life just draining from him. If it had come only two days later, he would have made it to college and been working on the art degree he wanted so badly, for at this time students were exempted from the draft. He would have been safe from Vietnam's explosive hell of bombs, bullets, and fear.

At home, we all knew men who had come back with tales of the war—of crawling through mud-swamps and living in foxholes. Emerson Manning, who had been in the Kirby gang which we had fought as children, told of the brutality—of this real war, and how the smell of blood rising from the ground every time it rained made you taste the thick saltiness of your own mortality. Many had to fight to maintain a sense of humanity. Along with nightmares of misery, suffering, and death, the influence of narcotics and drugs added to the turmoil. The trust of women, the innocence of children were made foreign on many levels. These men were taught to kill without question and eventually without guilt—to separate self from other selves for their own survival. Those who would not make this separation went crazy and died a little more each time they killed. When they came home, their families and friends had to share hearts, minds, spirits with them until they could heal and revive their own. Sometimes this took months—sometimes years. Sometimes it never happened at all. When the tour of duty was over, the men were given a seventy-two-hour deprogramming period and set free to go home to their healers, who all too often understood little of what these men had undergone. And sometimes a psychological rigor mortis had set into the tongue, and the stories never got told. At home such men could be doing something as simple as leaning against a pillow when they'd feel sand bags taunting their backs. They could be playing cards and suddenly see the Queen of Spades as the bitch, Miss Liberty, who had tried to plot their death. Or worse, they could be sweeping the front porch and look at you through the foliage as if you were the enemy. The men who went off to this undeclared hell were never the same when they came back. And some of them, like Stickman, another childhood friend, never came back. I was frightened for Houston. And I didn't like to think about it. He didn't either, and so, a little after his Washington assignment and as part of my graduation present, and before I went off to start school at Tennessee State University, he invited me to see how Washington, D.C., "Chocolate City," parties. I suppose this was the only way that we could make sense of the conflict of experiencing a new and promising beginning in my own life coupled with the possibility of Houston going off to war, which produced a sharp sense of life's fragility. What we had named in our defiant abandon, the determination to dance the sun up, was in reality our assertion of our life and youth against this very pronounced threat of danger and death.

"There's so many changes," Houston said, as we walked Washington's crowded streets sightseeing. "And so fast," he said, pointing out the White House, an enigmatic symbol that left the two of us standing there uninspired. "Stella, I'm telling you, though," he said, pumping himself with confidence, "they can send me down in the middle of hell's fire and I can still come out surviving. Send me to the furnace—I'll still survive!" In a moment, the seriousness melted into a smile again.

"I think I remember that tale in the Bible," I said, laughing. "Shadrach, Meshach, and a bad Negro, right?!"

"Huh, I am a bad Negro! Me and Abednego, too. The fires in that furnace didn't touch him and those fires in 'Nam ain't gonna touch me neither," he boasted. "Huh, the ladies take to me, Stella," he said as if reclaiming some vital part of himself that he had let go of during his three years in the monastery.

"They know what's bad! I'm glad God didn't want me in no monastery! Too many ladies would be out there crying!" We laughed at this, putting whatever fear was in our souls to shame.

Then I remembered a little something that I had bought for him in my purse. "Look at these poems," I said. "I got some Nikki Giovanni for you! I got some Don L. Lee!" I said, already bopping my head to the rising rhythm. "Inspiration for the weary."

> change.
> like if u were a match I wd light u into something
> beautiful. change.
> change.
> for the better into a real real together thing. change,
> from
> a make believe
> nothing on corn meal and water. change.
> change. from the last drop to the first, maxwellhouse
> did. change.

I was dancing the piece by now, and Houston was laughing, snatching at it greedily from my hands, ignoring the passersby shaking their heads at us.

> change,
> change was a programmer for IBM, thought him was a
> brown computer. change.
> colored is something written on southern outhouses. change.

"Where do you get this stuff?" he said, long enough for me to snatch it back.

> change.
> change nigger.
> saw a nigger hippy, him wanted to be different, change . . .

"Give it here, Stella!" he said, peeling my fingers from around the crum-pled words. "Give it here, make-believe woman! I ain't seen nobody igno-rant as you," he said, smoothing out the paper, then finishing it silently. "Damn, I was going to school."

"You will," I said. "You will." We moved on, trying to cram as much in those seventy-two hours as the law would allow. I was staying with friends of the family, Jenny and Mary Bennett, and met as well some of Houston's other friends from the base. The apex of the entire weekend, though, was being at a party and looking out across a crowded room, and seeing, for the first time, what had to be none other than my soul-mate.

Houston had gone to get a drink, and suddenly there was this incredible creature, this wonderful man, holding me in the mystery of his gaze. No words, no thoughts, really—only the black earth inside me quaking, and the heaven-wind between us becoming our breath.

"Hello?"

It was Houston grasping Princeton's hand, breaking him from the spell. "I see you two have met."

Princeton mumbled some burdensome words. My own reached the edge of my tongue and dissolved. Houston laughed at us, then dispelled the awkwardness.

"Estella's not my lady, man," he whispered. "She's my sister." Then he stood back. "Princeton Walls, meet Estella Conwill."

Aretha was singing, "If Ever I Would Leave You," and the two of us floated into the first dance. Before the music's end, I was in love. I would see him again. I had to. There was no way we could experience this and not see each other again.

I left Princeton Walls and Washington, dreaming of next time. I tried explaining it to Momma, who had fallen in love over several unfold-ing seasons, and then to Gert, who tried to cushion me for the possi-bility that I might never see him again; that perhaps it was an evening to simply cherish. I didn't even mention it to Lyda, who had obvious-ly heard and deemed the whole thing nothing more than a crush. I stopped trying to understand. I knew by then that love chooses its own occa-sion, sets its own time and place, performs its transformation precisely the way it wills. I knew it could come like wind, from out of nowhere, beautiful, empowered. And despite their veiled expressions, I knew that they knew that I knew. I'd run to the phone every time it rang, hop-ing it was Princeton calling the number I scribbled on a handkerchief before boarding the plane. I'd have to catch my breath before lifting the receiver to say a calm hello. He did call the day after, after hours of waiting, and promised definitely to see me again. I was getting ready for college, and he wasn't due for a leave any time soon. By September, we had written dozens of letters, and I was overwhelmed now by my intense feelings for him, my anticipation of starting college, and my growing anxiety over Houston's soon-to-be-released new orders.

Houston called saying not to worry, he had a few months before being transferred, and then he would possibly be sent to Korea, to the demilitarized zone, not to Vietnam. No sooner had that been cleared up than William called from San Francisco saying that he had received his summons, too. He had decided to leave the seminary after eight years and, despite having filed for conscientious objector status, had received orders to report for physical examination. His orders were on one level even more unnerving, because one thing was sure regarding William: he would not be writing anybody from any military base in Texas or Washington or Vietnam. He had no intention of fighting anybody's war.

This transformation had been prompted by the clearing of that jungle in the back yard long ago. He intended to go on and obtain a master's degree in psychology at San Jose State and become the healer he had vowed to become. Either that, or leave the country for life.

"Why would I want to go all the way over there to kill somebody?" he said. In words reminiscent of Muhammad Ali's, he added, "The Vietnamese haven't ever called me no nigger. If I was going to kill, I would've started right here on the real battlefield." I wondered how far into Canada I would have to go to visit him, because I knew that he meant it.

While Houston, in time, wrote home about the unbelievably high ratio of Black soldiers going to the war zone, William wrote home saying that he had sent his income tax payment to the White House addressed to the president, proposing that his taxes be used to free the Black prisoners-of-war at home. I supposed this would cover the Black Panthers, the Students for a Democratic Society, the victims of poverty and civil rights atrocities. Momma handed me the letters and sighed.

"They'll be all right," she said. And after a moment more of reflection, she added, "They both already are." I hugged her, then left to read my letter from Princeton. A few minutes later, she knocked at my door, inquiring as to my well-being, unknowingly intruding on the moment.

"Everything OK?"

"Uh-huh . . . He wants to be a journalist, Momma."

She smiled. "Yeah, you told me. And what have you decided about your major?"

"Literature," I said. "That's a good major, don't you think?"

She nodded, smiling again.

"I'm glad to be going to school away from home. I mean, I haven't seen anything, you know. Gone anywhere."

"Estella, some poets don't go any further than their own hometown. You've been to Cincinnati dozens of times and up to Michigan to see the boys. We've been all up through Canada. It's not how far you go. It's how deeply you know that counts."

"What's deep, Momma?" She didn't make the slightest attempt to answer.

"I went over to the Louisville Art Workshop," I said, referring to the newly established Black visual artists consortium, "and they read my poetry and made it sound like it was out of some Cracker Jack box! 'Ain't you mad?' they said. 'Where's the mother-you-know-what in this poem?' they said. 'It's good, but it would be a whole lot better if you put a little gunpowder in it. This bastard raped your grandmomma!' they said like I knew nothing at all . . ."

"Estella, you don't have to write that way to be a poet."

"I know that, but they paint that way, and they have such a bond, such an awareness."

"What do you want to know, Estella?"

"Everything, Momma! Everything! Listen to this," I said pulling out LeRoi Jones's poem.

> Poems are bullshit unless they are
> teeth or trees or lemons piled
> on a step.

And this," I said, throwing that poem aside and reaching for the next. "This is Nikki Giovanni. These are poets for change, revolutionary poets, foreseers of the future. They know something," I said. "I just want to know what they know. I missed something going to Rosary."

She looked at the poems. These were not scripts that were familiar to her, though from the arch of her eyebrows, I was sure that she understood the subscript well enough. "Whatever it is you're searching for, you better make sure that's all you're getting."

"OK," I said, knowing she was referring to my choice of college. All over Black America it was known that "unless you've partied at Tennessee State—you've only partied second-rate!"

When I finally arrived on campus, the first thing I did was look at all those beautiful Black students—mingling, coolly meandering, talking that talk, ready to both book and boogie. This was definitely my world.

Across the street was Fisk University. One of the slick brothers said, "The line between the schools separates the poor from the privileged, true Black from not true Black. In this 'Black Is Beautiful' new day, the meek, along with the sleek, are inheriting the earth!" Some people hearing him applauded, and he bowed. It didn't matter that I didn't know a single soul in that place. I hadn't felt so at home in a school in years.

I sighed. I'm gonna be just fine, I told myself. These were the same words I'd said in response to Momma's earlier "Study hard now . . . and remember home." And her favorite reminder for any of us when leaving the house, "Remember who you are." She had made it sound as if I was entering the island of lotus eaters, where the native herb causes folk to lose all instincts for remembering. "Of course I will remember," I said. I had no idea that in just three short weeks I would be right back home again.

That first week I moved in with a hip crowd; indeed, the undisputed hippest. My new friends, Shaneequa and Samantha, knew the campus and town like one does the jungle of one's own back yard, and they were always eager to play. They had been coming to campus weekends for two years now, and they were pretty, popular, and could get in anywhere. When I asked my roommate to join us in one of our "harambee" get-togethers, she lowered her timid eyes and declined. Before I could insist, Shaneequa and Samantha hurried me along. "Conwill, some of the gatherings will be private—especially the one Friday night. We can't invite just anybody," they whispered. "I'm talking fine, fine niggers, child. Football players, basketball players, and all kinds of players. The conscious ones, the unconscious ones. The brothers who deal, child. All the bad ones. And we are going to par-tay!"

When she wasn't at classes, my roommate stayed in most of the time. "What's out there?" she'd say in her old folk's voice. "Nothing! . . . and if you knew what I know, you'd stay right here and study." On a level, some of what she said rang true, but it also sounded stale. Her comrades were similar. Mostly they enjoyed being left alone.

I had spent the first week running to and from offices between classes trying to get confirmation on my scholarship. From the first day, some discrepancy had existed. By the second week Momma would end up sending some money. I may have gotten a full-page send-off in the Louisville newspaper, "Miss Exposition Goes to College," but there were still all kinds of confusion about the scholarship when I got to school.

"Forget about that," Shaneequa told me. "Think Friday night. Think party! You down for that, right?"

"Yeah," I said, ignoring the anxiety. It was deeper than homesickness. The school's orientation had actually disoriented me. They talked about the majors in terms of how much money was to be made. A man put four different figures on the blackboard. "If you teach, you get this. If you do business, you get this much, and if you do law, in time, you get this. And if you become a doctor, you will, oh boy, be making this much."

"I'm down for the money," Shaneequa said. "Aren't you?" But I had expected the man to say something about service, consciousness, Black pride, nation building—something. I did not understand that for many of us within this first generation up from sharecropping and cotton and tobacco fields, the calculation of future earnings was a necessary consideration. Many of these students and their parents were investing in a college education on the expectation that this investment would gain interest for them. I, on the other hand, had been given a measure of freedom. Grandma and Grandaddy had already experienced owning property. Momma and her sister had already been to boarding school and college. So for me, college was not about making it. It was an opportunity to be fed, to reflect, to synthesize and have the time and space to began a new creation. Classes weren't what I expected either. There was no critical analysis of Black writings. Just more of Hemingway or whoever else was revered by the white establishment within which the students would have to succeed to make money. This curricular omission of Black people's lives would soon explode into Black student demands for the establishment of Black studies programs across the country. But at this point, it certainly had not and I felt outdone.

Betty Jo, I know, was not experiencing any of this at Western Kentucky. I was alone in my disappointment. She had not expected to find in the university greater exposure to Black people's histories, our struggles and accomplishments.

The longer I stayed, the more convinced I was that I had made the wrong decision. I wanted to write and tell Houston that in our "basic training"—his in the military, mine on campus—we were both being socialized to accept servitude, to perform for those who controlled the purse strings in this country. More miseducation through education. Nobody here questioned the superiority of white folks; after all, they were the ones with the money. I was getting more depressed. I kept thinking about the demonstrations at North Carolina's A&T. How four students had sparked the Civil Rights Movement, how they had gotten the people together, knocking on the doors of the dorm and rallying others to join the boycott. How the campus had risen to the call and challenged the system. I wanted to see something relevant. I wanted to grow in knowledge as the proverb commanded: "Listen to counsel—receive instruction that you may eventually become wise." If I couldn't do that here, then why pay the tuition? Why even stay? Why continue being hypnotized, traumatized, by all this, not knowing which parts of all this newness I would even choose to become? I wanted to experience some die-hard Blackness.

"Don't worry," Shaneequa told me. "Some of the ones in the movement will be there." My hopes quickened. I was ready to pursue my dream again as one would the sweetest berry in the thorniest bush.

"You'll be thinking you're in Negro heaven!" she said. "And they gonna love you."

I laughed and said, "I'm already in love. I told you that."

Shaneequa raised her brows into a Mount Everest arch.

"Child, you hook up with one of these players and they'll have you throwing rocks at that nigger next time you see him!"

"Impossible," I said, laughing, "but I do want to meet them. Why aren't they on campus? Why don't I ever see them?"

"It's kind of gone underground now," Shaneequa said. "You'll meet them, don't worry."

It was an off-campus party, by invitation only. When we first arrived, Shaneequa had to say the password "deep" to get in.

"How deep is it?" asked a smoky voice from the other side.

Shaneequa's answer: "Deep enough."

Moving in with the others, I descended the stairs, scratching my stockings on the wooden panel. Bending down, I could smell the sweet cherry and musk incense coming toward us. Save for the black light, the place was barely lit. Stevie Wonder's "Signed, Sealed, Delivered" was throbbing from the box. Every corner had bodies mingling, couples grinding, some joking, some smoking. Shaneequa and Samantha introduced me around. Many of the people I met were older men who had come back to school after the war, matured from the Vietnam experience.

After a few exchanges I moved about, checking out the huge posters on the walls. They could have been a visual litany of saints. Malcolm was there, his pantherlike eyes quickening me to the urgency of the times. Stokely Carmichael had his powerful fist lifted in the Black Power salute. Rap Brown seemed caught in the middle of pronouncing the words "Revolution, now." LeRoi Jones's "S.O.S." poem was almost audible from the wall. The poet Sonia Sanchez and the musical group the Temptations were there, as well as Nikki Giovanni. I stopped at John Coltrane and read the inscription: "A Love Supreme." "I've never ever heard that piece," I murmured. "He is my favorite," somebody said. "Of all those up there, he's it."

I turned to see an interesting-looking older Black man standing beside me. "Really," I said, and within minutes we were talking about Miles, Ahmad Jamal, Count Basie, and other greats. "You're hip to the Count?" he said, and I nodded my head and smiled, remembering the night he played at the Expo.

Shaneequa saw us and came over. "I see you two didn't waste any time getting to know each other." Then she bent over and whispered, "Girl, this nigger here is gold. You're bad. You know what's happening." Then she winked. "Just don't stay in one spot all night."

"By the way," he said, extending his hand, "my name is Mo; that's plain M-O, initials to my name. Only my enemies call me Melvin Oliver; now that's Oliver. And I certainly wouldn't want you in that category. I've been all over the world," he told me. "Made a lifestyle of moving on." He had lived in Africa, South America, Germany, and Japan. He had witnessed the liberation of Ghana and the inauguration of Kwame Nkrumah, and he even wore the matching pants and shirt popularized by the president. Mo definitely was one of the main players that Shaneequa had referred to earlier, and his presence fascinated me. His hair was thinning a bit, but he managed an Afro and his beard had streaks of silver. The chain around his neck held cowrie shells. I looked hard at him and wondered what he was doing here in the middle of a party of coeds, most of whom seemed half his age. Before I found the words to ask, the energy from his eyes had gathered on to me. "And what about you, my sister? Why have you come here, I should say, to this hellhole?"

Was he talking about the party? Before I could figure, Samantha and Shaneequa were back.

"What's this nigger telling you?" Samantha asked.

"That they awarded him the keys to the city of hell?" Shaneequa chimed in, laughing.

"Believe him," Samantha said. I looked back at Mo. It was like trying to make out a camouflaged man in the middle of an outback. I couldn't tell who he was. Could he be the berry inside the thornbush? Or was he a rattler on a limb? "Whatever you're searching for, honey, make sure that's all you're getting." Mo recoiled and Shaneequa reached over and took a swallow of his drink.

"Did he tell you he has fucked in all fifty states—except Alaska?" she asked, chewing on the ice and swaying to the music.

"As-salaam alaikum," I heard someone say from over my shoulder. The new arrival interlocked his hands with Mo's.

"As-salaam your lekum," Shaneequa played.

"Hello, Shaneequa," the brother said. Something was definitely going on between them.

"Look," Shaneequa said, "I want you to meet somebody." I extended my hand.

"Abdul," he said, shaking my hand.

"Estella is a poet—as in Nikki Giovanni. She needs some truth to write about."

"Shaneequa, don't play games with me."

"I'm not playing, Abdul."

"Later, sister.

"Later?" she said. "Later? You been hounding me about Islam and you here hanging out yourself?"

"You disrespecting me, sister, and yourself," he said, taking the drink from her hand. "If you don't want Islam, that's your business, but don't come questioning my integrity and don't play with my faith."

Shaneequa looked confused. I know I was.

"I can stay a Christian and get high," she said.

"But you won't be with Abdul," he said. Then he turned to Mo. "Man, we ready to burn."

"Then let's do it," Mo said.

At that, Abdul, along with another man, began stretching masking tape along the edges of the windowsills. They sealed the front door. I could feel Mo's eyes on me. I tried simply staring back into them, but the green and black ambiguity there was too unsettling. I turned and looked at Shaneequa.

"What are they doing?" I asked.

"You'll see," she said, her voice lifting over the music.

"Hey, sister—mash the trash and have some hash," some skinny, beady-bearded brother said as he offered me an ashtray with one hand and a joint with the other.

"No, no thank you," I said, but he kept standing there.

"Do you mind?" he asked, nodding for me to extinguish my cigarette. "'Cause when we blow, we want to be able to know it."

I put my cigarette out. Mo reached past me to take a joint. I had seen people smoke a little marijuana before, but I had never witnessed a real "get-down-get-you-right-reefer" party before.

"Ah-ha!" Shaneequa exclaimed, peeling back the oval rug, pulling out a joint. "Look what the Easter Bunny left this time. She lifted the telephone receiver—another one under there; the bongos on the floor—another one there. They were planted everywhere. All you needed was a good imagination and a decent reach.

The smoke curled through the air, crawling hypnotically to every corner of the room. Samantha was already going under. A woman named Nefertiti was blowing circles around Abdul's nose while he sucked them lustfully from the air. Shaneequa tried to play it off but couldn't. "Damn him," she said. Another couple was kissing in the corner, blowing hot pleasure into each other's mouths. General, another brother, was entranced, his feet moving in sync with some unheard martial song.

I had never seen so much smoke before in my life. "They could throw us under the jail," I said.

"They can't come in here—no search warrant."

"Besides," Mo interjected, "we already in jail—Brother Malcolm hipped us to that." The smoke wasn't just filling the room by then. It was filling my head.

"Turtle Island is Alcatraz," Mo said. "America is a prison and we all do life!" The smoke was trapped in the top of his chest. He passed his joint to General, and then with his next comments ventured into some grounds that were off-limits to General. "Course, some of us get let out on probation to run the prisons in the 'Nam."

General responded as if he had been ambushed. "Man, don't say that word. Vietnam is to be forgotten." He spoke coarsely, exhaling as little as possible. He held in the remaining smoke until his eyes watered and his lungs gave way to uncontrollable coughing. When he finished, he looked at Mo. "This some good shit, man."

Then he looked at me. "Don't worry, momma—they ain't coming in here. No can do." With a heavy sigh, he reached under his khaki jacket and placed his thirty-eight revolver on the table. "Don't mean nothing." My heart pulsated wildly inside me. I could almost smell the metal of the gun. With the force of his disturbed state of mind behind that gun, any one of us could be dead in the next second.

"No can do," he said again. "They ain't that crazy, the bastards—besides, we ain't doing nothing but forgetting." he said. I knew he was the one who was crazy. "Hey, momma, ain't you got something to forget?" he asked. Absolutely crazy.

"Is that damn gun loaded?" I asked Shaneequa.

"Hell, Estella, everything up in here is loaded—including all us niggers," she said, focusing in on Abdul, who was coming toward her from across the room. Before I could say any more, they were dancing, wrapping themselves around one another.

"Man, everybody's got something to forget," Mo said, answering General's question.

"Shaneequa, can I talk with you," I whispered.

"Yeah," she said, "just be cool a minute. You said you was down with it."

The mood was changing right in front of me, to say nothing of what was happening inside of me. I tried to play it off. To look normal. To act as if this levitation was my usual mode of mobility. The couple on the couch were getting up to go into the back room. Two horny-looking guys were staring straight at me and rubbing the inside of their thighs to the music. This place is damn crazy, I was thinking. How am I going to get the hell out of Dodge City with the door double-sealed that way?

"Hey, brother, who let that bitch in here?" General asked Mo, pointing straight at my uneasiness.

Mo lied. "Man, I don't know, but find out and put both the muthafuckas out of here."

"Wait now, brother. I don't have to be no bitch and none of those other names either."

General cursed his way across the floor, murmuring, "Yeah . . . same shit . . . and all of them brothers don't have to be dead either . . . doctors, warriors, generals . . . everybody over 120 IQ they put on the front line."

Mo's eyes never left me. He took another draw and held it in for a long time. Then he exhaled it slowly, in my face.

"Don't," I said, fanning the smoke away with an attitude.

"I don't—believe—this—shit," he mumbled to himself, attempting to caress my hand. "Dance with me."

"No, I just want to leave. I want out, brother."

"Why the hell did you come?" he asked, biting down hard on his lip. He had floated into some fretful zone, his eyes red now and raw looking.

What was I supposed to say—"Because Shaneequa invited me? Because you brothers were supposed to be conscious and able to create with me something powerful and bright? Because I was looking for real-life images of a particular beauty that I had only imagined up till now?" I felt stupid and intimidated. I had no idea how I was going to get back to the dorm or even through the door for that matter, and I didn't know what might befall me. Oh, Mary, I thought, your child done messed up now.

"Why the hell did you come?" he repeated. "How the fuck you plan on getting out of here without breaking the seal—on the door, that is."

Everybody started laughing.

"Wait a minute, wait. I bet," he said screwing his coarseness into my privacy, "I just bet you ain't never given it up before."

"This is dumb," I said.

"Naw, you ain't never had none!"

The laughter exploded this time even louder than before. But I was determined not to be the fool even though I felt quite foolish.

"Look," I said as if asking him to read my lips, "even if I was to give it up to you, I still wouldn't be getting none!"

"Wo-o-o!" the crowd cried out. The women fell over laughing like the justice itself had been some kind of dope. Even Shaneequa came up for air.

"I'm out of here, Shaneequa," I said, knowing retaliation was sure. I snatched the door and all hell raged forth.

Nefertiti pounced from the floor, the horny leg-rubbers snatched back the door, and General grabbed hold of my sweater with both hands, yelling, "Damn double agent!"

"Brother, I'm leaving." He snatched my sweater almost all the way out of my hand. "No can do! You in here now—don't go breaking the fucking order!"

"I don't want to break the order, that's why I'm out of here."

"A fucking smart aleck. That's what you are. An insubordinate fucking smart aleck!" he said, keeping an eye on his gun and yanking the sweater completely out of my hand. That's when Mo said, "Brother, stop it. Come on General, man. Let the sister go." He nodded without even giving up a glance, and I stepped out the door.

"And you," he said to Shaneequa, "get your ass on out of here too for bringing her up in here."

Shaneequa came out behind me and we started walking home. Samantha stayed.

"Child, you sure messed that up," Shaneequa said. "That was my best chance."

I didn't say anything.

"I don't blame Samantha for staying. You done blown it, child, for me."

"Go on back then, Shaneequa. I was on my own anyway."

"Yeah. Nothing from nothing leave nothing."

We walked the rest of the way in silence, the late fall wind forcing some of the lingering foolishness from our lungs and filling mine with both resolve and fear of what I had to do. Upon reaching the dorm, I said to her, "Shaneequa, I've seen enough. Tennessee State isn't for me."

"Estella, it's just a matter of getting used to it. Give it time."

"I like you, Shaneequa. And I like Samantha, too, but this isn't what I'm looking for."

"Exactly what are you looking for?" she asked, and I was speechless, thinking of Mo, General, Samantha, and all that had happened since I had come.

"I don't know."

"Girl, they'll look at you like you crazy if you go back home."

"I know," I said, not knowing how to deal with that either.

"They'll think you just couldn't hack it!"

"I know, I know, but I've got to go."

And so I did.

It took me three days before I called Momma. It took practically that long to get the reefer from the contact high out of my system. I thought of Houston, getting ready to fly helicopters in Korea, and I wished that he would be spared some of the brokenness that I had witnessed here. And I thought of William, who refused to go to Vietnam, and I realized that none of us would ever truly be untouched by the anguish of this war.

Even though I could not articulate it at that time, when I looked into the eyes of these men who had deliberately participated in death rituals for their own survival, I entered spheres where our connectedness had already been disrupted. In place of the openness, there was a distinct vulnerability and aggressiveness about these men who had experienced that severance.

But I had seen something else in the faces of Shaneequa, Mo, Abdul, and General that had allowed me, even in those brief moments, to see things from their point of view. I found my own vision challenged and enlarged. General was more than a shell-shocked soldier who had lost his grip on reality. Even in his insanity he understood that the gifted are practically always targeted for some kind of annihilation. And Mo was not simply a roaming hustler sugar-daddy pimp. He was also a genius at understanding the territory of the human psyche. He had roamed its fields and valleys enough to know its seasons and anticipate some kind of harvest, even if he was not entitled to it. And Shaneequa was not just a good-time girl ready to turn in her religion, reason, and rights for the attentions of a man. She was also a young woman, testing the boundaries and borders of life and wanting it all.

I had come to this territory having charted my way through the dream of wanting to find sustenance for my evolving Black woman self that I was consciously trying to construct. I found other seekers who were at various points in the formation of their own identities.

While the exposure had challenged my parochial thinking of culture and womanhood, it had also affirmed my freedom to choose the kind of Black woman I sought to become; one who would risk entering new landscapes—whether jungle, garden, war zone of racial confrontation, or militant's camp—and who would leave them if necessary for the achievement and clarity of the vision of who I am in the world. As I rode the train returning home, my memories began to merge like fatigues into the Kentucky foliage, blending into an unknown dawn.

5

TELL MARY NOT TO WEEP

The first three weeks after returning home from Tennessee State, I felt drained and distant. Momma understood. "Child, don't worry about it. You did well," she said. Betty Jo invited me to Western's homecoming, but that wasn't exciting. Neither was the invitation from others at Eastern. What I needed was a good night's sleep, a deep blue velvet, and a moon-spun dream.

A silvery web glistened in space, its symmetrical lines like some ancient temple. A familiar yet unidentified voice was weaving the words from Ecclesiastes: "There is an appointed time for everything. And a time for every affair under the heavens. A time to be born, and a time to die. A time to plant and a time to harvest." There was no particular vibration from any singular verse. Each bore the same significance as the next in an even poetic timber. "A time to kill, and a time to heal."

It was more than a filtering of unresolved fears. It wasn't about Houston's new orders to Korea. Nor did it feel as if it had anything to do with Sandy, who was getting married in two days. Although I remembered every part the next morning, I couldn't catch the meaning. I pulled out the Bible to see the words. "A time to tear down, and a time to build. A time to weep and a time to laugh." Could it be that life just pulled one big joke on me, I murmured, and I have yet to find it funny? One day I'm off to be a revolutionary, and the next I'm back home with no direction for my life save for working day after monotonous day for an insurance company, stamping "Paid" and writing meaningless dates in little "time to weep" burial books. "That could very well be your problem," I said aloud.

"What?" Joe asked, passing my bedroom.

"Nothing," I said. "It's just the dream again. I can't tell if it's a time to seek or a time to leave it alone."

He reached for the Bible. "Stella, I don't know why you left college, really, but maybe they should've written in here 'time to quit,' too. I don't blame you. I want to quit myself."

What was he talking about? He was a high school sophomore, barely fifteen. He had spent a year in the seminary but had come home to attend Flaget Catholic High School.

"I'm sick of it," he said. "I got cut from JV basketball and here Spivey's bringing home trophies. I ain't even got my biology book. Somebody stole it. One of the white boys, they said, when I found it thrown in the toilet. I wish I could go to Central or Shawnee, or one of the other public schools. I sure don't blame you, Stella."

I told him that I hadn't *quit* quit, that I was going to take classes in January some place in the city. No, I wasn't going to forever stamp payment books for people waiting to die. Plus he wouldn't be able to do even what I was doing if he quit.

He wasn't going for it. "I'll get another paper route. I'll paint pictures and sell them." I looked at him doubtfully. "I never get to do nothing. You know how Momma is. Guy, right next door, gets to go out all the time and I'm breaking to get in by eight. Guy's got it made." This was not the time to tell him that Guy was just another teenager trying to make his way in the world—insecure, bluffing, taking on generally more than he could chew for a sixteen-year-old with two false teeth already, his front ones having been knocked out in some duel before we met him. He spent a lot of time cracking on a lot of people. About the only thing he couldn't get away with with Spivey and Joe was making fun of Uncle Gene's lisp and playing the dozens on Momma.

"Guy's father don't put him through all that just to get out of the house! Momma doesn't understand," Joe said, trying to keep the tears from coming. "She ain't no man. She ain't no Daddy."

Joe was only four when Daddy died. He couldn't even remember him. And though he could remember Uncle Gene, our godfather who loved him like a son, he wouldn't allow himself to do that for long. Uncle Gene had driven us to the seminary that year to help him get settled, and he took us back again for the first visitor's weekend. Visiting Joe at the seminary was nothing like visiting Adolph and William, who seemed to have the air of young monsignors. Upon seeing us, Joe lost all holy reserve and crawled happily from one family member to another in pure abandon. He and Spivey, who had been like twins, punched and wrestled, headlocked and hugged till they were outright stupidly blushing. Our Aunts Evelyn and Edith, my father's sisters, who had come down to be with us from Chicago, laughed that day like I had never seen them laugh. It must have conjured up for them memories of my father's own childhood, the glowing faces of these two children too free to pretend. When it was over and it was time to leave, Uncle Gene got so choked up seeing Joe crying there in his rearview mirror that he crashed into the tree behind us. He turned off the ignition, and we jumped out and began grabbing on to Joe all over again. He was embarrassed by now. Momma told him that he didn't have to stay, that the door to home swings both ways.

"I know, Momma. It's just that I think God wants me to finish out this year."

"God is mighty understanding, son," Uncle Gene said. "You can come home with us now if you want to." Joe was already straightening himself up, tucking his tenderness behind a show of toughness, and saying to Uncle Gene that they would surely go fishing when he did come back home. Spivey turned away and walked to the car as if he had lost his best friend.

"You left school," Joe said, looking straight at me. "And I'm leaving, too, soon as I hit sixteen!" I was speechless. "Some people say you quit 'cause you couldn't hang." I bristled but kept listening. "But I know it takes guts to pull out of something you're already in. I quit the seminary and that took guts, just like your quitting must've taken some, too."

"And a little fear," I admitted for the first time.

"It don't matter. I sure the heck don't blame you. Everybody don't have to go to school. Daddy didn't. Jesus didn't either," he continued. "Mr. Ferman might let me work the store.

"Mr. Ferman?"

"Yeah, " he answered. "You got to get your own hustle when you a Black man."

When Joe came home at the end of the year, so many things had changed. He felt left behind, not having started with the freshman class. Everywhere he went, he was in Spivey's great shadow. Worst of all, Uncle Gene had died a few months earlier from kidney failure.

Uncle Gene had come into our lives many years earlier. "While we were sleeping in the womb" is what he used to say. He was best man at Momma and Daddy's wedding and was Adolph's godfather in baptism. A few years after Daddy died, Momma asked him to become more active in our lives. So he would come by the house every day after work, bringing his signature peanut brittle, the laughter that was the punch line to all his jokes, and a compassion that would rival any saint's.

It had happened so quickly, his passing. One day he was walking into our house saying, "I just love the smell of chili," and the next he was lying propped up on a steel gray hospital bed, speaking of death.

The doctor left his room after telling him as carefully as one could that he was going to die, and soon. Momma and Molly and Tom Elery, friends of the family, had stood outside the room.

Uncle Gene called out to them. "Come in . . . come on in." Momma and Molly tried to bring in a sympathetic warmth, but he cooled it. "I don't mind that I am dying. I do mind that the stranger with the white pad in his pocket had to be the one to tell me. I thought we were closer than that!"

Momma tried to explain that the doctor felt he should be the one to tell him. Uncle Gene looked at them sadly, then pulled himself up. After staring out the window, dealing with the stark reality, he turned again to them.

"All right," he said. "All right. But it's not time to start mourning yet."

He came home and threw the grandest going-away party ever. He invited all his friends and spent the evening talking, reminiscing, eating his favorite potluck of chicken, yams, potato salad, and greens, with chili as dessert.

Uncle Gene called me to his corner, saying how nice it was to see everybody together that way. He had a definite connection to a lot of people and was always connecting one to another—passing on some story gotten from one of the ladies whose houses he painted, or some truth learned from his friend Thomas Merton at Gethsemane or from some brother sharing his path on the street.

I was kneeling next to him, suddenly barely able to look into his eyes.

"You know one of the good parts?" he said in a weakened voice. "I mean, besides not having to feel bad all the time?"

I shook my head, trying to hold back the tears. "No, tell me."

"I get to see my mother again," he whispered. "I haven't seen her in so long."

"This is getting spooky," Spivey said, leaning beside me, not knowing how else to handle it. "I'm going before the white horse comes. I'm leaving." I tried to reach out to touch Spivey's hand but he pulled away. "Tell Momma I left with Jim." He turned to Uncle Gene, saying, "Bye, now. See you later."

Uncle Gene went to God a month later on the very day he had asked to go. Joe had missed the gathering. He had missed holding Uncle Gene's hand, missed the blessing he had given, and, except for coming the day of the funeral, had missed saying good-bye again.

I didn't know what to say to Joe, but I knew I couldn't mention Uncle Gene yet—though I remembered now clearly that the voice in the dream was his. I began telling Joe how special he was despite what was happening at school. That he was the only one in the family not named after somebody, which gave him a kind of distinction. That Momma and Daddy had designed it that way. No, she hadn't told me that, but I knew she had raised him in honor of Daddy. I didn't know where this was coming from—overhearing too many conversations perhaps—but I went on because the words kept winding themselves out now from some blue familiar space. Surely I must have dreamed this telling, or maybe I was even dreaming it now. Joe listened to every word until his eyes were filled to overflowing. He tried wiping his tears away, but now they would not stop coming. They salted his whole face until he finally gave in completely, weeping uncontrollably until the laughter broke loose.

"I think, I got it," he said, gasping for breath. "I understand, I'll be all right. In other words, I'm tough."

"Yeah," I said, hugging him. Then he turned to leave. I sat there now, thinking only of Uncle Gene. That evening, Joe bought me down a pen-and-ink drawing on poster paper.

"For you," he said. I looked, and my dream was transformed into a beautiful web of words taken from Ecclesiastes.

"This is wonderful," I said, grabbing him around the neck.

"Dance on these lines," he laughed, wrestling free from me. Then hearing Guy, he left to get the door. As I moved from line to line on the drawing, I gained clearer remembrance and unexpected release. The words themselves and Joe's response to them in this form gave me a larger context of the soul's journey than the narrowing space of my return to Louisville.

"You still ain't got it?" he asked, coming back into the room.

"Yeah, it really works this way," I said. "What's up with Guy?"

"Nothing," he answered, but that wasn't true. Ever since the first day he had moved there, something was always up with him. I remember when he had first moved here, he'd said, "This is mine," as he stripped the blossoms from the dogwood tree. "My daddy bought it."

That evening, he told Spivey and Joe that a friend was driving as far as Covington, and there was plenty of room for them. He promised they would be back before eight. They were both anxious to go at first, but then Spivey changed his mind. "I don't know, man," he said. "I'm staying."

"Come on, Spivey," Joe insisted. "Nobody's gonna even know we're gone. We gonna run by Cincinnati, man."

Spivey started to go. He knew how much Joe wanted to see the seminary again and check out old friends—especially Marc, his white friend who had visited us for a weekend the previous summer—as many of my brothers' seminarian friends had before, but he had ended up staying a whole month. Every time he called home to his parents, he would beg to stay longer. After the fourth week, they demanded that he catch the next bus straight for home or they'd be after him the next morning.

"Naw," Spivey said. "I'm staying. Tell Whitey I said, 'C-o-o-el, man.'" Then he came on back in the house. His basketball team was leaving town for a tournament at eight that evening and he would relax till then.

That night, Momma was the only one home, because I had gone over to Sandy's to spend the night and help with preparations for her wedding the next day, Saturday. Around eight o'clock Momma began looking for Joe. His curfew came and went. She called Gert to see if he had stopped over and had forgotten to call. No Joe. In another half hour, she called next door to see if he was hanging out there. Nobody knew a thing. In a hour, Momma had started calling around to his friends' homes. Then Gert came over. She and Momma got in the car and went to the basketball court. Nobody there had seen him. Then down to the West End Theater. They came back home, unknowing, frustrated.

I can imagine now the concerns and fears that might have gone through her head. All the things that might happen to a Black boy of fifteen at two o'clock in the morning in Kentucky.

"Lord, have mercy," Momma whispered again.

She pulled back the curtains. Mr. Eaton was coming home. In a couple of minutes he would be knocking at the door, looking for Guy. There had not been a word.

Gert got the Yellow Pages and began calling local hospitals. There were no reports of anyone fitting either of their descriptions.

Momma sat clutching her rosary beads. "This just isn't like him," she said. "When he gets here, he'd better have a good explanation."

Then, somewhere between the whispered "Hail Mary" and "Our Father, who art in heaven," Momma closed her eyes and there stood Uncle Gene. She said that he had been there, right there before her. He had looked at her, straight in her eyes, and told her gently, gently, that he had come for Joe. "He'll be with us now," Uncle Gene said. "Don't worry, he'll be all right."

It could have been a dream, a doze-off-deep-in-the-meantime dream, but, even so, it had happened. She finished her prayers determining not to mention it at all to Gert, surely not with so much still in the air, surely not her baby boy.

She looked at the smiling photographs propped on her desk and the newspapers left from Joe's morning delivery. Then she went to answer the phone.

There had been an accident. Joe was in critical condition at Good Samaritan Hospital, a few miles outside of Covington. Momma called over to Sandy's and asked Mrs. Reed not to tell me until after the wedding. She didn't want me to come. Within a short while, she and Gert were at the hospital. They walked in to see him together.

Momma told me later that it was horrible. There were tubes running everywhere and his skull was fractured. He was unconscious. There was no way she could take it. She walked out the door, fell to her knees, crumpling. Adolph, who had just turned the corner, caught her and helped her into the waiting room. The priest came and anointed Joe. Momma got up to go back in. She held his hand, talked to him. She told him that she loved him, that everything would be all right. She asked him if he heard her; if he heard her, then squeeze her hand; if he wanted her to pray with him like they used to, then squeeze her hand. There was, she said, the slightest pressure. Holy Mary, Mother of God, pray for us sinners now and at the hour of our death. Amen.

The day after Sandy's wedding, Mrs. Reed came home from the early Sunday Mass and stood before me with Sandy and said that my baby brother Joe was dead.

What was she talking about? Joe dead? I had just left him. Joe. We had played out a dream together. Dance on these lines.

"Estella, baby, did you hear me?"

"Yes," I said. "Where is my mother?"

I left their house, running toward mine, Sandy trailing behind me. I cut through the park, past the swings and the courts, down the sidewalk and into the heaving wind. It was all full of chants, sacred songs we had learned as children. It was the requiem, too heavy and too much for Joe, even with children singing it, oh Jesus, even with little angel voices.

Spivey came home and ran upstairs and stood there, wasted. There was Joe's bed just like he had left it, the Ban-Lon shirt he had changed before going, the basketball they had played with together forever, the stations on the wall he had helped paint bleeding through the coat of white paint that covered them. Within moments Spivey was back downstairs, bolting for the door. Gert tried to embrace him, but he jerked away.

"Let him go," Momma said. He ran to Mrs. Reed's and stayed there.

Guy had made it through the accident without much physical harm, but he was still in shock. When I went outside, he came to me clutching something in his hand. Joe's shoe. He looked up at me helplessly, and we wept together.

Then I went back into the house and I stood there looking again at the picture that Joe had drawn. I was glad that he'd had the opportunity to see the pattern in his own life. Most of us spend our lives just redrawing our pattern to gain greater clarity, to make our purpose more distinct. Joe was fortunate enough to have achieved that vision and was called out of the wilderness.

On the morning of the funeral, Momma gathered my brothers and me together in her room to pray. I remember her hands, how hot they were, how utterly soothing. Then we opened the door and went on to the church. I sat in the car, in between Spivey and Houston. Momma sat in between Adolph and William in the seat in front of us. Lyda had flown Aunt Scottie and her children back from California. The church was already packed. Many of the boys from Flaget High came, as did the children from Immaculate Heart School. They sang beautifully. Father Simon came back to give the sermon. As he walked to the pulpit, I thought of his passion and resurrection plays that had already prepared us for this moment—for the hope and belief that our souls joined with the divine spirit of Jesus will find their fullest joy.

Father Simon looked deeply into all of our eyes as he talked of love, of searching, of innocence and sainthood. He told us that sometimes God calls us because we've done all that we were supposed to do. And other times God calls us to keep our innocence from being tainted by the world. But all the time God calls us to stand before the throne and to give account for all our seasons in the Ecclesiastical web of life.

6

OVER MY HEAD I HEAR
MUSIC IN THE AIR

Princeton called from Washington. It was good to hear his voice. He told me that Houston was coming home on furlough after Christmas and asked if he could come with him.

"Tell me it's too soon—" he said, but I cut him off.

"Actually, it's right on time. It'll be great to finally see you again."

And see him I did, as he came to the door, warm, tall, and as beguilingly handsome as the night we met. He kissed my cheek and I introduced him to the family. He talked with Momma and Spivey while Gert followed me into the kitchen to get drinks. "Child, you got yourself some fine-looking man there," she said.

"She just met him, Gertrude," Lyda said, all the while peeking into the front room.

"Look, honey!" Gert said punching me. "He even got ol' Aunt Lyda's eyes bucking! You know he's something!"

"That girl's crazy," Lyda said, fanning her away. "Is he nice? That's the question."

"Do you think," Gert said, "Stella Marie would be silly enough to bring somebody by here to meet us if he wasn't nice?"

"He's wonderful, Lyda. Come and meet him."

Princeton charmed them. There's no other way to put it. He charmed them and practically everyone else that visit. We spent the weekend partying with Houston, Spivey, and friends, but mostly laughing and talking and gazing into each other's eyes. There were other whole worlds there, where time had no relevance, and voices other than our own were too distant to even hear. We could talk about anything—my disappointment with Tennessee State, memories of Joe, hungering for justice, being in love. The weekend ended before we would ever have let it go, and in a short time he was going back to the base.

Princeton came again and again to see me, each time more tender than before. He'd catch the military plane down to Louisville almost every three weeks, and when he ran out of leave it was horrible. Late-night calls ended too soon and letters wouldn't come fast enough. I wrote more frequently. He would answer, begging me to keep missing him until he could come again. Once he sent a sheet of paper with only the word "love" written on it. This had to be the most incredible man in the world, I thought.

When we finally saw each other again in late March, we fled through the airport into each other's embrace. Then at the movies, in the streets, wherever we went, all we could do was touch—his fingertips along the line of my lips, the heat of his breath moving literally through my skin. We would laugh at nothing, argue over trivial matters only to be drawn into each other's closeness again so we could kiss again, taste again, the intoxicating sweetness.

Young, crazy, craving lovers, we sat once in the late winter's park kissing, hugging, touching, and missing till we sweated like summer in July, till the clothes we were wearing felt like a lie, till everything inside of us wanted to cry.

Trembling, I held his desperate hands, pulled him up from the bench. Heaven knows, we needed to walk.

"They got benches over there, too, Estella," he said laughing.

I had never known feelings like these before. From beneath newly discovered wings the soul of me was pulsating, compelling, practically yelling, "Come on, woman, and fly!"

"I do respect you," Princeton said, sipping kisses from my lips. "I don't know what more I could do to show you."

"Well," I said, taking it a step further than I ever had before. "It would be different if—"

"If what?" he prodded.

"If we were married," I whispered. "We're not even engaged."

I had promised myself, my momma, and all three of my aunts that I would do this right. I believed Princeton when he said that he was committed, but aside from the way he kissed and held me so sweetly, I had no other evidence. Actually, there were moments when that was about enough for me, but then it would have broken Momma's heart, and she had already been through enough. And as much as Aunt Gert teased me, she had taken her time to break down in her own way what she thought about premarital sex.

"Child, I'm gonna tell you. It can get mighty hot down in the old Sahara. You thank God that you are normal and able to feel that way. But when you out with somebody that you really love, like I was with your Uncle Herman, you need more strength to maintain. All I can tell you is to keep your head clear and say your three Hail Marys before going out with him. That, dear Stella, will get you over. You know, when I went to Chicago and lived at the women's residence, I had a couple of boyfriends," she said. "And child, some of them will tell you anything. One of them told me that if he didn't do it, he would get sick! Imagine that. All I'm saying is, they say all kinds of things. That same man told me that he had talked to my priest and that he had told him that in our case it was all right. I let him go. I knew he was lying then. Child, if he cares that much for you, let him marry you first."

Princeton looked at me. "If we were married?" he said, clearing his throat. "Baby, listen to me. You are all I ever wanted. Part of me is already married to you."

I kept listening, wanting for him to make plenty good sense, but he ended up repeating his words as if listening to himself say them.

"Part of me is already married to you."

"What part?" I asked, half jokingly.

He laughed. I guess I did too, a little. It took away some of the tension.

"Look. I'm flying down here every chance I get for the past I don't know how many months. I'm staying right at your house. Your family likes me. I like them. And I love you," he said, slipping his arms back around me.

"Yeah," I said, cuddling more into the serious detour he had just taken. "You do know a lot about my family. Tell me more about yours."

"What's to tell? Mom lives in Memphis and my dad in Chicago."

"What's your mom like?"

"Mom is Mom," he said, seeing what he would add to it. "She's a lot like your mother. And some like you, I think."

"What about your father?"

"That's another story. I haven't seen him for a long time. But I know that they felt like this once, and ran off and got married. His people didn't like it and got the marriage annulled. It's all back then now. Water under the bridge."

"I hear you," I said.

He left for Washington that evening with me whispering into his ear, "Give some thought to what we talked about, OK?"

"I will."

It was another two months before I saw him again. Neither of us brought the subject up directly. We hemmed and hawed, talked about our tomorrows, but never quite said anything.

Meanwhile everybody was curious. Momma's statements had progressed from "Be sweet, now" to "Remember, Estella, to keep yourself to yourself, now."

Spivey would signify whenever he knew Princeton was coming by imitating Momma's tone precisely but substituting certain words: "Keep your little fast ass to yourself, girl!"

"You need help," I'd tell him.

Gert, of course, didn't mince words.

"He keeps running down here every time we look up. Houston's over there in Korea. What's the man's intentions?"

"Stella's just nineteen," Lyda interjected. "She just started school." The argument between them was already on. "I'm just asking what's the man's intentions? The girl's in love. And you can't just ignore love."

"You do if it means getting your education."

"I ain't never finished school and I did just fine," Gert said.

"That's you," Lyda said, "you and Herman. A man ain't always gonna stand beside you."

Princeton would, though. I was sure of it. What we had was just incredible. Momma chimed in with, "I know I was sure blessed to have my degree after your daddy died. I could make my own way. Ain't nothing like getting your education."

I didn't respond, but I could have told them that the courses I had enrolled in did not include one Black writer or one authentic Black thought. It was nothing like the Black collegiality that Momma had experienced at Municipal College or what Lyda had at Kentucky State. It was just more of what I had learned at Rosary. The Black students were few and the white ones spoke to us only when necessary or if we were willing, as some Blacks were, to be their clown or mascot. These terms of entry were unacceptable to me. I simply went because the job at the insurance company was putting my mind to sleep. Anyway, the people in the registrar's office had actually told Momma in my presence that I wasn't college material, by their standards, that I should start out with twelve credits to see what happened.

I had met a girl from Vietnam at school named Sue. Her eyes were so much like Joe's that it amazed me. All the people she loved were a world away, she told me. She wanted to make something of her life, she said. We lunched together, and her enthusiasm for the opportunities of this nation fascinated me.

"I cannot understand why more of your people do not take advantage of them," she said, now sounding more like the people who had sponsored her stay than her own self.

"You just got here," I said. "We've been here over three hundred years. The only reason any of them would want to take us into their homes would be to clean them up. Besides, you're leaving after a while. It's not like you've come to stay or set up household next door." She nodded. "There's just so much excitement I can generate behind this. My momma is a teacher and two of my aunts are, too. They still have to deal with injustice. Education used to be the path, but I'm not so sure it is for me anymore." I laughed a little. "Not unless they come a little more clean about Columbus in that classroom and admit that Thomas Jefferson, bless his soul, had a proclivity for the enslaved clitoris." Sue frowned at first and then looked shocked, not knowing at all just how much she looked now like Gert.

I may never finish school, I thought. Lyda and Gert can argue about that till the cows come home. I was going on with my life.

Now Sandy joined in the conversation about Princeton that Gert, Lyda, and Momma had continued. She leaned in close and whispered, "Girl, every time I see him he's somewhere with his legs crossed. What's up?"

"Oh hush, Sandy."

"I'm serious. I know the subject's come up by now."

"Yeah. But you know I can't just do it."

"Well, no. You know I ain't saying that. I'm saying it looks like somebody ought to be saying something. I mean, aside from Aunt Gert in there. I know she's told you the Blessed Mother and the bride story by now?"

I shook my head. Gert had obviously told Sandy the same tale during her courtship with Wayne. It seems there was this woman who lived on the same floor with Gert and Scottie at a women's residence in Chicago when Scottie was working on her master's. The woman was wild as a cootie bug, Gert said, just a-jumping from bed to bed, just a-testing and a-tasting, and when she finally found who it was that she wanted, she had the biggest wedding that you have ever seen. She had a train on her dress that was still stretching to the back door of the church after she reached the altar. She had a veil on her face like nothing had ever been lifted or even peeped at. Under that gown she had a corset on her butt that was two sizes too small to help take some of the roll out of her experience. Anyway, when it came time to present her bouquet as offering in front of the Blessed Mother's statue, the flowers just up and wilted.

The details on how long this took were never clear, but the fact is that they did wilt and that the folk on her floor were all saying that without the blessing, the marriage would last no longer than the honeymoon.

I looked seriously at Sandy and said, "Oh no, dear sister, the plot thickens. When Aunt Gert told me the story, she made it sound like our Blessed Mother had changed the poor flowers into cockle grass! I suppose that's better than kicking them from the vase!"

We laughed, but I knew that this was serious, that marriage was sacred, that the two becoming one is no less than a miracle performed by souls who stay open lovingly to one another regardless, and that the power I had within me to procreate was a tremendous one, with responsibilities I could not even fathom then.

"I love him, Sandy, I do."

I continued going to classes and studying for exams, but the real exam was inside. I wished Princeton and I could spend more time together, yet when we did, it only intensified the situation. I hated being away from him and dreamed of going up to Washington as his wife.

He had about nine months before being discharged, and afterward he wanted to play basketball for the University of Missouri. I wanted him to do whatever he wanted, but I wasn't going to visit him on campus forever. It was too hard, this long-distance waiting. It didn't make sense. Marriage made sense. I thought about finances for a second, and about building on the courses I was already taking for another second. But mostly when I thought about the future, I thought about going to him.

The next time Princeton got a leave, he let it go, saying he had gotten an extra job. His late-night phone calls shortened, too. No, nothing was wrong, he'd say. It was that his money was tight. His letters became less frequent. He said that with the job there was less time to write.

I didn't understand. He had never acted like this before. Maybe I had been too forward, I thought, but then suddenly changed my mind. The moves we were making were forward. Why not put form to it? If this was what I wanted for the rest of my life, why not make provisions for it?

"What?" Sandy said. "You proposed to him?"

"No, I didn't propose. I just brought up the subject."

"You didn't even make it sound like it was his idea?"

"Sandy, he's not stupid."

"That ain't got much to do with nothing. Write that in one of those poems. When you dealing with a man, you got to at least give something up."

"I do. I give him my love."

"Right."

I went back and read his last letter again. It sounded so clipped: "... coming ... soon ... want to talk about something face to face. Even though we have been apart for longer than we've ever been, the time was necessary," he wrote. "We need to look very seriously at our relationship. We'll talk more soon. See you Friday after next, same time. Love, Princeton."

I kept seeing us laughing, touching. I could almost feel him there. "Baby, we gotta do something," he whispered.

Oh, God, I prayed, please help me. I know I don't know anything about being a wife but, please, just teach me."

I made a novena—saying the rosary and going to Mass for nine days. When Princeton visited, we came into each other's arms more cautiously, kissed curiously, then went silently to the car.

"It's so good to see you," he said.

"I'm glad you came," I replied. "I've missed you."

"Have you?" he asked, searching my eyes looking for who knows what.

"Yeah. I did. Did you get the leaves that I sent?"

"Yeah. I got them. From our tree, right?"

"Yeah. The new ones haven't come on yet. This one was red from the winter. Late spring, you know."

"I know," he said. "It was still nice to get it. And the lipstick kiss on the paper too, Estella, that was nice," he chuckled, "real nice."

"Thanks."

We rode listening to the radio. I don't know how it happened but Aretha's song came on, "If Ever I Would Leave You." The words seemed to have turned on themselves, like maybe the singer was looking for a time to leave as opposed to denying there could ever come a time to leave. I found that I didn't know what the song meant.

"Estella?"

"Yeah?"

"Do you know," he said, smiling now, "that you had me kissing that paper?"

We looked at each other, and the shadow disappeared.

"You had my 'gotta-have-you-baby' in-love behind laying up in the barracks, kissing a piece of paper 'cause your lip prints were on it. You know I'm in trouble."

We couldn't stop laughing.

"I had to think for a second. Now suppose one of my main men came in and checked this? I'd be looking pretty bad. 'Man, I seen Walls lay-ing in the bed kissing paper kisses!'" he said. "You know I got it bad."

I told him how I had tried once to lick the glue where his tongue had been.

"You definitely got a problem," he said, shaking his head and going into the house.

"I been thinking a lot about us lately," he said after he had gotten set-tled. "And I really want us to be together. Now, I know how you feel about all that."

"Yes."

"And I've been thinking a lot about that, too."

"Uh-huh."

"And I'm trying to give you the respect that is due you."

"I know."

"No, Estella. Let me finish."

"OK."

"I can't see living my life without you. And I've decided, baby, that I'm asking you, Estella, will you marry me?"

"Yes," I said joyously, "yes, yes. And I will love you, Princeton, forever."

We talked with Momma and started planning right away. At first we said the engagement would last till Houston came back from Korea. And then we said six months and then, nah, we dropped down to three. We had one season to plan, to get the gown designed and the bridesmaids' dresses made, to save the deposit for our apartment and one month's rent, to get the invitations printed, and then there was the cake, the photographer, and money for the first month's food. I would have to get a job when I got there. And the plane tickets back to D.C.—the moon and the honey.

"Are you sure three months is long enough?" Momma asked. "You know there are those pre-Cana conferences at church." And she had wanted me to get in at least another semester of college. I promised her I would find a college somewhere.

"The question is, is three months short enough?" Sandy teased.

So we went to the priest and he told us all about marriage, and the Church being the bride of Christ, and one of the speakers at the conference talked to the men about foreplay and Princeton said he didn't need no more lessons on that. They talked to us about commitment and lifetime giving and taking, and then an older couple told about hardships, horrors, and hope after marriage. They warned us that it was not always going to be easy and sometimes we might not even touch. I could not imagine that. When I told Princeton about that meeting, which he could not make, he laughed. "You laying there next to me and we not doing it? Where do they get these people?"

I kept going to the meetings between going to Molly's to get fitted for my dress and making arrangements for the reception. A doctor came to the third meeting and told us about female and male anatomy. He also told us a tale about a man and a woman who married and the next morning the wife came out to join the husband at the table and said to him, "Honey, you were really great last night." First he kissed her and then he slapped her, saying, "The kiss was for the compliment and the slap was for knowing the difference." The doctor told us that we should bring forth children, but he also told us about the rhythm method of birth control based on your body temperature.

"Your body is always hot. How the heck would you know the difference?" Princeton said.

"They've got special thermometers, plus, you know, I can almost always feel when I'm fertile."

"I bet you can," he said.

I still had to buy Princeton's ring. He wanted a yellow gold band. I could not find one simple enough, precious enough. How did he ever find mine? And we still had to find somebody who could play Schubert's "Ave Maria" the way it's supposed to be played when I presented my bouquet to our Blessed Mother.

In time, thank God, we were ready. The morning of the wedding, I moved joyfully down the aisle, looking through the veil into Princeton's loving eyes. This was the man I would spend the rest of my life with, the man whose children I would bear, the man I would love and love and love.

"Do you take this woman to be your lawfully wedded wife . . ." And I disappeared—became wind—seeped into him—floated around through his thoughts—his being—then slipped back out through his breath.

"I do."

Now there was no veil between us. Our lips touched and we became flame—burning into smokeless blues that cast no shadows. And the fire spread across the altar—our touches scorching the six bridesmaids, our embracing emblazing our mommas and the whole community of lovers. We were a myriad of mounting fires that were really only one fire. And the aura of our light was more light—more endless light divine.

"I love you."

And a shower of sun rays cooled us as we ran outside the church and rice sprinkled down around us and danced through the flowers of my white lace dress. And inside the reception room were gifts of celebration: crystal—china—silver—matter that has moved from formlessness to form—all given in celebration of bonded love.

"When I saw it, I thought of you—"

"I really hope you like it."

And a special keepsake gift: a wishbone—wrapped in a ribbon. Momma's friend Mrs. Ray had saved it from Momma's wedding shower over twenty-five years ago. The women at her shower had touched it with wisdom and good wishes intended to extend to her progeny. I held it close and showed it to Princeton. His fingertips brushed my smile.

"Beautiful smile . . . beautiful . . ."

"Would you look this way, please . . ."

And suddenly I became a rolling teardrop that rippled into a river that spread into an ocean of joy and I was deeper than I had ever been before— and all the lovers began swimming in our dreams and then the camera flashed and I blinked back, and Princeton and I stood smiling into each other and standing before a three-tiered wedding cake.

"May I have another piece of cake so I can put it under my pillow? I want to dream of my future husband."

I watched as Betty Jo, my maid of honor, carefully wrapped the slice of charmed cake in a napkin with "Princeton and Estella Walls" inscribed in gold. Mrs. Reed took the knife from me after the first two slices.

"It's your wedding day, honey, I'll do this."

Joy had me. All the happiness of my nineteen birthdays came wheeling into one. Princeton and I embraced again, then we slipped away.

7

MY LORD, WHAT A MORNING!

We spent our Washington nights in bliss and our days waiting for night to come again. I'd rush home from work, prepare surprise meals, light scented candles, then wait anxiously for the sound of his key in the lock. I'd open the door wearing a negligee that could just about drop itself to the floor, and the smothered chicken and rolls all glazed with butter would go forgotten. The maple nut ice cream or whatever flavor he had would simply go melting in the bag. Marriage was wonderful.

We'd wake around midnight ravished with hunger, and stuff ourselves with food and each other's stories, while trying to keep our laughter from filtering through the walls. About a month after moving to Washington, D.C., Princeton came home with news that couldn't wait. He was getting an early discharge—in fact, three months earlier than anticipated. That meant we could leave Andrews Air Force Base in just two months and he could start college in January as opposed to the following semester.

Princeton's version of how short a time we had to wait took the form of a hundred shorts after that. "I'm really short," he'd say, and I'd respond, "How short are you?"

"I'm so short that if I were to sit on a street corner curb, with my legs dangling down, my feet still wouldn't touch the ground!"

"That's short!" I'd say, and then continue, "He's so short that when the doorbell rings he's got to jump up seven feet just to look out the peephole."

"Baby, that's not short. That's squat!"

That night after dinner, I gave him a preview of his final day in service.

"It's just a little production," I said, seductively. "Call it a short." Dressed in his Air Force uniform, I stepped out from behind the bedroom door and began to striptease for him.

"Take it off. Take it off. Take it a-l-l off," I sang, undoing the already loosely fitting clothes, then sliding them across his sweet, mounting pleasure, until, in a most incredible turnabout, layers of illusions began giving way in his eyes, exposing the beauty of his soul glistening before me, the vision entrancing me even in my dreams.

"I didn't know you were that crazy," Princeton said to me the next morning over black coffee.

"Before last night," I said in a whisper, "I didn't know you at all."

Within weeks we were packing to go to Columbia, Missouri, where we would stay in married students' housing. We moved in next door to a Jewish couple. The husband, John, was studying law and the wife, Becky, was expecting a baby. We laughed when they told us that the last two couples who lived in our apartment had a baby within twelve months after they moved in. We told them that we both intended to go to school. That Princeton was on a basketball scholarship, and after a semester, I would enroll too. Becky looked at me playfully, signaling otherwise.

When our boxes were moved in and the cabinets all scrubbed down, Princeton and I blessed the apartment. I had brought holy water from home and sprinkled it generously to the corners of every room. We asked God to bless this place, to make it a fit and holy dwelling. I asked for grace for us to grow and love each other like this forever.

"I am so blessed to have you," Princeton said after we finished. "That was nice. I'm glad we did it." He looked around the room. "You know that poster your mom's friend gave us for the wedding? Let's put it where we can see it from the bed," he said, lifting it from the box.

"When did you get it framed?"

"Ah-hah," he said, then went on to read it.

A gracious wife
delights her husband,
Her thoughtfulness
puts flesh on his bones.
A gift from the Lord
is her governed speech
And her firm virtue
is of surpassing worth.
Sirach 26

We hung it on the wall, assembled the bed, turned off the lights. The next morning John and Becky told us that the last couple who lived in our apartment kept up such a ruckus that other students in the building couldn't study. Their lovemaking was so fierce on their rickety old bed that neighbors on both sides and below could hear them all night. And sometimes, John added, the poor slats just gave way and everybody in the building was laughing at them. Then one Christmas, the neighbors took up a collection and presented them with a brand new bed.

"Why is he telling us something like that?" Princeton asked.

"I think he must be trying to study."

"I think he's nosey as hell," Princeton said. "Becky's all right, but he's a jerk. The couple may not have been able to buy a bed. They may not have had the money."

"I know," I said. "I know."

I got a job working at the university pharmacy, dispensing narcotics and barbiturates to the hospital floors. I assembled them into trays to be given to the head nurses and registered their numbers in the records. I also passed out prescriptions through a window that on every first of the month framed docile, lethargic faces of housewives who came in for their legitimate fix. These were not urban women hunting for heroin or looking for a legal ride on the white horse but haggard-looking white, middle-aged farm women, depressed, disenchanted with life. Their eyes held a wretched loneliness that I could hardly bear to see. They would hand over the prescriptions without speaking, or even blinking. Some of their drugs were serious antidepressants. How did they come to this? What had happened to them? The pharmacists knew most of them by sight. "We don't treat them, Estella. We just fill the prescriptions."

At other times, some of the students came in needing medication for muscle strain, colds, or whatever. I was glad to see them, glad to be working at the university, and proud that my husband was among them.

"I'm doing this for us," he'd say, and on my most tired day, that would be enough to make me smile. And yet I wished that I was already one of them, with enough money earned to enroll in classes. I would read Princeton's books at night and help him write his papers. I'd type them and quiz him for exams. And I'd do most of the household chores to make sure he'd be free to do well in his studies. I understood that we were building a future together, that he was going to be a first-rate journalist. Sometimes while he studied, I'd write poems about love, about the women's faces I saw at the pharmacy or about one day getting a phone so we wouldn't have to use the corner booth. Princeton was diligent. We were determined that basketball was going to be a means toward education, and education a means toward our future.

"Maybe if they had hobbies—" I told Princeton, referring to the faces in the pharmacy.

"Ain't that much hobby in the world," he said. "Not if they are as bad as you say."

"Well, maybe if they talked to each other," I said.

"They live in isolation," he said, "too far apart."

I looked out the window at the couples moving here and there. White, almost all of them, busy unto themselves. Jake and Terri, a Black couple, lived in the building across the street. He played football and the pros were already talking to him. I was glad they were there. Even though we saw them only occasionally, and Terri sometimes would call Jake out for spending more time with his white female tutor than he did with her, their presence was comforting.

"Do you know what that fool John said to me?" Princeton asked. "Something stupid about Blacks on sports scholarships rather than academic ones. You know he was cracking, don't you? Hell, like I don't have to maintain my B average. Like whites are the only ones who have to think, or can for that matter."

"John is out of a Cracker Jack box. Some folk have a problem recognizing intelligence outside of white skin. And when they do, they're scared of it. You've got a good mind, honey."

"Yeah," he said, letting it pass, "because look, come here, I've got an idea right now."

He kissed me tenderly.

"How's that?"

"Brilliant," I said, but neither of us could take it further. We were just too wrung out even to move. Then, for no apparent reason, Princeton looked up and said, "Speaking of brilliant, where did you put the study sheet we were doing last night? It's the last midterm. I can't afford to mess up. It's nowhere to be found. Coach is on me like white on rice. Last thing I need is more pressure."

"Here," I said, handing it to him, passing over his insensitive comment.

"You've got to get more organized. The sheet is mixed in with the bills, your poems, the newspapers. You've got to get it together, Estella."

I was tired and knew he must have been too, but I couldn't help thinking, "Girl, you definitely married yourself a prince, a royal pain in the ass."

I sorted the papers. The week had been a blur, so cluttered that I felt as if I were the one taking the exams. Three nights straight spent typing his papers past midnight. And him coming in from practice too pooped to even talk. And now, instead of celebrating, we were revving up for—what?

"I mean, other women do it," he said.

"Other women like who?"

"Come on, Estella. It's just a matter of organization."

What had I been doing all week? I mean aside from cooking, typing, supporting, and holding down a full-time job?

"I'm tired," I said, restraining myself. "I'm really tired. I'll get the rest of this straightened out in the morning."

Then we both turned to each other and said at the same time, "Look, baby—" and "Yeah." We agreed even without words that rest was what we needed. We flopped back against the sofa and into the Smokey Robinson tune on the box. We were just beginning to let down when the doorbell rang. It was Becky wanting to know if we wanted to come over to watch the game.

"No, thank you," I said. "We're laying low tonight."

"Tell John I said we can catch the one tomorrow," Princeton said, and Becky turned sadly and left.

"What's the matter with her?"

"Just lonely."

"How do you know?"

"I just do."

Seconds later, John was back.

"Come on, Princeton Walls. It's the weekend. Two dollars says Nebraska wins."

Princeton and I looked at each other. We smiled and went on over.

Before the evening was over, we had argued over the game, finished two batches of buttered popcorn, and gone on to debate politics.

Dr. Spock's baby book was amid several in a neat pile on the coffee table. The debate began with that, I think. Becky had read it several times. It had made sense to her. But John was swearing off it because Spock had gone on to counsel and aid draft evaders. Even though Princeton had been in the service, it was not like either of us was in love with the war. It was clear to us by then that Dr. King had been right in his stand against the war.

Princeton and John went at it, as usual, with me joining in on the side. Occasionally I would insert Becky's opinion, shared with me earlier, because she rarely did it for herself.

"Like Becky was saying, it makes sense that somebody dealing in babies and generations would be concerned about war on the planet."

"Becky said that?" John asked.

"Yeah, she did."

"Well," she said, almost squeaking, "I was just thinking—"

"Maybe that was the problem," John said laughing, pulling her into his side like he had just found his lost rib. And to my surprise Princeton looked at me as if I had laid an egg. When Becky snuggled beneath John on the couch, everybody seemed less anxious.

"So," John was saying, "you're telling me you think the students at Harvard were right protesting the ties to the military industrial complex? How can you say that?"

I got up with Becky to help with snacks. Certainly the attempt by the men to exclude us from the political discussion was nothing new to me. I had seen its variations since the earlier times of being shut out of the jungle by my brothers, and this one here was no less annoying.

"Are you OK?" I asked Becky.

"Yeah, sure." she said. "It's just that sometimes I miss my mother. Maybe that's also why I bought the book, you know."

"Yeah.

"I mean, she's coming after the baby's born. John's mother is coming too."

"That'll be good."

"You know, all while I was growing up, we read together. We'd discuss books that we'd buy almost every other week. We did other things, too," she said, smiling a little and rubbing her hands around the baby. "We'd fight like any mother and daughter, but we did all kinds of things together—reading was what I liked most."

As she spoke, the life came back to her face. This was what had first attracted me: her happiness when engaging ideas. That, along with the extraordinary respect she had for the written word. Most of my friends would listen to me read my poetry. If they were touched by the reading, then the feat was accomplished. Handing the script to them would be like handing somebody a musical score. Whether they could read the music or not didn't matter. It still had to be played by me if it was to be fully shared. Becky, however, would inevitably go beyond my reading, almost demanding to see the evidence of what was spoken, the inscription itself.

"My mother bought novels all the time, and poetry, and how-to books," she said. She was almost laughing. "She would look up a question in the book and stay there until she found an answer. I miss her."

"Why don't you go home to see her?"

Her face dulled again.

"No, I can't do that. I have to be with John. He's my husband."

"Well, why don't both of you go together?"

"No, you don't understand. I have to be here with him."

"I hear you," I said.

We went back into the front room. Our husbands continued talking about Nixon, then Cambodia, then all the Blacks newly elected to congress, including Edward Brooke and Shirley Chisholm. John looked at me finally and said, "Now that's the system working at its best, don't you think?"

"Three hundred years and letting three people enter is the best equality the system's got to offer?" I thought. Maybe we should have stayed in Washington at Resurrection City with the Poor People's Campaign and camped out in tents rather than come here to school.

Becky offered me popcorn. I took it and chewed down hard.

"You people have to admit it," John repeated, "that's the system working at its finest."

You people, I thought. He was looking for Becky to back him up now since nobody else did. But a strange thing happened this time. It wasn't as dynamic as John Carlos and Tommie Smith raising clenched fists in the Black Power salute at the Olympics that year, but it was powerful. That extended silence—that use of it as something other than acquiescence—was provocative. Seconds later, words came.

"John," she said, "I can't understand you."

She did everything but say, "Remember? I can't think."

Within a short while, of course, we were leaving to go home and closing the door on the thick anger behind us. But some of it was still with us, emanating even through our silent hot breath against the Missouri cold as we huddled to press the key into the lock.

"Estella, what did you say to that woman?"

"I didn't say anything."

"No, something went down in the kitchen, and I think you had something to do with it."

"Princeton, I didn't say anything."

"I hope not. Jews have their own way of doing things. And I sure can't say it's all bad."

"What? The way he talks down to her? This is not a particularly Jewish trait. It's universal."

"She's his woman, Estella. They understand each other."

"You're siding with John, all of a sudden? With Mr. Future Prosecuting Attorney of the World?"

"See, you're taking this way out of proportion."

"How am I supposed to take it?"

"You're talking that Black crap all the time. The sisters in the struggle, as you call it, would know how to take it. They know about backing their man! You take the parts you want to deal with out of this Black stuff, don't you?"

"What's that supposed to mean? I take what I think are the best parts, yeah!"

"You can't go around trying to change everything, Estella!"

We could hear John and Becky through the walls. They were arguing, too. I could hear him hushing her, telling her to lower her voice, telling her that I, Estella, was completely out of control and that Princeton was a decent enough guy but, after all, a damn jock! "Two niggers! Don't you ever side with anybody against me. Ever."

"And there you have it, ladies and gentlemen of the jury! You're defending someone who doesn't even respect you," I said, hating the crack in my voice, in our togetherness. Our first argument.

"I'm not defending that know-it-all son of a bitch! And I don't need respect from him. I need it from you, damn it."

I stormed into the bedroom. He had cursed at me. We had lifted our voices against each other and the world was falling apart. And none of it made sense. I mean, we barely knew these people. We barely knew them, and yet our disagreement over them had set in bold relief something playing just under the surface of our developing life together—something that we'd have to deal with. But I didn't know where to start. I fell across the bed, crying.

It was frightening to feel the hurt and anger from the same source that had given such joy. He was sitting in there thinking heaven knows what, and I surely wasn't going to ask. After all, he was the one who had cursed at me, had sided with Perry Mason, and was now signifying by playing Aretha Franklin's "respect when you get home." Give me a break. I blew my nose.

He turned the record over. Drums mostly. "You always talking that Black shit," he repeated.

Please. I'll tell you what's crap. We don't even have a phone. I'd rather have gotten a phone for two months than those stupid-looking matching winter jackets any day. Huh, every night complaining about Coach. Of course Coach is talking down to you! What did you expect? For him to say, "Mr. Walls, would you please run three laps around the gym?" Baby, wake up and smell the stinkweed! "Coach" might even mean "massa" for all I know. If I look up the word "massa" in the dictionary, they might even have a picture of Coach up underneath it. Tell him to give you some respect, not me! I'm the one who loves you, you jackass!

Footsteps. Shadow of his feet on the other side of the bedroom door. Maybe he's come to his senses. Huh—he leaves. Probably has to use the toilet and too proud to come in. Oh, pee on yourself! He's sitting back down on the couch. I'm gonna take up my own collection from the neighbors for a new one that doesn't squeak! What? He's leaving. That's OK. Go on. I'm sick of fighting with you. The needle's stuck on the record. "Other women do it." How insensitive! That's all they have to do, too, crawl up underneath their husband's haunches. He's back. The record's off. He's sitting back down on the squeaky couch. Wait. Nothing.

I hold his pillow. No comfort. It makes me nauseous, so I throw it to the foot of the bed. I get up to go the bathroom, look at my face in the mirror. Pitiful, so pitiful that I sit on the toilet and cry.

Oh God. He's saying I disrespected him. What did I do? Strange how anger diminishes everything to an unpromising present. "I like that purple gown on you, baby." Huh, next time I'm going to get some pajamas with feet in them! Make it so you can't touch none of me. I go back into the bedroom, stretch out on the bed.

I don't know, maybe I should cool it. Maybe he does need more respect here since he's not getting it in the world. Maybe with all the pressure, we should just work this out. We really should be celebrating. All the papers and exams are almost over. I can find a better way to tell him how I feel.

I got up to go to the door. When I turned the handle, I discovered that he was turning the outside knob simultaneously.

"Princeton, baby, listen. Let's me and you talk, OK?"

We did and afterward promised never again to go to sleep angry and have the sun come up on all that red. We wanted peace again, yes, joy again.

The next morning, we also made a kind of peace with Becky and John. We were on our way out to a restaurant. I didn't want to eat. I didn't even want to smell food, but I wanted to be with Princeton. We saw them in the parking lot, and for the first time John seemed at a loss for words. He stumbled over phrases till the comments finally ironed themselves out, mostly about the weather. And Becky was acting a little like him.

"How are you?" she asked.

"I'm fine," I said, smiling. "Your husband still owes my husband two dollars on that game."

"Yeah, man. Give me my money!"

John paid up, and Princeton reminded him that the reason Nebraska won was because it had better strategy, not simply strength—brain, not simply brawn.

"You just might have something there," John said. "You just might."

Princeton laughed and told him, "Yeah, man, I got your money!"

We all laughed. Then Princeton and I went to the restaurant with our two extra dollars to spend. When we walked in, I felt as if I had entered a cloud. The place was drenched with odors. Egg smells and bacon smells and sweat from a dozen armpits and disinfectant from the vomit-colored floor all came rushing upon me.

"Oh, God," I thought.

"What's the matter?" Princeton asked grabbing hold of me. "I think you need to sit down."

"I think I need to leave."

"Estella, what's the matter?"

"Wait!" I said rushing to the bathroom. I barely made it. When I had finished spitting up, I rinsed my mouth and came out.

"It's all that butter from last night," Princeton said. "Are you OK now?"

"Yeah, I am," I said, but inside my head was swimming.

How was I going to tell him that there was life growing inside me? A little person made of our love, our life together. On the way to the car my fingers were counting the days, the weeks to see how far along I was, counting, trying to figure the time of conception, the time of birth. Princeton kept talking. I kept losing count. The idea was too big to hold anything else in my head. I was a mother, a mother, for how long now? I was trying to figure how many months I could work up to the baby's birth.

"What?" I said to Princeton. I didn't know what he was talking about. Oh—the final exam. "It'll be fine." If my count was right, I could make it through the summer and a little into the fall. I put my hand over my stomach, smiled a little, then felt the stinging in my eyes. How would he react? We had talked about waiting at least a year. I decided to wait until I got home to tell him. No, I'd wait till after the exam.

When I told him, he was dumbfounded. He didn't say anything at first, then he smiled strangely. "A baby? You mean I'm going to be a father? You've got a baby in there?"

"Yeah," I said. "I do."

"How do you know? You been to the doctor?"

"I went last week during my lunch break. The doctor laughed and said it was too soon to tell and to come back in a couple of weeks."

"So you really don't know, then."

"Yes, I do."

"Why? Because you felt like throwing up in the restaurant?"

"No. Because remember that night of nights that you told me, 'I don't care if we make triplets, baby, let's chance it'?"

"That wasn't me. It was you!" he said, laughing. "And don't say it too loud. Three really would be more than we could afford."

We laughed and began dreaming. Was it a boy or a beautiful girl? A girl would be smart, have my eyes and his mouth. A boy would be handsome and have everything like Princeton but his feet. He was sensitive about them. In fact, he slept in his socks our first night together, not wanting me to see them. It reminded him too much of the hard times, the year his shoes were too small and his family couldn't afford better and his toes stayed crammed. I didn't care. They were part of who he was and I loved them.

"Definitely your eyebrows," I said.

"And definitely not your nose," he said, laughing.

"Not my nose?" I said incredulously. "That's the cutest thing on me!"

"Oh, no, it's not."

"Yeah, right."

We found that the baby was due the last day of September.

We shared the news with family.

"Ah, this is great," Momma said. We had slipped into calling her Lu then. I think Spivey was the one who started that. Spivey got on the phone and said, "You sure didn't waste any time!"

Gert was so happy that she cried. Princeton's mother was over-joyed. "You mean I'm going to be a grandmother? I'm too young to be a grandmother," she teased.

"Well, seven or eight months from now, you'll be older," Princeton said. "And there will be a little one in the world calling you Granny!"

"Oh, my goodness," she said. "We'll have to come up with something better than that."

"OK then, Gramps," he said.

We wrote the rest of the family but knew that the news would be old by the time they got it. We got a letter two days later from William, who had obtained his conscientious objector's status and was working in California, and one letter from Houston just two weeks after I had written him, even though it came all the way from Vietnam. That in itself was worthy of celebration from everybody, since his leaving had been such an upsetting event for the family and his letters were so sporadic. Wouldn't it be incredible if Houston wrote he could make it back to the States by the time the baby was due? Adolph left a message for us to name the baby after him, whether a girl or a boy, because he was becoming a priest and was not going to be having children. Can you imagine a little girl named Giles Adolph? or Gilsetta Adolpha?

During the next week I got weaker. It was the nausea. Every time I would eat or smell something, it would simply come up. Nothing stayed down, not toast, not even crackers. I kept going to work and losing weight instead of gaining. I turned the pages of Becky's books and understood that some of this was normal, that it was supposed to subside. But it never did. It just got worse. The doctors gave me medication for nausea and it came up too. There was a little knot where the baby was supposed to be and the rest of me began to look skeletal. Then the dizziness came and continued to worsen, and on the way into work one Friday, I grabbed hold of the railing going into the building, grabbed hold of the outstretched hands reaching out to help me, and felt the daylight fading to night. Breathing deeply, my head held low, I fought to stay conscious and barely managed.

The doctor checked my vital signs, took a blood count, and refused to let me go home. I leaned up from the gurney and bent over the vomit bowl again. It was horrible. Morning sickness had gone into the afternoon and evening. I was throwing up seven to eleven times a day and gagging all in between. I couldn't stop the spit from forming in my mouth. Whole boxes of tissues gone in a day. Then more endless gagging. I had forced myself out of the house that morning, hoping that the routine would help pull me out of it, that the fresh air would enliven me, but it did everything but that.

"You're dehydrated, Mrs. Walls. The liquid in your body is low. Your blood test shows you are anemic and you are certainly malnourished. No, you may not go home."

"I didn't say go home—I said no phone."

I couldn't speak, not really. At any rate, no one understood what I was saying. Between my trying to hold my head up and trying to form words through the vomit and spit, nobody knew what I was saying.

I stayed in the hospital for almost three weeks. No medication worked. They kept saying that after the first trimester the vomiting would stop, but there was no sign of it letting up. On my second or maybe third day there, I lifted my head from the pillow and, above the overwhelming loneliness of the room, heard Momma's footsteps coming down the hall. "Lu!" I said, knowing that sound was hers, that the rhythm of those heels ringing high above the others was definitely my momma's. She was coming sure and real any second through that door to see, yes, God, about me. Her perfume and deep momma scent was practically there in the room. Even the spit under my tongue stopped its pumping for that exact moment.

"Hello, sweetie," she said.

I hugged her and wept. I buried my face in her bosom and could feel the cold still on her, and the welcome warmth underneath. It was so comforting. I was a little girl again, safe in her arms. Then I was reaching again for the dish.

"There, there," she said.

"They've brought in a team of doctors, Momma. Nothing works."

I didn't want to start complaining. I was so glad to see her. Princeton was, too, because my sickness was also wearing on him. He came evenings and said little. Not that I could talk, but I did miss seeing him.

They fed me glucose through my veins, gave me medication for my kidneys and bladder. They were concerned about anemia but couldn't give me iron. There was no way it would stay down.

Momma stayed until I was discharged. The vomiting hadn't subsided, but I could hold my head up and walk a bit. She cooked a meal that evening and the smell of the broiling meat in the pan made me think of hell. The blood smell seeped through the walls, under the door, and into my lungs and stomach, where it literally wrung out my intestines.

My poor baby. I was afraid the violence would force my baby out.

That night I tried eating cracker crumbs, hoping that if I placed the crumbs on my tongue they would melt and slip in and my stomach wouldn't know and would let them stay. No such thing. There was as much eruption from the crumbs as from the spoonfuls. This was crazy, Princeton said. So I tried eating slowly, regular mouthfuls, and hoped that some of it would stay down. Maybe.

Momma left, and in a couple of weeks I was back in the hospital, this time staying only a week. The doctors were humbled by their inability to do any real healing, and I was humbled by my dependence upon others to meet my basic needs. I was able to keep the vomit down to only four or five times a day and gained a few pounds of weight at last. By the end of the semester, Princeton and I left to spend the summer in Louisville. Princeton could get a summer job there that paid more, and I could absorb the energy of home.

I knew that more than blood was being transmitted from me to my baby. I wanted my rhythms right for the baby to feel positive and safe and not come out on an adrenaline high or a depression low. Going there helped. I was close to family and closer to the sun, with which I felt a special affinity by then. It could have stemmed from my being away from it so long during my hospital stay, but it probably had more to do with my conceiving during the time of the sun's own "conception." I rejoiced with it as my baby, who I felt must have been a girl, took form, kicked, and jammed, oftentimes waking me in the night to join her celebration.

At summer's end, Princeton went back to Missouri. I begged him to stay and have Coach register him, but he had to go. The baby wasn't due for three weeks, he said, so he left.

That night, despite my efforts to strain into some logical consciousness of time, the remaining three weeks seemed forever. I still had images of lying almost lifeless with plastic veins extended from a bottle into my flesh. I could still hear the voices floating around from five months ago.

"If you don't get better, you're going to lose the baby. At this point, Mrs. Walls, to be perfectly honest, our major concern is you."

But even then I knew our baby was going to be fine. Even when I had to go back into the hospital, I felt that even through my suffering my baby was being blessed. Even when my ankles began to swell and dehydration caused my body to moult, and I vomited blood, I kept on fighting. I knew that my baby was going to make it.

"All I'm asking, Mary, is that she make it here a little earlier." I pulled the covers over my head and cried.

And the spirit voice inside that usually speaks only in quiet began struggling through my noises. "God doesn't ask more of you than you got strength enough to handle."

Who wanted to hear that? I wasn't asking for strength. I was asking to have my baby. So I got loud and drowned out the spirit voice. "Ask and it shall be given you," I cried. "I want my baby to be born now."

And my words became a midnight moan that slipped into the silences of dawn, and I could feel the dreams for that night still seeping out through my tears. Soon enough, I heard the sun humming, but still I didn't move. I lay listening to my heartbeat against the bedsprings.

I could hear the clock, bringing me back from my timelessness. It was at least two hours before anybody else in the house would awaken. The house was exceptionally full. I was not the only one beginning a new cycle. William had not yet begun his classes in California and was taking a vacation. Adolph, who was changing to the archdiocese of San Diego, had stopped by on his way to a retreat at Gethsemane. Houston was home on leave, having finally been discharged from his tour in Vietnam.

Two nights before Princeton left, we had all gone to the airport to celebrate Houston home. We waited at the ramp for him to round the corner. It had been a year, and now God was restoring our brother to us. Two dozen people must have passed before we finally saw him, moving sluggishly, frail body sunken inside the dark green khakis. We were sucked into his drain momentarily, then broke out applauding, waving, screaming his name, "Houston! Houston! Houston!" over and over in joyous triumph, releasing a healing even before we touched. Momma, Gert, and Lyda enfolded him, and I squeezed in among them, the baby inside leaping in excitement.

"What happened to you?" he said, reaching out to touch my roundness.

"Jet lag," I said, managing a laugh, then wiping my mouth of the saliva. "Flying too high, I suppose."

"Don't get too close to her, man. She spits," Spivey said. "Man, it's good to see you."

Our cycles of renewal had coincided. It was the first time in a long time that we had been together, feeling the newness. Spivey was starting his first year at Western Kentucky University on a track and field scholarship. And Momma was celebrating her first-month anniversary, having married Walker, a kind man with a hefty humor. He had changed our mother's life and allowed us to see her in a whole new light.

I lay in the quiet, trying not to move, managing to keep the nausea down. I stuffed my rosaries under the pillow.

"Little one," I whispered, "what kind of dance is that you're doing all night? Butt over here. Leg over there. There you go again. That's better. Your daddy's gone but he'll be back. Those others are all your uncles. The one we're making so much fuss over is your uncle Houston. I told you, he introduced me and your daddy. He's a little quiet now, but give him time, huh, the doctor's talking three more weeks before I see you, little sweetie. But you know by now, don't you, that he ain't the boss. Almighty God is. When you get here, remember that, OK?"

The churning started. A pocket of spit was filling one side of my mouth. Another day in the life of Elephant Woman, I sighed. I opened my eyes, rolled out of the bed, and headed for the bathroom. And that's when the miracle happened.

There from between my legs was the warm welcomed stream—the footwash on Holy Thursday again—hot summer rains making me dance again—endless tears of salvation bathing my face with a holy forgetfulness of everything save for only that which is needed for birth. My hands trembled upward and the joy screamed out of me.

"Momma! Wake up! The baby's coming!"

My gown was clinging to my trembling legs. From the adjacent room Momma threw back her covers.

"Sit down, sweetie," she said, spinning in circles. "You don't want the baby to fall out on its head." I ran to the bathroom and lifted up my gown. "Thank you, Jesus!"

I stood in the middle of the tub just listening as the fluids danced out of me.

"I'm getting a towel. Tell her to sit down," I heard Momma's voice whir through the hall.

I stepped out of my gown and wrapped the blue robe around me. Houston knocked at the door to ask if it hurt and I was stuck in a grin so big that he grabbed my hand and we danced like children around the hallway.

"Lord, bless them," Momma said, and Houston yelled up the stairs to William.

"Come on down here, man. We uncles! The gates is wide open and we coming through!" Then he turned to me, laughing: "I don't believe I made it home in time for all this." Lyda appeared there, beaming—somebody had run next door to get her.

"Take us to the hospital, Walker," Momma said. "There's no way I can drive."

"I don't want to go to the hospital right away, not now anyway," I said, my laughter trailing off a bit, but just as quickly the lilt was back. "I've got to get in touch with Princeton!" I must have believed he could blink himself here from five hundred miles away, simply because he said he would.

"I'll send him a telegram," William said.

"Girl, you better come on here and go."

"Carolyn, Betty Jo's cousin, said that they made her walk around forever when she came in early. I can walk around right here." I wanted to put off going to that hospital for as long as I could. Momma's face fell into disbelief.

"It'll be all right," Walker said, consoling her.

"Why are you doing this?" Momma asked.

"Because, Momma, I don't even hurt. You said yourself that the first baby has plenty of warning."

She and Walker looked at the water traces smeared across my ashy feet.

"I think you've had your share of time and warning," Walker chuckled.

"But my feet—I need a bath." Surely this had to be done. I settled for a quick wash-up, and we piled into two cars and rushed down to the emergency room at General Hospital.

They rushed me through the halls in a wheelchair. Momma wouldn't let me walk. Streaks of white uniforms came flashing by and corners of walls came spinning around, and red arrows came rushing down the floor, pointing to "Emergency."

"Guess why she's here?" William said from behind me. The nurse looked up from her desk and down at my roundness, then greeted the expectant tribe. Gert worked in the emergency room and she came flying down the hall.

Within moments I was readied for examination. I held on tight to the sheets, shivering as much from anticipation as from the cold. My eyes wandered across the room and landed on the illustration of the uterus on the wall. I focused on a chart of dilation measurements . . . a quarter of an inch . . . a half inch . . . and on to full dilation. I wondered how far along I was. I wanted Princeton to be with me—maybe not in the delivery room, but close enough for me to hear him call our child "the most beautiful baby," or better still to hear his utter speechlessness.

My doctor came in and asked me the usual questions. I had to wipe my mouth clean of spit before almost every answer.

"Any pains yet?"

"Yes, sort of like menstrual cramps."

"When did they start?"

My mouth ballooned out with spit and I reached for a tissue. "My baby's going to be all right, isn't she?" I wanted to hear him say it.

"Yes, he/she's going to be all right," he chuckled. "He/she's just fine."

"I'm glad." It didn't matter whether it was a girl or a boy. The nurses came in and moved me to another room.

"May I see my mother?" I asked. I wanted her to come in and do something—hug me, maybe, or rattle off an African proverb like "Children are the reward of life." She came looking a lot more relaxed than she had at first. "Did you try to reach Princeton again? He should be there now." He would have to turn right around and come all the way back.

Momma nodded, then began to unhinge my earrings and slip off my wedding rings.

"I'll hold on to these for you," she said. I stared at her for a moment.

"Momma?" I whispered. "Momma . . ."

I wanted her to say something—something that would keep the joy and wonder there but take away a little of the scare. And if there's such a thing as an heirloom smile, I think she gave it to me—the one Grandma must have given her years ago.

"Momma," she whispered back.

8

GOD'S GONNA TROUBLE THE WATER

Having Patrice for a daughter made me new. I looked into her eyes and my own vision expanded. I touched her hands and felt strength come into my own. She moved through her first year, grabbing on to our smiles, laughing at anything that moved, talking about Sunlight, her doll, and pointing to her daddy's face on television.

We had gone back to Missouri after her birth, but Princeton's scholarship hadn't increased and my job simply wasn't enough, so we came back to Louisville, found an apartment in the West End, and began looking for jobs. I found one working as a secretary. Princeton had gone for interviews at various businesses, but he hadn't gotten any offers. I suggested that he try one of the local television stations since that had been his interest in school. The riots of the sixties had made the need for Black reporters more obvious, but he was reluctant to do so, having had only two years of college. "It doesn't matter," I said, reminding him of the reading I had given on one of the talk shows. I knew there was a big difference between performing a poem and seeking a job there, but for heaven's sakes, it was 1970.

"You see those ashes down on Twenty-eighth Street?" I asked. "Do you think the brothers who did that are going to seriously talk to reporters about why? What would the reporter say? 'Excuse me, could we get a quick shot of these flames in the background while you explain why you're doing this?' The media can't afford to get caught off guard again. They need Black reporters, I'm telling you. They may not know it till they see you, but they're not exactly dumb. Besides, something good ought to come from all that." I kept ironing his coat while Patrice grabbed hold of his tie and babbled.

"She said, 'You'll be a hit, Daddy!'" I said, laughing, and he indulged the possibility through her.

"Yeah, 'NBC news!'" he said. "I heard her!"

"Tell him, sweetheart, that the man interviewing him probably won't have his degree either," I said to Patrice.

"Yeah, but he's white," Princeton said.

"Yeah, but he's not the boss," I reminded him.

"Yeah, but nobody's rioting now."

"Huh. I can solve that problem."

"You're nuts."

"Nuts!" Patrice said clapping her hands, falling back on her behind.

"I don't want to just be a Black reporter."

"What else you gonna be?" I asked, thinking of Langston Hughes's "The Negro and the Racial Mountain." "Look at this," I said, pulling the piece down from a shelf. "Langston's talking about a man who said he wanted to be a poet, not a Negro poet: 'We younger Negro artists who create now intend to express our individual dark-skinned selves without fear or shame. If white people are pleased we are glad. If they are not, it doesn't matter. We know we are beautiful. And ugly too. The tom-tom cries and the tom-tom laughs.'"

Patrice fell out laughing. "Tom-tom laughs, tom-tom laughs."

But Princeton didn't laugh.

"Estella, you know what I mean. I want to be a reporter. Not a Black reporter. Not a white reporter. Just a reporter."

"I hear you."

"Journalism is not art. It's journalism. Who. What. When. Where. How."

"Princeton," I said, "relax. It's going to be all right. You're handsome. You're articulate. You've taken courses at one of the top journalism schools in the nation. You wrote pieces for the newsletter in the service. You're good, what more can I say?"

"G-o-o-d." Patrice was clapping her hands and losing her balance again.

"When is she going to walk?"

"When we stop picking her up so much!" I said.

Princeton got the job, and after a while he learned that, just as I suspected, many of his co-workers did not have a degree either. They had been trained for their positions and were willing under the circumstances to train him, too. There was no such opportunity in my field of interest; I wanted to become an English teacher. So I set out to continue my education by transferring to the University of Louisville and arranging a three-day schedule so I could substitute-teach on the other two days. Afterward, I would pick up Treecie, as we had started calling Patrice, and begin work all over again with her. She was growing fast and telling everyone, from her sitter to strangers at stoplights, all of our business. At six o'clock, I would stop whatever we were doing and sit her on my lap to watch the news. At first, Princeton was behind the scenes, filming or gathering information for stories. But one day he called saying that he was finally going to be on-screen, standing in front of the camera, holding that mike in his own Black hand and changing the face of journalism in Kentucky. My fingers were shaking like crazy as I dialed to tell Lu.

One other older Black man had done it before in the heat of the riots, but he was mostly on radio now. I could still remember just a few years earlier when seeing ourselves on the set was cause for urgent announcement: "There's a Black person on TV! Come on down, hurry!" Feet would scurry from all directions and we'd stand breathlessly before the TV, our eyes transfixed. It would be the Supremes on "The Ed Sullivan Show" or the Jackson Five or, later, Martin Luther King, Jr., and then Carl Stokes talking about the inner city's challenge. If it had been one of the buffoon or mammy roles presented in the white movies, we wouldn't have even bothered to call. Nowadays mostly, the Black images appeared as part of the coverage on crime. Seeing Princeton standing there was indeed a mighty triumph for the Black community.

We celebrated for days. All the overtime had been worth it. All the extra time spent away on Saturdays learning the workings of the profession. All the frustration of waiting and wanting, of enduring ridiculous comments from the people with whom he worked. "You're better, but you still sound Negro." He had gone for voice training, to learn to speak in another accent, a more Midwestern accent. They didn't call it that, but that's exactly what it was. The people training him at his own station couldn't hear their own Kentucky twangs, couldn't hear the wind from the Appalachian Mountains or the Mississippi Valley blowing through their own hot breath. I could hear it as they spoke on the air and at parties at our home and when we visited their homes for cocktails.

In the end, Princeton sounded more like Walter Cronkite than they did. He had cursed the mockers in that accent until he got it down. But the film would always show his sweet cinnamon complexion five shades darker than he really was. His colleagues seemed never to know how to adjust the camera. They laughed at the film and apologized.

But the Black people in the community loved him. They recognized him right away.

"Ol' Princeton Walls is making news."

"That's that colored boy on Channel Three. That's the only channel I watch now. He sho' talks nice," some of the older ones would say.

"Man, I didn't know the dude was so dark. They had my man looking like Tar Baby!"

"Child, that man is fine!"

"Uh-uh-uh."

He only worked harder. At least, that's what he told me he was doing— working hard, working late. By his second year, he'd started coming home once in a while with alcohol on his breath or his dinner already eaten. And he had started to become more irritable. He wasn't advancing the way he wanted, wasn't getting promotions or raises the way he deserved. And we seemed never to have enough money to do much more than pay bills. We were pinching pennies, but it never seemed to help.

The people who called in to the station were not those in the community who looked upon him with such pride. His editor was cutting out the meat of his stories, and they often ended up saying something other than what he saw.

"Maybe you need more space," I said. It hurt to see him going through such changes. "Maybe you should propose something different. Plant a seed or something. Remember 'On the Road with Charles Kuralt'?"

"They'd never go for that. Not coming from me," he said.

But he and Benson, his white partner, talked about it. Benson presented it to the director, and within a month they were out on the road covering the news throughout the Kentucky-Indiana region, doing feature stories on ordinary people doing extraordinary things. "WAVE Country," it was called, after the TV station name. The beginning of his third year at the station was great. He and Benson were on the road together, bringing to the greater Louisville viewing area stories of Appalachian theater groups, of folk who made their living off the river, of a couple who ran a radio station out of their basement for the local town, of folk who trained Thoroughbred horses for racing. Once they even spent a week on Muhammad Ali's mountain in Pennsylvania while he prepared and trained for his next fight.

But after a while the program was cut, and Princeton grew even more frustrated. I suggested he sign up for a couple of evening classes, and he did. In fact, we were in one class together. My schedule had changed since I had taken a part-time teaching position at Immaculate Heart of Mary School, and I had enrolled in two courses. He joined me in the second one. But he simply couldn't take it. "It's a sacrifice," I told him, "for the degree. And you learn more about how these people think." But it was useless. It felt beneath him now. Besides that, he didn't know when his schedule would change. So he quit and became more strange. He was quiet, aloof, as if he were hiding something. When he felt me looking at him, he became defensive.

"What's the matter?" I asked.

"You need to get off my case!"

Numbers scribbled on scraps of paper had appeared when he emptied his pockets.

"It's contacts for a story! Do you think I'd be so stupid as to have some woman's number flying out so you can see it?"

But it wasn't just that. His whole manner had changed. His clothes smelled different, and the last two Thursdays he hadn't come home until midnight, though he knew he'd promised to keep Treecie while I went to class. If it hadn't been for Lu, I would have missed an exam.

"Maybe you ought to see if Lu can keep her on Thursday nights. I need some time off," he said. I agreed to do it. Maybe if he were freer, things would be better.

"And to make up for missing Thursday," he said, "let me take you out this weekend." We had not been out in ages, and I welcomed the chance.

We went into Joe's Palm Room because I wanted to go there and not to some "little quiet club" on the east side, as he always preferred.

"It's just so noisy," he had said to me when I suggested Joe's. "I won't even be able to enjoy you." But I insisted. I wanted to go to where they were playing rhythm and blues, where I could see friendly faces and feel the vibes that were more my match. I had been in his white world, supporting him, for so long. When we walked into Joe's, I could have sworn that the place quieted, that the singer got a piece of the song stuck in her throat. Princeton tensed up but with feigned coolness pointed to a table in the back.

Was I paranoid or what? Had it been that long since I'd been out? Did my dress look mammy-made or something?

The waitress smiled at me and said, "Princeton Walls, how's it going?"

We ordered drinks, but suddenly I could not stand him, could not stand the way he wasn't looking at me. The betrayal was all over his face. Lies were stuck to his eyes like thick gray cataracts. There were two women, one in each corner, and from the way they were looking at me, I could tell that I was trespassing in their territory and interrupting their insidious agendas. One of them angrily locked eyes with him while the other one swept her gaze dismissively over my person. Neither of them could have been as disappointed, mad, or hurt as I was.

"Princeton, what's going on?" I said.

"I told you it was crowded," he said. "Let's go."

He threw the money for the drinks on the table. I tried to fight back my tears. I trusted him, had trusted him, and what had he done? Betrayed me. Some kind of way he had betrayed me.

"What?" he yelled in the car. "After all we've tried to build together, you're accusing me of something? Suppose I said that about your Thursday night adventures?"

"Princeton, you know that's not the same thing."

"Look, I told you, sometimes I stop in there to wind down after work. I get a couple of drinks, then come home. Big deal! This job carries all kind of frustration," he said. "People look because they see me on television. You know that, baby. Where's the trust? Your vibrations, as you call them, are not always right."

I almost felt ashamed of myself.

"I wouldn't do anything to endanger our relationship, our family," he continued. "I love you and I love Treecie. I didn't even want to bring you down to Joe's."

My impulses changed again. I didn't believe him at all. And it hurt so bad to feel that way. As if I had to choose between what he was telling me and the truth of what I was feeling inside.

A few days later he came home late again. Late, loud, and wrong. He accused me of confusing what he had told me about when he would be home. One thing led to another, and in the heat of the exchange he struck me.

I couldn't believe it. At first the blow descended upon me like some screaming bat bursting out of lower hell. I must have been in shock. I mean, nobody had ever really attacked me this way. And yet he was doing it again, shoving me into the corner, taking out his Black man frustration on me. Everything inside me began dying.

Patrice started crying.

"Oh, my God, she's awake," I thought, tearing myself from the corner, straightening my face, then rushing to see her. I stood there rubbing her back until she was asleep again. Then I locked myself in the bathroom.

"Estella," he said, "look, I'm sorry."

I leaned against the door and sank to the floor. "My God, this is crazy . . ."

"Estella, open the door. I want to talk to you, baby."

Talk to me? With what, your fist? You two-timing double-crossing low-life bastard scumbag.

What on God's good earth was I to do? I couldn't take the baby out in the cold in the middle of night—to go where? Couldn't tell Lu. Her knowing right now would only intensify everything I was feeling and everything that I knew and didn't know at this point. There would be no hiding place, no gathering time to prepare myself to look directly upon this raw, strangely pulsating wound of my life. And Lord knows, if Giles Adolph and the others knew that Princeton had beat me, they would gladly sacrifice his life. A year away from the priesthood or not, Giles Adolph Conwill would most reverently kick his sorry ass to kingdom come. And Houston, oh, God, was completely unpredictable. I couldn't allow myself to even think of his response.

"Estella, I'm sorry," Princeton said through the door. I had to figure what to do on my own. "I—I didn't mean to hurt you. I didn't, baby. Let me see you."

I could still feel where he shoved me. My face was stinging. The least he could do was drag his bully bad ass on out of the house.

"There's just been so much pressure at work," he said.

"I don't want to hear it."

"And you keep pressure on me at home . . ."

"Yeah, it's all about you."

"And I'm trying to keep our marriage together, but I keep fucking up. Estella, you didn't do nothing. It's me. I got a confession to make," he said. "Can you open the door and just listen? It'll help clear things up if we just open up and be honest, OK?"

What the heck was he talking about now? I kept the door locked and ran some bath water.

He kept apologizing, talking about there being nobody for him but me. And hadn't we come through Washington together, and all that sickness when I was pregnant with Treecie, and she made it through just fine, and hadn't he been there for me in the move back home? We had been there for each other, even when the white folks jammed him up on the job, we had made it through the crap. He said that he depended on me, he loved me, but this time he had really messed up.

"Estella, please open the door, I want to tell you this face to face."

I did, and got not only an apology but a confession of an affair. "I been with somebody and caught something, baby. And I think you ought to go to the doctor."

"What?"

"I'm sorry," he said, and turned around and left.

What kind of pain was this that I was feeling? Deeper than the blows he had just rained on me, deeper than any pain I had ever known. My heart was suddenly too small for its cavity. It was swelling fast within me, birthing some misery so wretched that I could hardly believe it. The wretchedness itself, it seemed, was now turning to eat the very heart that had given it life, first the fat and firm of it, then the beating lobes and all the secrets inside the chambers, then the tissue of our promises, the tenderness of dreams.

I was a desert. Tears would not even flow. I sat in the rocker, staring at the darkness till dawn. Why did he do this? What doctor could cure this feeling? None could even begin to.

At dawn, I took Patrice to day care. There was no sense trying to think through classes. I was changing the sheets when Princeton came in. He apologized again and told me his doctor wanted to see me. He said that many couples have a problem of infidelity and that was no reason for them to break up. That it could make them stronger, make them face their problems. Come, he said, and talk to the doctor. So I did.

The doctor was kind. He gave me medication as a precaution, although there was no evidence it was needed. He talked about open communication and caring, about the pressure of professions and the need for understanding, about the pain I must be feeling. I told him how much I loved this man, that he was who I had wanted from the first day I met him, that his dreams had become my own, that I didn't want to leave him after four years, but I just didn't know how to be with him anymore.

Princeton and I went home and began working things out. We made new promises, new plans. I prayed to God that we could grow from this, but it was hard. The trust wasn't the same. It was taking so long to get it back or have some new form of it come forth. But soon enough, I guess, I was better. At least this was out in the open. At least we weren't lying. But, oh, God, that seemed so little to settle for compared to all that we'd had. The thirst stayed inside me. The drought never subsided.

Then, just when we seemed to be changing seasons, it happened again. I was pinned between him and the bedroom wall. This time, thank God, Patrice wasn't home. Crying, I ran outside and kept running. He was mortified, concerned about the neighbors. He didn't know where I was going, so he jumped into the car to follow. After a frantic chase he caught up with me, calling out through the window to please come in and talk to him. We don't have to take our business out into the streets, he said. I swear, he told me, I'll never do it again. As God is my witness, he said. And I went back to the car thinking of the vow we had made before God, of Patrice being raised without her father, of how much I wanted him to be whole again, of how much I wanted our marriage to work. I reasoned that this wasn't Princeton. This was not the man that I had fallen in love with. I thought that if I could just cover us until the madness was over, we would live again.

I didn't know how to deal with what was happening. I knew, however, that I had to find a way. My poems helped. They'd resuscitate me until the next sadness. But the metaphors weren't enough to deal with the madness. And worse, the poems led me to cut myself off another way. When the Black Student Union asked me to do a poetry reading, I found myself not reading any of the poems that cried out for help. I couldn't turn him in that way. So I stopped sharing the poems that expressed my real feelings and eventually stopped writing them at all.

One day I went to get away from things and think at the water lily pond in Chickasaw Park, but I found that in the late fall, all that was there were leavings, upright stems where the blossoms had been. Huge, heart-shaped leaves, split down the middle, lay scattered upon the waters like so many broken hearts. I stared down at them in horror.

That spring, I went to the annual Black Family Conference held on campus and sponsored by the Pan African Studies Program. There I heard Preston Wilcox talking openly about abuse. He said that we Black women participate in our own destruction by not dealing straight up with these brothers. That we help them to destroy us if we assume the position of victim. He planned to hold a second workshop in the Black community, he said. He wanted to be able to reach more sisters who needed to hear his message. I followed him to the new site like a broken-winged bird, still longing, still remembering flight.

People talked, but nobody admitted anything about their own experiences. Lots of statements were hypothetical, or of the "I know somebody who" type. But it felt reassuring just to hear it being talked about. And one thing became clear to me: I did need to talk about it.

Eventually, I told Sandy. She wasn't surprised. She said I had changed so much since I had gotten married, that I could hardly move without Princeton, that everything seemed filtered through his eyes, that if she were to ask me how I was doing, I would have to ask him first.

I hadn't realized that I had changed that much, or that my love had become both blind and mute. It took some time before I figured out the true meaning of the Sirach quotation on the bedroom wall. The oracle was not proposing muteness but governed speech, tempered by understanding and clear expression.

Sandy told me to look at the good side. "At least he told you to get checked. Many men don't even do that," she said.

Soon, Princeton and I went in for marriage counseling. I wanted to make it work. He basically went along. He hated exposing himself and having to face another man, especially a white man, about his shortcomings. Besides, a man, he believed, was supposed to deal with his own business. We had to face all the obstacles Princeton set up before we could get down to work. Never mind that the white male counselor had his own limitation in regard to women, particularly Black women. The things that I celebrated were often perceived as problematic and vice versa, particularly questions having to do with my relationship with my mother. And he didn't understand our particular insight into America. On top of all that, this was just one more bill to be paid.

My family knew we were going for counseling, and Lu was glad. She had pulled me aside many times to tell me how much I was slipping away, but I couldn't see it. When I told her that I might have to stop school to meet our budget that semester, she offered to help with tuition. But I was so discouraged about our marriage, our budget, and the seemingly irrelevant classes in the brochure that I began to wonder if school was even worth it.

The first two days of class had been such a turnoff that I went back to register and had my major changed—to anything other than literature, I told the Black woman behind the desk, to anything other than white male writers pontificating about their privilege and arrogant professors looking down at you over horn-rimmed glasses and all but smirking at your contribution to class discussion. I didn't need discouragement at home and at school too. I had tried, every semester, to take at least one Black course as my elective to make my required literature load more tolerable. The professors in the English department seemed awfully underexposed to Black literature, and even to the ideas and needs of Black people. No Black student had finished a literature degree in anybody's recent memory. There had never been any Black teachers. And many of the white teachers seemed to never understand my hunger. Having no access to Black women writers in the literature curriculum was an incredible deprivation for me as a student and as a writer. This was a formidable obstacle. And the injury to me must have been deeper than the discrimination Princeton faced at the station. For my major, I would have to sit in literature courses that didn't even acknowledge that a Black woman had ever picked up a pen. It was frustrating. It was like looking into a telling pond and hoping to catch a glimpse of your foremothers' faces that would help reveal your own, but seeing instead yet another white man's stark reflection recalling all the endless genealogy of composed white male writers whose demeanor gave no hint of the bewilderment that must have sparked their creativity. The first time I dreamed it, I screamed. Even awake, I could still hear the water's murmurings, moans from some spiritual.

I wondered, too, about the white students. What were they possibly getting out of these classes? The burden of having their cultural superiority affirmed? The burden of having to compete? The burden of knowing themselves already irrevocably eclipsed by their ancestors' "masterful" literary achievement? Perhaps it was the impediment of being mocked by the masters who conspired to impose the daunting conviction that the best had already been written, that no greater achievement was possible. Some of these students appeared quite content. They no doubt were the ones who could see themselves in the teacher. The classroom itself was the telling pond that assured them that in a few years they would be standing at the podium—not even to surpass the one standing there but simply to become him. These were the four or five out of thirty-five to whom the lecture was directed.

The day I dropped English as my major, I left the registrar's office and went down to the lunch table, where the Black folk were due to gather. I was almost the first one there. Somebody else's belongings were on the table. I saw beneath a deck of cards a copy of Maya Angelou's *I Know Why the Caged Bird Sings*. Whoever it belonged to was probably in the lunch line. The title kept resounding and wouldn't leave me alone. By the time Yolanda made it back to the table, I was well into the second chapter.

"This is heavy," I said, hardly looking up.

"Go ahead," she laughed. "Don't mind me. I done already read it twice." I read the entire book that night, laughing and weeping, and in the morning I was in the registrar's office again, changing my major back to English. I wasn't leaving literature. Literature could be wholesome, healing, relevant. Maya Angelou had suffered, endured, and transcended. She had been raped at eight and had survived. She had borne a child at seventeen, two years younger than I was when I had Treecie, and had survived.

Angelou's tale didn't just give a view from some high Pisgah, nor did it simply show the way out of the wilderness. It showed the artist's struggle to come through. In that light, I could remember the same kind of saving revelation that glimmered from other texts, the brightness that had drawn me to the literature major in the first place. It was no small wonder that Emily Dickinson's poetry was dismissed in the classroom. This dismissal was characteristic of the treatment of art that exposed the artist's own struggle, and in Maya's autobiography, both were combined. I would continue to draw from writers like Dickinson, Sylvia Plath, Thoreau, Anne Frank, and Henry James. But having encountered this reflection of my Black woman artist self, I would search for her in other courses.

I paged desperately through the college catalogue. I knew that there were no Black literature courses in the English department, but I did find a course called Women in Literature, offered by a Lucy Freibert. I added her course to my other requirements. For the first time I saw Nikki Giovanni's work included on a literature syllabus. On the day I joined, just after the professor had announced the good news and begun reading Giovanni's poem, "Ego Tripping," one of the graduate students protested, I am sure with the blessing of many of her peers and faculty, that she absolutely resented "having this street razz passed off as decent literature!" Dr. Freibert watched the door slam. This graduate student was not disrespecting just Giovanni but all the thirsting students who had come to share this trickle of water in the wilderness. I held my breath to see what Dr. Freibert would do, to see if she would cower under the pressure, to see if my two dollars of lunch money would go to change this last reprieve of a literature course to heaven knows what. A moment later Dr. Freibert was drawing in breath from the four corners of the earth, lifting her arms defiantly, and finishing the poem: ". . . I mean I can fly like a bird in the sky." Thank you, Jesus, I signed triumphantly, for this one woman's courage.

A few mornings after that, Lu called to say turn to Channel 11.

"What are you doing?" Princeton asked, seeing me switch from the all-important Channel 3.

Good heavens, it was Maya Angelou, strong, empowering, wise—all that I wasn't, all that I wanted to be. This was a poet. This was life and literature.

"This is the reason I changed my major back to English," I said, wanting badly to share my excitement with him.

"You'll never get out of college at this rate," Princeton told me. "If you do elementary education, you'll be teaching your own class at Immaculate Heart in a year."

"It doesn't matter," I told him. "And I don't want to teach part-time elementary school anymore. This year at Immaculate Heart has been good, especially since it was my school, but I want to go on, get my master's, and maybe teach at the junior college."

"Wait a minute," he said. "You never said anything about that."

At counseling session the next evening, he told the counselor how unsettling I was, that I had a perfectly good job teaching part-time and seemed to be enjoying it, and "out of the blue she's not getting a teaching certificate anymore. We can't afford this, and I'm sick of her changes!"

Changes? I was the only one who had been constant, coming home every day tending Treecie, preparing incredible meals on the budget we had, turning on the set religiously to watch his news report so I could give him feedback, then waiting forever for the sound of the damn key

in the door. "And I'm sick of her distrust!" Women had now started calling the house all the time. "I'm just letting off steam, that's all! Yes, at
two in the morning!"

I signed up to teach another year at Immaculate Heart and, without
noticing it, changed my clothes to a basic black. I called Houston, now
in his third year at Howard University, studying art. He was in the womb
of Afri-Cobra, African Commune of Bad Relevant Artists, one of the major
artistic components of the Black Arts Movement that began in Chicago
and branched out to various sites across America, including Howard. When
I spoke to him, I found that he was not only changed creatively, he had
fallen in love and was bringing Kinshasha home that very weekend. "Estella,"
he said, "I swear this is the woman." Shasha was beautiful. They arrived
at my door earlier than expected, and the surprise made the meeting doubly enjoyable. She was an artist too and from the first moment of our meeting felt so like my kindred spirit that we skipped all the formalities and
started simply laughing together, me pulling out old family albums to share
and my Aretha Franklin and Nina Simone albums, and Shasha unwind-
ing from her magical straw bags great splashes of purple and orange kente
prints to wrap the first geles upon my and Treecie's heads. Just like that
for a moment, I felt restored again. I stood before the mirror taken aback
by my own radiant image glowing in the reflection. "Purple is good," I
said, practically blushing away from the glass. "Orange is good," Treecie
responded, hugging into Shasha's embrace. I found out all that Houston
and Sha were doing at Howard and how much in love they were.

I wanted Princeton to just see them this way and be renewed by their
example, too. But he was working late, and when he came home he showed
a defensive arrogance toward Houston. Houston, in turn, showed a veiled
contempt toward him, even though I had never mentioned the fights.
A few months later we went to Kinshasha and Houston's wedding in D.C.,
but Houston and Princeton were never the same as before. Later,
when we all went to California to celebrate Adolph's first mass,
Princeton swore that all my brothers were crazy, especially William, who
was supposed to be getting his doctorate in psychology at Stanford.

Our conversations stayed full of tension, and our silences were
worse. One night, as I had done so many nights before, I crawled out
of the bed, my soul aching, and stared through the window at the darkness. My God, what on earth am I to do? I cannot live this way. I turned
that night for whatever and all the reasons and looked at him sleeping

there defenselessly before me and, in an unguarded startling rage-filled moment, understood completely why God had given the fifth commandment, "Thou shalt not kill." After all those months, those years that I had spent trying to prevent my brothers from knowing and acting out their potential for defense, I discovered that same power within myself. While it scared me to know that I could take him on, take him out in his revealed vulnerability, it also empowered me. I recognized that the impulse to fight for my own life, to defend myself, to kill and not be killed was there. I was the same soul of the little girl who had fought when being taken out of the jungle, the same fighting spirit of the schoolgirl who had refused to turn the other cheek. But more than the role of sister, or young Black Catholic schoolgirl, this socially constructed role of wife demanded a surrendering, a relinquishing of my very power and entitlement. In my willingness to surrender, I had expected a reciprocity that didn't materialize, but now I was confronted with the rage that did emerge. I fled the room trembling, and the next morning I gathered up Patrice and simply left him, the rosary in my pocket held tightly inside my fist. I carried with me not only a lingering intimidation generated by Princeton's violent outbursts but also this seedling recognition of my own potential. This recognition was too embryonic to bring forth a vision of what to do with my life, how to spiritually, emotionally, and economically sustain it, but it compelled me to establish some boundaries so as not to unleash a destructive retaliatory force.

He found me a few days later in a room at the house of one of Sandy's friends. He begged me to come back and promised things would get better. We would talk things out more, spend more quality time together. He would be more honest. Perhaps, I reasoned to myself, this was simply the hard part of marriage that is so much spoken about. But the soul of me said no, this is not marriage at all. But I needed more time to figure it out. It had only been a few years. Perhaps? So I went back to him. A season later, I was pregnant and feeling doubly trapped.

I made it past the spastic vomiting and was doing miraculously better, moving into my sixth month, when suddenly my water broke. At the hospital, the doctors put a gas mask over my face and I began to give in to the drowsiness. Suddenly, I decided that if my baby lived for only a few struggling moments, I wanted to see it alive.

"How about that," somebody told the anesthetist. "She's back." And the mask was placed back over my face.

The next morning, I woke in a hospital bed. The shadows moved around like mourners. Between knowing and not knowing, I floated on a hope.

"Mrs. Walls," I heard from the lady holding blue papers before me. "These are notices for release and documents to be signed as to how you want us to deal with the baby." My heart slowed, then sped up full rate.

"The baby?" I said. "Aren't you even going to tell me about it first?" A red shading crawled over her skin. Aware of her carelessness, she asked gently, "No one's been here this morning? Your doctor hasn't talked with you yet?"

I turned to the window. "No. Please go away."

She apologized.

"Please just leave me alone," I said. She closed the door behind her.

I tried to unscramble my feelings. Sorrow, yes, but first there was relief; relief from a painfully depressing pregnancy that had kept me in the hospital off and on for six months. Then sympathy for my baby, and next, a slouching feeling of inadequacy. I hated the order in which I felt these things. It seemed quite unmotherly to feel for my own self first, to have one single self-indulgent moment where the mourning is just for me. Not for the baby that died, not for the mother that lost the baby, but for the wounded, bleeding woman who had lost pieces of herself in this process. I sped through the first impulses toward healing, through the attendant guilt, and skidded into honesty. Even though this truth would later moult to make way for a new one, at this moment it was as bright and naked as any I had seen. I was alone because I was alone. There is no sharing of real and personal experience. To expect understanding was unrealistic. I would manage on my own. Momma had never miscarried. None of my friends had either. If they had, I didn't know it.

I closed my eyes, rummaging through the memory of my last hospitalization two months ago, how sick I had been, how depressed, my arms so bruised and tracked with needle marks there was no place left to stick anymore. They began looking at my ankles to see where the tubes could be fed in. The doctors were all talking at me; nobody listened. My stomach heaved, my mind snarled. All I could feel then was grief, unrelenting grief, and I wanted out of this flesh that caged, that tortured me, that wouldn't let me speak without vomiting, walk without falling over, that wouldn't let me think or pray or be. Earlier that morning, Momma and Gert had brought Treecie to the window so I could see her, but I couldn't even brace my legs to stand. When I made it there with the nurse's help, Patrice seemed to be waving to all the windows, waving even perhaps to the wind. She had no momma. I had not held her in weeks; I had not held myself in months. God, she deserved better. That night I had decided to strip myself of this living death and go naked back to eternity. I knew suicide was forbidden, but I had searched for a way around that. I concentrated more than I had ever done before as my spirit resolved to die. As I drifted off to sleep, I remember thinking, it is done. Native Americans do it in their departing rituals and so can I—and once out, I will never ever come back.

The following morning, my first moment of consciousness was so glaring that I wanted to curse the sun. I was still trapped in this flesh, this pitiful, pitiful flesh. My spirit raged fitfully inside my agonizing body. I opened my eyes to the wretched familiarity, the stupid cart just as I had left it, the funky spit bowl, the needlepoint picture hanging crooked on the wall bearing the words, "Jesus knows our every sorrow."

"Then why don't you help me!" I screamed, flinging my vomit dish at the picture and knocking it from the wall. "Why don't you just take me," I cried, "and stop messing around!"

"Estella," I heard. "Estella!"

It was Grandma's voice, clear, unstrained, deliberate.

"God writes straight on crooked lines," she said. Then it was over.

"What's the matter, Mrs. Walls?" the nurse asked. "What happened to the room?" I wiped my tears, shook my head. She checked my vital signs and seemed to panic. A doctor rushed in, responding to her call. "God writes straight on crooked lines?" I thought but dared not, even in my confusion, utter the words aloud. They examined me frantically. My blood count was low, they said, so low that it was a miracle I was conscious.

They told me I would have to have a blood transfusion.

"I don't know what happened between yesterday and this morning, but there's a drastic difference and it's serious," the doctor said. I waited for Lu. She was the only one I'd tell this to. Of course they had already prepped her.

"Momma. I'm so glad to see you," I said.

She shook her head sympathetically.

"I just wanted to go," I told her. "I got so depressed." I went on to explain that Grandma had come, that she had actually been in the room.

"My poor baby," she murmured. "It's not going to be this bad all the time. Look, honey, at the good parts. You've got a beautiful little girl, a husband who loves you." There was a shadow over her face that I had not been able to see before then. It was the same one that came for brief moments whenever she remembered Joe and had to hum her way back from the hurt.

"Momma," I said shaking my head, trying to confess not only my desperation but my impulse now toward renewal. I didn't want her down because of me. I tried to say, I know I needed faith. I know, too, that I had cut God short, throwing the vomit dish against the picture.

Momma was reluctant to talk. She was following the nurse's warning that I was depressed and needed care. But for me at that moment, care meant understanding what I had experienced.

"Lu," I said, holding her face in my hands and speaking more deliberately. "Grandma came. She said these words: 'God writes straight on crooked lines.'"

Suddenly the recognition was full in her eyes. She repeated the words, letting the water stream through them. "These words," she said smiling, "were the code your grandma and I shared when I was a girl." They signaled that a message brought by somebody was really from Grandma. For instance, if someone was sent to pick Lu up from school, or if there had been a change in plans, then the person should know this phrase.

"God is merciful," she said. "And yes, you must have faith. God is still on the throne and still has something very special in mind for you." We embraced, and in time I apologized to the nurses and the aides for the mess I had made.

I don't know what I thought would happen afterward, but I certainly wasn't expecting to miscarry two months later. I rather expected for God to move me through the hardship and bring my baby forth the way Treecie had been born. I was focusing on the notion of "writing straight" and had altogether missed the message, the "change in plans," that accompanied Grandma's words. Now, lying alone after the miscarriage, I understood. "I should have known you were double-talking," I sighed heavily.

Then I opened my eyes and reached for the mirror on the stand. I sat staring for what I thought was a private moment. Then I saw that privacy, being alone with myself, was almost impossible. My face was already so many faces before me. I was Momma right before Joe's funeral. I was all those drawn-faced women in my pharmacy window. I was Grandma, disappointed with the city tearing down her efforts to build. I was Mrs. Brown, who had miscarried, they said, all of five times until she lost her womb. And yet, I whispered beyond the recognitions, I am none of them, none of them at all. I am me. If nothing else, my pain is my own.

When the doctor came in, the only thing I asked him was if he had tied my tubes like I had requested so I would never have to go through this ever again. My regular doctor, with whom I had made the agreement, had gone on vacation. This substitute looked at me without blinking and said no. I couldn't believe it.

"I looked at you, and you looked so young I couldn't do it," he told me.

Idiot. He had no idea what I had been through.

"You're twenty-three years old, for heaven's sake. I had you all prepped to do it, but something came over me and I couldn't."

I shook my head over and over again.

"You're young," he said softly.

"You don't know me," I said, accenting each word as if he couldn't hear. "You don't know anything about me."

He lifted the chart and began reading. "I know that you are Estella Walls, that you are married, have one child, a daughter. That there have been complications during this pregnancy and that you miscarried a child last night."

"Is that all?" I thought to myself "All?"

The doctor put down the chart. I could see the scribbling from a distance.

"That I miscarried a child last night," I repeated.

"I'm sorry," he said, but I waved him away. "You're young," he continued "If you want to make the arrangements after you heal, you can still do it."

"My doctor said it was an easier procedure right after the birth."

"But this wasn't a birth in that sense, Mrs. Walls. If the baby had lived, I perhaps could have seen it, but nobody counts on these things. You are young," he said.

I asked to be left alone. As old and worn as I felt, I would have likely died of natural causes if I'd heard him say "you're young" one more time.

About midmorning, Princeton came.

"Good morning, baby," he said, looking tired after being up half the night outside the delivery room. "You know?" he asked, and I nodded my head. "I'm sorry, Estella. I really am. There was nothing they could do." After a few careful exchanges, he left, saying he'd be right back. In that instant, the back of him seemed that of a complete stranger.

Minutes later he was back, tracing the wrinkles of my brow, trying to talk but unable to do it. He had been down to see the baby, he said. A girl . . . like Treecie . . . just like little Treecie . . . little fingernails . . . little hair. This seemed to be the first time that the baby was real to him. Unable to contain himself, he fell over my bed and simply wept—wept at seeing an extension of himself dead that way—wept at our love no longer being creative—wept for having overslept that morning—wept. Then he held on tightly to me. I mostly held on for his sake. The real me inside was simply looking on.

He asked what I wanted to do with the baby.

"Nothing."

Even though I believed a spirit had lived inside the body, I didn't want a funeral rite. I didn't want to see her. I wanted to move on—cut the umbilical cord, dispel the afterbirth of this experience, and begin healing.

"You don't want to do anything?"

"Nothing."

Princeton just looked at me.

"Nothing?" he asked again, and this time I didn't even look at him. Momma came in after a while. She had been keeping Treecie, and she'd had to wait for Gert to get home from her night job before coming. She kept Treecie thinking that Princeton would then be free to see me. I didn't tell her otherwise.

A couple of days later I came home to Lu's house. Patrice was waiting for me there. I saw her coming toward me and thanked God aloud for such a gift, such a precious, precious gift. I held her head in my hands, rubbed her arms and her fingers all over again. We snuggled into each other on the couch and stayed there all afternoon. Shortly afterward people started coming by with sympathy and, they said, understanding. This community was determined to have some ritual, though I saw no need for it. I didn't want to go through any more mourning. I would rather have stayed there forever in that nothing space where the flowering had ended and no promises could ever be made or broken again. Deborah came by and said she understood and Betty Jo said she understood and Momma's friends all said they understood. One woman even came to tell me that she had not miscarried but aborted and, indeed, she understood. They sounded like changeling echoes of one another, and I wanted them to stop.

Then the ultimate happened. Momma sat down beside me to say, "I understand." I cried out with anger and confusion: "Momma, please don't say that. Just say 'I'm sorry.'" I was sitting, still feeling the milk seep out of my hurting breasts for no baby. "I just don't need this," I said. She left me alone in the living room and went back into the kitchen.

I was sitting, still looking out the storm door, when Mr. and Mrs. Brown drove up. He stayed parked. She came up the walkway. She didn't knock, as she ordinarily would have. She just opened the door and stood looking back at me. And while we stared, I remembered her childlessness, that she had miscarried five times and still had not one daughter or son to claim, and I braced myself for another "I understand." But she didn't say that. She simply reached out to me through all that distance, held me in her arms, and cried. She cried until her tears baptized and claimed my waking flesh, until her warmth and wisdom seeped deep into me like rain into parched land, until the soul deep inside poured forth its own waters. Then she held me back away from her. We were two again. We dried each other's tears, and without a word, she turned around and left.

Raven Woman. That's what she was to me. Not in the tired sense of all the death associations we make with the bird but in the restorative sense. Mrs. Brown came to me like the raven did to Elijah in the wilderness. She fed and strengthened me when I was desperate and dying. And for this I am grateful.

Estella at age five months, 1949.

The wedding of Estella's parents, Giles Adolph
Conwill and Mary Luella Herndon, Louisville,
1944.

Estella and Spivey, 1956.

The Conwill children, 1959: (left to right) Houston, Joseph, Giles Adolph, Estella, Spivey, William.

Estella after winning the Miss Exposition crown (with the second- and third-place winners), 1966. (Photo: *Louisville Defender*)

Estella with Patrice, age nine months, 1970.

Patrice with her great-aunt Gertrude Herndon and grandmother Luella Conwill.

Patrice with her aunt Kinshasha, 1973.

Patrice at her graduation from Indiana University, with Estella, late 1980s. (Photo: William Conwill)

Family and friends at Dominic's baptism in Louisville, 1985: (back row, left to right) Estella, Patrice, Aunt Lyda, Giles holding Dominic, Lucy Freibert, Faye, Amy Brown; (front row, left to right) Alyson Brown, Giles Burgess, Aunt Gert.

Dominic at age two, 1987. (Photo: William Conwill)

Dominic with his cousins Giles Burgess, Mondlane, and (front) Justin.

Family picnic in Central Park, 1993: (left to right) Houston, William, Estella, Spivey, and Giles.

Three generations of women at the Studio Museum in Harlem, mid-1990s: (left to right) Luella, Estella, Patrice, and Kinshasha. (Photo: Giles Conwill)

The collaborative team of Houston Conwill, Estella Conwill Májozo, and
Joseph DePace. (Photo: Jules Allen)

Dedication ceremony for the "Rivers" cosmogram honoring Langston
Hughes (see floor) at the Schomburg Center for Research in Black Culture,
1991: (foreground) Chief Howard Dodson and Jean Blackwell Hudson of
the Schomburg Center. (Photo: © Lee White)

Crossing the Whirlpool Bridge into Canada, led by Harriet Tubman's great-grandniece Berry Brown, as part of the "Stations" installation commemorating the Underground Railroad at the Castellani Art Museum on the Niagra River, 1993.

Opening ceremony of the "Revelations" memorial to Dr. Martin Luther King, Jr., at Yerba Buena Gardens, San Francisco, 1993: Estella pouring a libation, accompanied by Terry Richardson playing "Wade in the Water" on trumpet.

Luella Conwill and Kinshasha's mother Mariella Holman inside the "Revelations" memorial following the opening ceremony. (Photo: Houson Conwill)

Patrice and her fiancée James Lowe at the "Revelations" opening ceremony.

Estella and Dominic in the elevator of their Harlem apartment building, late 1990s. (Photo: © Petra)

Estella in her office at Hunter College, photographed by one of her creative writing students, late 1990s. (Photo: Gail Garone)

9

After Mrs. Brown left Lu's house, I sat in the middle of the back yard with my eyes closed, thanking God for such a presence. I could feel the sun on my face again for the first time in months. I could feel the gentleness of the breeze blowing the hospital stench from my pores. I could hear birds everywhere, their praise songs never before so clear. When I opened my eyes to catch a glimpse, I found the beauty of nature unexpectedly enrapturing me. The sky was the most incredible blue, and a radiance moved from the trees that left me breathless. It danced with the fragrance of honeysuckles and roses and violets. I was somehow inside all of it and it was all inside of me, the light everywhere glistening a heavenly gold. My soul trembled its recognition of God's pure and affirming love manifesting such wonder. Then, suddenly, it was over. But the touch had already taken. I knew joy was possible. And this gave me hope.

It was another two years before I left Princeton. And though I thought extensively about it, I still ended up doing it haphazardly. Nobody in my family had ever divorced, not in my twenty-six years, anyway. Scottie had undergone a separation once, but everybody else had stayed married— Grandma and Grandaddy, Momma and Daddy, Gert and Herman, William and his wife, and certainly Houston and Kinshasha, who seemed to be on a perpetual honeymoon. Uncle Gene had been married once for a year, they say, but had remained single after that out of respect for the church's stand on divorce.

But model or no model, I knew I had to deal with my dilemma before Patrice started first grade. I couldn't leave for me. But when I looked at Patrice . . . She was so beautiful. She was still growing, and I just didn't want her to grow up with the abuse and with the model of this sad, worn-down, depleted woman. I didn't want her to see me like this and to think that's what she should become. My mother had not given that to me to behold, and her mother, my grandmother, had not given her that to become. I thought I had no example of how to handle this and what to do. But I remembered the water lily. Like it, I appeared to be drifting alone in my predicament, but hidden below the surface was a root, the example of my mother's and grandmother's bearing, which anchored me. The memory of what my grandmother had given to my mother, and what she had given me, reminded me of what I was supposed to pass on to my daughter. I decided to leave so that I could regain that bearing. I saw a way of being independent and of building a network to sustain myself. This gave me a new appreciation of what I had seen in the literature. I realized then that for those women who didn't have the family genealogy or model for passing on strength, the example could still be found in literature. I realized why Nikki Giovanni had taken such pains to describe the role of her grandmother, Louvenia, in her life; why Margaret Walker Alexander, in "For My People," labored to bring forth a vision of hope.

On the morning that I left, I took Patrice to day care, then called my family to tell them for the first time about the abuse, Princeton's infidelity, and my decision to leave. Lu, Gert, and Lyda were not only shocked, they converged on my house in a lion's rage from three different directions, determined to help me pack immediately. Lyda, shaking her head in disbelief, saying, "Uh-uh-uh." And Gert throwing things into boxes, swearing she had no idea the bastard would turn out this way. And Lu just glad for my decision and for the fact that Houston, who had come with Shasha to Louisville for a year to finish an art commission, was now in Los Angeles at the University of Southern California, hundreds of miles away.

I had rented an inexpensive apartment on Algonquin Place. The windows were low and a bit vulnerable, but I had already gotten bars to make them more secure. They provided great light, and light was what I needed, I explained to Lu and Gert, not the leather sofa that was too showy to begin with, not the king-size bed with all the bad vibes and tears in the mattress, and not the overstuffed recliner, but the light, filtering through the new wide window into my yearning soul.

We were out before Princeton even thought of coming home. In the new apartment, we disinfected the cabinets and sinks. "This will do for now," they said, putting the dishes in place while turning phrases of my story inside out in utter befuddlement. They kept talking about it over and over, the way people do during mourning, asking questions that in fact made me relive, as in an extended death moment, my seven-year marriage. I knew then, on another level of recognition, that it was over. "You can get whatever else you need in here later," Lu said, but I assured her that I had everything I needed and that Patrice and I would be fine. And I looked at the little placard I had brought to put up in the new place. It read, "Seek ye therefore the kingdom of God . . ."

In the tradition of my grandma's garden I furnished the place with the only things that made sense to me, wandering ivy, cactus, and philodendron. I had emerged from the bewilderment of my stunted existence of not knowing who I was or what I was to become. These plants were a declaration of the identity I had chosen for myself. In the ivy, I saw the possibilities of growing around and beyond obstacles. The cactus was a reminder to protect the creativity within and to draw moisture out of the dry soil. And the philodendron was one that grew in my grandmother's garden.

I set up Treecie's princess bed in the bedroom the way she was used to it to give her some sense of security, but I got myself a single sofa bed. I figured a folding card table could hold our food and my typewriter as well as any dining set. I placed it before the window where I planted morning glories so I could see how they, in turn, climbed the iron bars to freedom. At the center of the room Patrice and I placed Amazing Grace, a discarded plant that we had hauled in from a grocery dumpster one day like it was a bit of salvation. On a drive home, Patrice spotted it. "Momma, can we take it home?" Like a child who asks to bring home a starving puppy, my daughter had the conviction that this scrawny tree could be nursed back to blooming health. It was potted and had a lot of height and few leaves. "OK, baby. Let's take her home. She looks like she can use some company," I said, watching Patrice's smile spread full across her face. We placed her in the center of the front room.

Neither of us thought it overbearing at the time, though Sandy and Deborah teased us about it being Christmas in springtime, asking when were we going to decorate the thing.

"We're not going to decorate it," Treecie told them. "We're just going to talk to her and listen."

"You've got my godchild talking about as off as you," Sandy joked. Then Sandy's expression got serious as she whispered, out of Treecie's hearing, that I'd better start talking to Princeton about some support. I knew I would have to do it, but I wanted to take one step at a time. I rather dreaded having to see him and appreciated the fact that he had not contacted me. "I'll talk to him, Sandy, when the time is right," I said defensively. I didn't want to feel his voice vibrating inside my head just yet, and I certainly didn't want him here in my space. I knew he would want to see Patrice eventually, but I was still sorting things through. No lawyer would even talk to me about a divorce without a little money up front, so I had to bide my time. "I've gotten this far," I told Sandy. "I'm sure more grace is coming."

One day shortly after this, Patrice and I rode up to the back of the apartment and saw two ragged-bearded men standing outside our window. Upon seeing us, they ran. I could see then that the window was broken, the bars were yanked out, and my plants on the sill were gone. Instinctively I pushed Patrice's head below the seat.

"Stay down, baby, no matter what," I said.

"Why, Momma? I want to see!"

"Hush and stay down!"

Crouched over her, I pressed down hard on the horn, trying to flush out whoever might still be inside. Within seconds the fierce daring face of a young Black woman appeared through the broken window.

"A sister in my apartment," I mumbled incredulously, getting out of the car. "What are you doing in my place?"

"Is this your place?" she said senselessly.

Jim, my neighbor, came out yelling, "What the hell! You want me to hold her?" But her dark eyes cut into catlike slithers. She was too dangerous to hold. Maybe a switchblade in her Afro, a razor in her sock. With the deadbolt on my door, her only exit was the window.

"I'm the hell out of here!" she said, her long lanky body curling through the window. I hadn't even noticed the blue car beside me until then. She jumped in and sped away with her get-away woman, shouting,

"Somebody must've beat us to it! Her shit is zero!" In that instant, I felt stupid for endangering Treecie's life by confronting her. I scribbled down the license number and pulled Treecie up from the floor.

Miss "her shit is zero" had torn through my ivy, knocked down the cactus, and scattered my papers everywhere.

"Call my daddy, Momma!" Treecie cried.

"Baby, we can handle this."

"Uh-uh. Tell Daddy so he can get the crook! " I calmed her, then called the police. I also called Sandy and her husband, Wayne, to help with the window. When things were settled back to some semblance of normalcy, I tucked Patrice into bed. As I was tiptoeing from the bedroom, the doorbell rang.

I looked through the peephole. It was Princeton. I forced myself to calm down. What did he want? Who told him we were here? I drew another deep breath, then opened the door. He asked if we were OK, if the burglars had taken anything. I shrugged nonchalantly. "Treecie said they took her finger paint."

"May I see her?"

I didn't want him in there. I didn't want his scent crowding my space, and all those ghosts that were his baggage, taunting, torturing, yet refusing to show face. I didn't want those negative vibrations robbing the room of its peace.

And I didn't want to wake Treecie either, so I allowed him to go quietly into her room. He touched her face. She smiled "Hi, Daddy" in her sleep. He kissed her, whispered something, then tiptoed out.

"It's hot in there," he started. But his words waned, perhaps remembering his comfort in the suburbs. Then his eyes flashed down at my hands. The ring was still there. I had thrown the wedding band into the weeds one desperate night, but the diamond I had saved, maybe to give to Treecie. His eyes moved from the ring to around the room.

"Still prefer to plant your own," he said with stale nostalgia. I wanted him to leave right then, to go on and take all those signifying ghosts thriving in the hell wind between us right on out with him.

"What kind are these?"

"Morning glories. Why?"

"Morning glories are weeds," he said sarcastically, and I could feel the sword taste coming back in my mouth again, the steel replacing my pupils, and the iron taking over my marrow.

"This is not what we need to be talking about, Princeton, and you know it," I said, unwilling to continue the charade. "But if you want to play it that way, why not ask about this Venus's-flytrap? We both know a bit about this. This plant sits there with its leaf wide open and inviting, looking like it's going to be loving, and as soon as the little creature lands upon it, it stifles and devours it!" I was referring not only to myself being caught in his lies so many times, but to him, who was now caught in an obviously not-so-surreptitious relationship that had drawn, it was rumored, an engagement from him. I thought of how little had changed between us, of all the hurt and anger I still had to get through. I hadn't grown one damn inch! Despite the separation, prayers, and hope of moving on, it was only a physical move. I hadn't gone anywhere!

My God, I thought, moaning my way through the funk, it's like I'm living some gut-bucket blues song that keeps rounding itself out. There's no real transcendence. Where the heck is that part in the song when all my striving finds release?

I truly wanted to go on with my life.

"Look," I said to Princeton, who stood there trying to read my changes. "Would you like some tea?"

"Yeah, Estella. I would," he said. Neither of us wanted to engage in an analytical discourse on the significance of the Venus's-flytrap.

We did need to talk. I was barely making ends meet. I was struggling to stay in school. The rent was paid, but food was a definite challenge. I'd go to the open-air market and buy two bags of vegetables for the same price as one in a supermarket. Three dollars' worth of gas for the piece of car I had left me measuring the blocks to school, church, and Lu's house. I would pick up Gloria, another student, on the way to school and she'd hand me bananas or a share of cornmeal while scooting onto the seat. We'd look out for cops who might stop us for the loud muffler or exhaust fumes. I was sure he wasn't dealing with anything like that. Since we hadn't been to court, child support hadn't been determined, and he certainly wasn't meeting it on his own.

Just a month ago, I had come home to no lights and no electricity. I hadn't enough gas to make it to Lu's and the service station was already closed, so I sat on the front steps humming some rarefied version of "What did I do to be so black and blue?"

"Why didn't you write them a check, Momma?" Treecie said.

"It's going to be all right," I told her. I had gotten my check that day, but that wouldn't do me any good now. I searched the catch-all drawer, strung together three extension cords, and plugged them into the hallway outlet. Like Ralph Ellison's "Invisible Man," I found a little reprieve. I put Treecie to bed and studied for my exam. If I could get through the final lap of my bachelor's degree, things would have to be better. I could work on my master's degree, perhaps even teach freshman composition at the university. Dr. Lucy Freibert, from whom I was taking another wonderful course, and Dr. Sena Naslund, who conducted a creative writing workshop, had both told me a week earlier that I had a real chance. At first, the possibility of teaching there at the university was almost inconceivable, for all the usual reasons. I would only dare tell Lu and Gert when it was definite.

The next morning I went to the gas company and had to wait in line. There were at least fifteen people ahead of me—mostly Black women who had their own pain or embarrassment or anger. Nobody was talking. I turned to the woman beside me.

"Kinda reminds you of the song, 'I'm glad man didn't make sunshine—'cause he might not let it shine on me.'" She chuckled, and the one beside her laughed too. We began sharing stories of what we were doing when the lights went out. One was watching "Days of Our Lives," another was away at work. Still another was giving her husband a haircut with electric clippers. He ended up with half a Mohawk cut, which she said would set next year's style. One old woman with a porkpie hat pulled over her wig pushed her way to the front. "Let me see the manager," she told the clerk. "I come to collect my profits! I know I got shares in this place. I been paying in for thirty years! Miss one time and poof! They do this all the time in the Black neighborhood and we the ones who got to see each other in the dark!" Everybody fell out laughing.

Indeed, Princeton and I did need to talk, I thought now as I opened the cabinets to get down the cups. In some African communities, after divorce the women of the family would break those household items intimately shared by the couple. Nobody had broken my cups, and I hadn't broken them either. I was sorry now that I hadn't left them in the old apartment.

What I needed was a new vessel into which I could pour my feelings for him and see them take new form. I got down two mugs.

We sat sipping in silence. My diamond sparkled as I lifted my cup. Oh, that it could have been like the ring of Solomon. His had the power to compel the demons to identify themselves, make themselves visible, and tell of their antidotes. If only I could compel these ghosts to come out and make themselves more visible. If there were just the two of us there, maybe more would have been possible. But the room was always crowded. The ghosts were always there, and since for the most part the demons refused to identify themselves, and since we didn't take the first step of naming them, they continued to harm us.

When Princeton did speak, he told me he still wanted to help make Treecie's way. After we agreed upon an amount, there was nothing else to say. "Too many things stacked against us," he said, brushing his hand painfully across my hand. When he finished his tea, I opened the door and he left.

I sat for a few minutes rocking and wiping away my tears. I went to turn on the radio, but it was filled with too many love songs. I turned it off. I missed having a phone. I sipped my tea and started to say something to Amazing Grace but stopped, remembering that Patrice had said the plants had gotten so they'd quiver whenever we'd enter the room, the leaves of Amazing Grace especially, during conversations, as if the tree really was listening. I had laughed when she said it. I had told her many times before that it wasn't simply the tree that I was forever calling out to but what the tree represented. That yes, there were waterways along its rough limbs and a magical dance going on in its newly developing leaves— one that took from the soil and air and sunlight all that it needed and gave us back the very air we breathed. But the tree also symbolized the Holy Spirit who empowers us to grow, change, and know ourselves.

"The Holy Spirit is what makes us want to love," I told Treecie, who followed up with "Momma, do you love my daddy?" She always did have a way of bringing things down to the basics.

"Yes, baby, I do. And I love you and I love me, too."

Sooner rather than later, I thought, I will tell her about things like stone plants whose leaves are covered with tough brown skin to make them resemble rocks, plants that know the reason and rhythm of closing in times of drought, that show the beauty and protectiveness necessary for survival.

The next night, Treecie walked into the room and climbed onto my lap.

"I'm glad you love my daddy, Momma, because last night he came in a dream and said he loves me."

"Baby, that wasn't a dream," I said, and then went on to tell her that he had been by when she was asleep.

"Yeah," she said, "I thought so. And Amazing Grace was talking, too, after Daddy finished, right?"

I laughed. "That part was a dream, baby. It must have happened after Daddy left. What did Amazing Grace say?"

"Momma, that's what I was asking you. You were there."

I shook my head. "No, baby, I wasn't."

"OK, then," she said. "A momma that symbolized you, that looked just like you, was talking to the tree and listening. Now, what did it say?"

"I'll listen some more, baby."

"OK, then. Now, what did Daddy say?"

"He's taking you to the park tomorrow."

"Good. I want to show him the new window." She went on playing with her doll.

Momma, do you love my daddy? Patrice's question had sent me back to Grandma's garden. In that second cycle of seeing, I discovered new dimensions to the basics learned there. "Honor thy father and thy mother" wasn't simply about the necessity of me respecting my own parents but of teaching Treecie a healthy respect for hers. It was calling me now to strive as well to be a parent worthy of honor by instilling the right ideals in her. Indeed, the virtues of wisdom, understanding, counsel, and fortitude took on deeper demands.

I would, in time and by God's grace, identify the demons keeping me from meeting those demands. I would deal with my pride and rejection and develop a steadfast sense of my worth. I would face my jealousy of Princeton and his girlfriend by renewing my vows to the life within me. I would bring to my own career the kind of creative investment that I had given his. I would make new friends who would be loyal to me rather than to the material things I might or might not possess.

And because I believed in the power of forgiveness and the grace to seek enlightenment, I would in God's own time come to know the song of the sacred tree.

"Live!" it sings. "Live! Learn my ways and wisdom! I am Life! Everlasting Life! Secret of the pyramid. Blossom of the blues. Reminder of the rhythm. I am your good news. Joiner of earth and sky. Jammer of wind and fly. Water is my middle name. Taste the Light. I am the Flame!"

10

Coming forth as artist is akin to an instinctive act. You find yourself a butterfly wrestling loose from a binding chrysalis you may or may not even have been consciously aware of spinning. Suddenly the threads are too tight to be comforting anymore; the dark solitude is too full of radiant colors to be contained anymore; and the crumpled wings folded around your restless soul cannot endure the airlessness.

The fall of 1975 was a busy one. I was preparing Patrice for first grade, beginning my master's degree, going through divorce proceedings, and breaking the color barrier as the first Black person to teach in the English department at the University of Louisville. And along with all of that, feeling the strongest urge I ever had to bring out *Metamorphosis,* the book I had been working on for years. It was worse than bringing forth any one single poem. It had the force of all the poems behind it now, in much the same way that birth pangs could be equated with nine months' worth of menstrual cramps all rolled into one.

I took Patrice to school that first day, stared deep into her bright morning eyes, and for a moment her joy and expectation was all I could see. But in the brief seconds it took me to get back to my car and head toward campus, the *Metamorphosis* compulsion was back. "I can't do it now," I insisted. "There are too many things going on. And right now, I've got to think about teaching this class." My voice curled under as if trying to take back those last three words.

But already the overwhelming reality of "teaching this class" was before me. The world suddenly grew immeasurably bigger. Sitting wide-eyed at the red light, I began the unfailing ritual I used to make my chore more manageable. Yes, I whispered to myself, this is indeed the big bad world that needs transforming; America that still needs its trails blazed; the South that needs to join the union; the university that needs to be made more universal; and the English department that definitely needs to depart from its exclusionary ways. But more precisely, this is my class, with these particular students, through which a mutually positive, more humane course is about to be charted.

There. My ritual had worked. I now perceived that there was one small corner of the world that I had to transform.

The light changed, and I drove on. Why was the urge to publish so pressing right now? I thought to myself. Why must I do the book this moment? I could not figure it out right then, but it must have had something to do with the order of things in my own consciousness. Here I was with the opportunity to come forth as a teacher and I hadn't yet come out as a poet—my primary and strongest expressive self. Deep down, it was as if I knew that my own soul needed to be fed before I could truly give. It was paradoxical, this creative imperative. Outflowing, but also replenishing. Without writing, without creating, I know I couldn't do anything else right.

I parked the car and gathered my books, then walked into my classroom and greeted my students. Then I registered the shocked expressions on the faces of my white and Black students alike. This was the moment of crossing, the opportunity for transformation. It had definitely begun. But just as quickly, that first day ended. A statement of my mission, a few brief exchanges, the roll call and presentation of the syllabus, and it was over.

There was hardly time to reflect on what had just transpired or to pay much attention to the now seemingly dormant creative life sulking inside the chrysalis. Treecie would be getting out of school in less than a half hour. I made it there early and saw the other parents watching for the children's return. I thought of the nights Treecie and I had dreamed of this day, the tablets she had filled tracing her name, the pictures she had drawn of the school and the teacher she had never seen. The teacher was always smiling, and there were never any beds because there were never any naps. "You can't just sleep all the time," she had said. I sprang from the car and within seconds was standing among the other parents, trying to appear as normal as possible, feeling all the while the poet inside flexing from its hold.

As the children poured from the school, I caught sight of Patrice, obviously too full of the day's unfolding to maintain her strict position in line much longer. She ran into my arms, laughing.

"How do you like school?" I asked. She was grinning so widely it made me laugh, too. "Well, what did you do?" I asked.

"Momma," she said, "we told stories!" She rolled her eyes and giggled incredulously at my question as if to say, whatever else is there that could give such pleasure?

"Of course," I said, "of course."

"And we sang songs," she said, "and we ate cookies! Oh, and I drew this for you. A picture of us holding hands." Her teacher had written "To Momma" at the top for her.

"This is the most beautiful picture I've ever seen," I said.

"Even better than the one Houston made for your cover with the lady butterfly?" she asked.

"In its own way, baby, it is."

"OK, then. Now, what did you do in school, Momma?"

"I'm not quite sure," I said, studying the picture, knowing now how urgently I needed at twenty-six years to express something of the designs I was making of my life, and to address it "to my community." And so that afternoon, after Patrice and I celebrated, we went to see Randall at the press.

The press was basically a one-man operation in the heart of the community. People were always coming and going, leaving and picking up orders, networking and telling jokes over the loud noises and Randall's continuous prodding of both the machines and the signifying. He printed brochures for various companies and churches in the area. He designed programs, raffle tickets, and bulletins of all sorts and could be counted on to produce a most exquisite product. The only drawback was his timing. He nearly gave some customers heart attacks, getting the work done within an instant of the moment it was due. Even though it was aggravating, the community suffered Randall, especially since he often personally delivered the job, unveiling it like a precious work of art. And upon seeing the elegance of his design and printing, nobody followed through on threats to take their business "downtown to the white folks," whose work may have been more prompt but was never so exquisitely rendered.

Lu told me that she wouldn't bother with Randall if she were me. She said he was a likable person, a committed husband, and a very good father (indeed, she had taught his children years ago), but a businessman he was not. I listened halfheartedly. With all my rejection slips, I didn't care. The sixties were over. White publishers no longer found publishing Black writers lucrative. And the few Black publishers, such as Lotus, Broadside, and Third World Press, who had made it into the seventies were struggling to stay afloat.

Months ago, I had approached Randall about the possibility of getting a book printed. "I can make you a publisher," I told him, and he had laughed over the phone. Houston practically did headstands urging me to convince him, and Shasha anxiously pressed her head against mine at the receiver. "It will be an investment in the work of a local artist, an act of faith," I said. I assured him that I would pay him when the money from the sales came in. "Yes, I have a plan for that." The words came, unexpected and bold. He surely must have heard the voice change—Shasha was now smiling, waving me forward to weave the possibility. "A book author luncheon at Masterson's Steak House," I continued, "for which tickets could be sold. They could easily accommodate our one-hundred and fifty guests—covering the cost of the book while allowing the community to celebrate its own emerging artist." It had to work.

At first he gave me an outright "no," he would not be interested in making a contribution to the local artists' charity; then he told me that he wouldn't be able to do it right away because he was in the middle of his heavy season, which seemed to have extended throughout the year; and finally he told me he needed time to think about it. Meanwhile I kept going to the press and dreaming. I must have gotten addicted to the sound of the churning and the look of the print damp upon the paper— newly unfolded luna wings drying in the wind.

In Randall's earlier days, while he was a student at Tuskegee, he had written a bit himself, just enough to know that he should stick to reading and appreciating literature rather than writing it, he said. Langston's words rolled from his lips like music. He could do "When Suzanna Jones Wears Red" and make you see folds of silk. He could do "I've Known

Rivers" and make the ceilings leak, one brother had said. When I approached Randall this final time, telling him just how serious the matter had become, that I simply had to do this book in order to be who I was, he said unequivocally that he'd do it. At that moment, the life inside me expanded in a most marvelous way.

"This is wonderful!" I said. "I really appreciate this. I'm telling you, I do."

He nodded his head in acknowledgment and began handing me examples of different type fonts. Patrice was busy pressing little strips of cutaway paper into accordion-like folds, which she used for doll's legs. "You know," I said, still unraveling the meaning of what was happening, "for doctors and teachers, graduation is a kind of announcement of their availability to the community. But there's no such thing for poets. We ourselves have to show the direction we have chosen. That's kind of what this is about, you know." I stopped talking to see if he was listening—if he really understood what I was feeling and trying to express. There was a long undetermined silence.

"Like the testimonial in the church?" he added, without looking away from the metal fonts he held against the light.

"I think so," I said. "It must be like that on some level."

Randall smiled, his eyes turning full upon me. "It signals," he said assuredly, "that now the old folks can stand guard in a different way, offer some guidance, some patience perhaps, but some other help. It signals, dear woman, that the community has raised yet another one to maturity. And with that, we know we have nurturers and will grow and survive."

Now I was smiling. A couple of customers came in, and Randall whispered to me before I left, "Men do not light a lamp and then put it under a bushel basket"—quoting Jesus' words. "They set it on a stand where it gives light to all in the house."

"Thank you," I said, pushing my poems back into the envelope and feeling in my soul a readiness to proceed.

Since then I have recognized the artistic restlessness preceding emergence in dozens of other artists and have participated in the self-naming process, witnessing and midwifing the delivery of their first book, their first solo exhibition, or their first performance. Years later, when a young poet named Karen Davis sat in my apartment with the same unnamed tension, I recognized her need. I took the poems from her hands while continuing to listen to her talk, typed them out, arranged a mock book complete with cover and a title taken from one of her poems, *And I Wrote MY Name There.* When I handed it back to her, she cried. Envisioning the form gave her the impetus to bring the piece to fruition.

Witnessing my book come together filled me with such anticipation. First one poem, then another came off the press until half the book was printed. This letterpress printing was a very old-fashioned method in which only one signature or set of pages could be printed at a time because each plate had to be set up and broken down. I would take the pages home and dream on them. Each page furthered my emergence from the sack. When the book was three-quarters ready, and the plates of Houston's illustrations had arrived, I told Randall that it seemed we were close enough to begin planning the celebration.

"Go ahead," he told me. "Everything is about set. There's only three more poems to print. Then we bind them. Do what you got to do."

So I began pulling in folk to help. Andrew Jackson, an artist friend, designed posters; Gloria, another friend from school, helped make arrangements for the banquet at Masterson's Steak House; Dan Massie and Tai Wong sold tickets, which in two weeks totaled more than sixty-five. One week before the banquet, when I began showing up daily at the press to check on the progress, Randall assured me that I worried too much, the books would be ready, I should go home and do what I had to do. On the morning of the celebration, Houston flew in from Los Angeles on the red-eye and went with me to pick up the books.

Randall came to the door wearing the same black apron he had worn the night before when I left him promising that the books would be ready by morning.

They weren't. This is what he was trying to tell us with his mouth hanging open and no words coming forth: that the books were still in press. He said something about two more pages needing to be printed, covers not yet dry enough for the binding. If they weren't dry, they would smear, leave fingerprints. My "I am" statement started turning on itself. My public disclosure promised to become public exposure, the embarrassment of a person rising from the mourner's bench to stutter about some conversion unfinished.

I fought back the tears. One hundred ten tickets sold and he was talking about ink spots!

"What can we do to help?" I said, rushing in as if I knew what I was asking about. Throughout the whole week, when I had tried helping out, hoping against a moment like this, Randall had only humored me, offering me small chores like unwrapping paper or stacking empty boxes.

"Yeah," Houston said. "We don't need all five hundred books." We began stacking, arranging the sheets as quickly as possible, the way Randall had shown us.

"My estimation was off," Randall said apologetically, his fingers never missing a beat. "And there were two funerals this week. You can't count on people not dying or living." I pushed all the disappointed faces out of my mind, then shook away the jeering expression of one signifying poet who would surely have his fill of laughter.

I called my friend Gloria, and asked her to go to the restaurant an hour early to get an actual count. I called Lu, who had sold over twenty-five tickets to her friends, and asked her to get Treecie dressed.

We worked for two hours with Randall, but there was a lot more to do. I thought of the time I had gone to see Nikki Giovanni and how she had spoken of her own self-publishing and the necessity of getting the word out there. I thought of Haki Madhubuti, who had come to the Black Family Conference with trunks of books on his back to make sure his publishing ventures were successful. I thought of poet after poet and wondered what their publishing tales might be: broadsides on a single sheet sold for a dollar on the street, or books supported by wealthy Park Avenue patrons, as in the days of the Harlem Renaissance? I wondered how many Ted Joanses there must have been crying out in deserts thousands of miles from their homelands, how many Gil Scott-Herons who self-produce, chanting over guitar sounds truth that is never waxed. I thought of all the poets on bar stools and the Alice Walkers slipping manuscripts beneath office doors and hoping.

Within an hour of the banquet, Houston and I left Randall to finish the run of the last page. We climbed in the car talking frantically about friends and supporters who would be readying themselves even as we were trying to do, the church folk, the campus folk, and the folk from the larger community. The gurgling motor choked in the middle of our prodding, and we turned simultaneously to each other and sighed, "The signifying poet!" Surely he would be there and turn this into a circus, this word trickster who could identify and magnify every glitch and shortcoming—who could undercut, overstate, poke fun, and exaggerate until you were two feet tall and caught in the snare of his humor. It was a shame to have to think about such a possibility. But pettiness could rise in fellow poets as easily as compassion. The envy is spun mostly by those caught in momentary disbelief in their own potential.

"Forget him," I said, getting out of the car. "Poets ought to be glad somebody's doing something."

"Yeah, he's the least of our worries," Houston agreed.

I noticed then that our hands were blotched with ink. There were smudges on our foreheads, cheeks, around our eyes. It reminded me of when Houston and Shasha had come home covered with paint, after finishing the last of eight murals for St. Augustine Church. The parish council had been divided on replacing the white images in the church with African ones, but the majority had agreed and the murals were exquisitely presented. Among their themes were "Worship and Praise," "Continuity and Tradition," and "Queens and Kings Arise!" The day before that exhibition, however, Houston and Shasha looked nothing like a king and a queen. They looked more like chief servants, which, I suppose, is what artists are charged to be. Healers. Hollerers. Stokers of the Flame. Bringers of the Image. The Markers. The Marked.

Coming in from Randall's, Houston and I decided not to tell Lu about the delay. But she saw our faces and knew something was not right.

"What's wrong?" she asked. We tried to put her off.

"No," she insisted, "tell me."

We did, and the pupils in her tiny eyes darn near disappeared. "This doesn't make sense," she raged. "He printed the tickets! He knew the luncheon was today! Everybody always said one day this would happen, that he would mess up and not be ready!"

"I know, Momma. I know."

No sooner had we gotten to the banquet than people began to gather. Many had bought whole tables. Lu's friend, Mrs. London, had come from church, along with Mrs. Boone, one of my teachers at Immaculate Heart, and Molly and Tom Elery. Even Betty Jo and her twin sisters had made it. Karen Davis and Mary Jefferson, two student poets, came to offer help. They were gathering tickets and helping to seat people when the gang from Nat's liquor store waved from across the room. They had met me one day when they helped push my car to the side of the road after it broke down, and had been faithful supporters of mine ever since. I could see Lucy Freibert, my mentor. Her smile was so full of pride that it made me want to look away. "There's a problem," I whispered to her.

"None that you are not able to handle," she said. "The poet in you can handle this." I checked my watch.

"Don't worry," Gloria said. "Randall's late, but he's always on time."

A newspaper reporter asked if this was the city's first Black book author luncheon. I wasn't ready for this. I invited him to stay for the meal and talk to me then. Turning to Gloria, I whispered, "I need a minute in the ladies' room. We'll have to think of an alternative in case Randall doesn't make it."

Too many eyes were coming my way. I felt like worming my way out of their midst. I tried thinking about my power to deliver the poems I had brought for the reading, and how any moment now, Randall would bring the books and I would spread my warmth and wonder across that room and transform it with my words. It wasn't working. God, give me strength.

"This is some celebration you're having," I heard behind me. Father Heitzman, the pastor from our church. After we embraced, he went to the center table.

The photographer began snapping pictures. Lu smiled graciously, then whispered to Father Heitzman, who turned shades darker while gritting his teeth. Seconds later, a parishioner greeted him, and he masked his disappointment.

In the ladies' room, I looked into the mirror until I could see the poet.

"It's your moment," I whispered, "whichever way it goes. The world out there is bigger than you even bargained for. Don't ever say again that I don't give you enough space." I laughed a nervous laugh, relaxed the tension around my eyes, lifted my arms up over my head and lowered them slowly. When I stepped back out into the banquet area, Houston stood before me with the sorriest look ever.

"Randall's sounding real doubtful," he said. "He hasn't even started the binding."

"OK," I responded. "We'll go on as planned. No use in everything being late."

Father Heitzman led us in a blessing. We bowed our heads, asking God's grace on this day, thanking Him for the delicious food, the occasion for fellowshipping and celebrating poetry. He took his time, asking that everyone be nourished by the sharing. With the meal started, I whispered to Mr. Crumes, my emcee: "I'll autograph the books and promise to mail them out within the week." In time, Houston began the dedication, asking Patrice and Lu to come forth. Patrice, for whatever reasons, didn't want to come. I didn't know if she felt shy or embarrassed about our dilemma. Lu had to practically pull her up from the seat. "In appreciation of the love you give and inspire, *Metamorphosis* is dedicated to you," Houston said to her.

Patrice heard the applause, smelled the flowers, and didn't want to go back to her seat. Everybody loved the ham in her, and it certainly eased the tension.

Before the reading, Houston and I took one last glance toward the door, hoping for a miracle, and who did we see standing there grinning, right on time, but the signifying poet himself.

"Just great," I mumbled. He was signaling behind the ticket takers, as if to say, "I know the poet. Estella and I are old friends." I waved him on through for free.

Then taking my first breath, I lifted into my performance with all the grace I could summon. I dedicated poems to the people to whom they belonged, and offered to all the best I could give. When it was over, I looked out at the crowd and promised that everyone there would receive an autographed copy of *Metamorphosis* as soon as I got them from Randall, who at this very moment was still printing out the last page. With one collective breath they sighed their disappointment and their compassion and began, one by one, to graciously stand up and applaud. And then, as if on cue, they began bringing up mementos for me to sign— posters, napkins, their tickets torn in two. And the signifying poet? Well, he found himself a poster and brought it up, too.

11

SOMEBODY'S CALLING MY NAME

The sense of rootedness and community that I felt at the banquet held me in good stead when a year later, in September 1976, Patrice and I packed up our belongings and, with U-Haul trailer in tow, headed for the University of Iowa. I was finally going to formally study the literature and history of African American people, finally going to tap a cultural root and draw out some of that long-craved elixir. I drove all night, wanting to accustom myself to the road when there was not much traffic. It was my first time driving alone on the freeway and maneuvering a trailer. I got lost more than once, and took it in stride until Treecie woke up no longer excited but crying out frantically from the back seat, "We're lost, aren't we, Momma?"

I blew out the unknown wind that had filled my lungs, pulled into a truck stop, and reread the map. Soon we were on the road again. And within a few more hours, dawn came rolling over the purple horizon, showing clearly that the Kentucky terrain had given way to rows and rows of corn. They at first appeared to me like so many graduates with golden tassels afloat in the breeze, and then like ancestors guarding and lending their grace along the path. The final image, that they could as well be vigilantes caught in the sun's revealing rays, I dared not ponder for long. We proceeded into the small, predominantly white Midwestern town with anticipation, with hope.

It was hard to believe that such a garden of Black resources existed in such a place, that there really was an Afro-American Studies Department, chaired by Dr. Darwin T. Turner and offering a host of courses on theory, criticism, literature, history—life. I knew that whatever we might have to bear here would be well worth it. While I held reservations about Patrice's school, I resigned myself to handle as best I could whatever might present itself. I knew we were leaving the comforts of family and community, but I knew as well that our real roots, with their regenerative possibilities, were embedded within our souls.

This notion was duly challenged by Treecie during the first episodes of Alex Haley's "Roots," which aired not long after our arrival in Iowa. When I asked Patrice if she wanted to watch the third night's episode, she answered by asking, "Momma, do I have to?" During the first two nights, while Kunta Kinte was in Africa, she had sat entranced by the unfolding of the narrative rich in ritual and cultural history. But once the episodes showing the capture of Africans by whites and the horrors of the Middle Passage began, it became too raw, too cutting for her six-year-old sensibilities.

"You don't have to watch it—but I can't tell you the truth about what happened to us any better."

"I don't know if I want to, Momma."

"We can stop and talk if you need to. No matter where the story is, I'll stop," I said.

"But, Momma," she insisted, "they whipped him for nothing and put sores on his back. They fed him leftovers all the time and put him in the dark."

"That's true, baby, and I can't say it's going to get any better tonight . . . it got worse for Black people."

I don't know if she even heard me.

"And they stole him," she said incredulously. "Like I belong to you—they took somebody who belonged to somebody else—that's stealing!"

"You're absolutely right, Treecie, but the beautiful part is . . ."

"They whipped him," she continued, "and tried to make him somebody different. 'Toby!' they said—'Kunta Kinte!' 'Toby!' they said—'Kunta Kinte!'" She was re-enacting the whole story. "It's sorta like—but not just like when I told my teacher that I like being called Patrice for real instead of Treecie for short."

"That's right, baby. What did she say?"

"She said that she thought I wouldn't mind it because you called me Treecie a lot at PTA conferences—but, Momma, that's just between me and you and, you know, family. She's not family. None of them at school are—except Tonie."

"It's your name, baby. You can decide."

Tonie was Treecie's only Black girlfriend there. Treecie loved her so much that she changed her last name for about a week to Tonie's, signing "Patrice Paul" instead of "Patrice Walls" on her papers. Oneida, Tonie's mother, told me that Tonie had done the same thing the week before.

"Momma, you read the book. Does Kunta Kinte ever get to go back home, or do the white people keep doing like they did last night ?"

I knew the story and was not going to clean it up. "I'll just tell you afterwards what happened," I said. "You don't have to watch, baby."

"OK," she said, hardly at all relieved, "and tell me if it's bad like it was last night—'cause if it is, I don't want to go to school tomorrow."

"Honey," I said, lifting her onto my lap, "I know it's bad, but what's this about not wanting to go to school?"

"Because," she said, "the kids will say it again, like they did today, 'Na-na-nanana. The white people won again. Na-na-nanana. The Black people lost. . . .'"

"Hellions!" was my first reaction. "Little white, wicked hellions! Like their ignorant-assed, chain-bearing mammies and pappies before them and theirs before them." But I couldn't say that to Treecie, to whom I had promised to give my best. How to tell her that these children were themselves victims of some offhand deliberate living-room sputterings by some not-so-well-meaning parents who practice a long tradition of domination that serves in time to deny them all of life?

"Baby, Black people didn't lose," I told her firmly. "And we're not losing now. The losers are the ones who hurt others. The people who free themselves and help others to survive are the real winners."

She wanted to believe it, but the doubt was too thick. How had they gotten to her after all I had done to nurture her self-esteem? After all I had done to cover her? Good heavens, I sighed, the wolves are already at the door. I thought about telling her that in "Roots" Chicken George and Kizzy did eventually find some victory, but that would have been too many generations away for her to appreciate my point. I was young myself and full enough of impatience to understand her feelings. The only thing strong enough to pull her out of this was a good dose of Harriet Tubman, and so I told her the tale for the first time that day. As I did, she read my face, hoping the contours would lead her to some place victorious.

"... Harriet would not stand for slavery and so she escaped. They had bloodhounds tracking her, and pettirollers roaming the weeds. They had posters offering forty thousand dollars to anyone who could bring her back, dead or alive. But they couldn't do it. She was just too bad. She made it all the way to freedom. And more than this, baby, she risked doing it again and again! Nineteen times! Coming back to help others escape. She chanced getting caught again. Facing the bloodhounds again. The snakes, the hunger, and guns again. Because she knew freedom was righteous!"

Patrice's eyes stretched in amazement. "How did she get past all those white people? Somebody must have seen her, Momma."

"Sure, people saw her, sometimes," I said. "But she knew how to disguise herself, sometimes as a man, sometimes as an old woman, they say, with chickens tied around her waist, stealing her way right in front of them, right on down the street. But even more, baby, she knew how to call on God. She sang the spirituals, you know. They aren't just ordinary songs," I said.

"Wait, Momma," Patrice said, squinching her eyes. "You're not going to say the songs made her invisible, are you?"

"If you're going to be smart, Patrice, I just won't finish telling you. This is true, little girl. I'm not making this up. Those songs are coded. They carry secret messages. While you're praising God and singing 'Swing Low, Sweet Chariot,' you're also saying something else."

"What?" she asked, leaning forward, and I led her on.

"Chariot rhymes with ...?"

"Harriet?"

"There you go! Swing low, sweet Harriet's coming for to carry you on."

"Neat!"

"And when she's singing 'Steal away, steal away, steal away to Jesus,' it had as much to do with going to heaven as Black folk stealing themselves back from the folks who stole them in the first place. And 'I Ain't Got Long to Stay Here' ain't just talking about leaving earth but the plantation, Patrice. Losers don't make no songs up like that, baby."

"I didn't say it, Momma. They did."

I sucked my teeth long and hard, insinuating that it wasn't even worth our attention, then I slipped into another tune.

161

"'Wade in the water,/ Wade in the water, children,/ Wade in the water,/ God's gonna trouble the water.' That wasn't only about baptism. Getting into the water was a way of hiding their scent from the bloodhounds. Go ahead, say it. Bloodhounds."

"Bloodhounds."

"Pettirollers." And she repeated that, too.

"And when they'd find a water well at the house that was said to be safe, they'd wait there in the weeds. I mean, they couldn't exactly come up to the abolitionists—that's the people who helped the runaways—and say, 'Hey, hello! I'm escaping mean old slavery. Can you take me in? I hear you on my side.'"

"Ah, Momma," she sighed.

"They couldn't do it!" I continued. "The whole thing would have been blown. People were risking their lives to take them in. There were laws against folk helping them. So they'd hide near the water pump and wait. They'd stay there till somebody came out to pump the water singing, 'Go down Moses,/ Way down in Egypt land,/ Tell ol' pharaoh to let my people go.'" I trailed off the song and looked into her eyes.

"Now what do you suppose that message is?" I asked.

"What, Momma? That it's OK to come out, right?"

"You're caught!" I said to her. "After all the dogs and the barking and the nights of traveling and the weeds and snakes and fear and hunger, you're about to go right on back into slavery because you can't read the song."

"Oh, no."

"It's not always the way it sounds, baby. You listened well but sometimes you have to know how to hear. Otherwise the whole thing goes over your head."

"I don't want to be caught. I don't want to go back."

"Then go down, Moses, till it's time to come out!"

She ducked down. I continued singing. She crouched as low as she could go. I sang another opening: "Amazing Grace, how sweet the sound/ That saved a wretch like me./ I was once was lost but now I'm found,/ Was blind but now I see.'"

"Now?"

"Listen, baby. See what's happening. 'Twas grace that taught my heart to fear/ And grace my fears relieved./ How precious did that grace appear/ The hour I first believed."

"I believe I can come out now.'"

162

"I believe you can, too." She hugged me, and I was happy to see her faith restored. "And when you're back at school tomorrow," I said, "remember that we won."

I held her a while longer, thinking of the paper I was planning to write comparing the film "Roots" to the book, thinking of how much I had learned since coming to Iowa. I had to balance my energies as mother and graduate instructor of the Black Poetry Workshop. When I participated in classroom discussions, the layered dimensions of my perspective almost always slowed me down, even as it quickened me. It made me think twice, sometimes thrice, when speaking, writing, or acting.

That summer, and for the next three following, I had the chance to participate in the Afro-American National Endowment Institute. Professors from universities around the country came to Iowa for intensive study of Afro-American culture. I was chosen by Dr. Turner to make summaries of their speeches for the annual report. As such, I had the privilege of attending all the lectures, even the closed ones. I gained understanding and came away with a heightened sense of accountability. Poet Sonia Sanchez talked about the function of Black poetry. Hoyt Fuller spoke on the challenge of publishing in the 1970s, Vincent Harding on the mission of the Black historian. Toni Cade Bambara on empowering Black people, James Farmer on the Civil Rights Movement. I heard Larry Neal speak on the Black aesthetic, Harold Cruse on the continuing crises of the Negro intellectual, Sterling Stuckey on Black folktales, and Leslie Hammon on "African Retention in Black Art." I heard Hortense Spiller, Margaret Walker Alexander, Robert Chrisman, and many others. I heard them challenging each other, even more intensely than my colleagues, Cathy Rosebud, Joe Henry, Dolly McPherson, Opal Moore, and Bob Douglass and I did after every class with Dr. Turner or Dr. Fred Woodard. The exchanges were exciting to witness, especially during this period of the late seventies, a period of metamorphosis from protests outside to transformation from within American institutions. It was good to see Black intellectuals probing the conditions, theorizing strategies, exploring options, and charting new directions for growth in the trenches. True, Martin was gone. And Malcolm, Medgar Evers, Fannie Lou Hamer, Lorraine Hansberry, and others were gone as well. But through these sessions it was evident that the struggle continued. People whose writing I had read in class were standing before me breaking bread. This is what I had been looking for ever since I left Holy Rosary Academy, what I had wanted at Tennessee State and had hoped for during the entire eight years it had taken me to complete my B.A. Furthermore, through the International Writers Workshop and especially through Peter and Mary Nazareth, who directed it, I got to know writers from all over the world. Most rewarding was the opportunity to share with such giving African writers as Ernest Alima of the Cameroon, Bessie Head of Botswana, Ama Ata Aidoo of Ghana, Atukwei Okai of Ghana, Okot p'Bitek of Uganda, and Fatima Dike of South Africa. Learning the works of different thinkers and gaining a sense of our historical struggle made me proud, and at the same time it humbled me. If I had not known before coming to Iowa that Black people were winners, I would have known it after this immersion in the study of Black culture and life. I could better understand the job we each had to do, regardless of where we were or how we did it.

In time I became more interested in the wisdom that Black narrative offered in its various forms, in songs, in telling, and in texts. I wondered about other Harriet Tubmans, about other Black women's lives untold. What had been their strategies for survival? After much gathering, Kunta Kinte's story had been literally broadcast to the four corners. What about other Black lives that were female and artistic? What were their struggles and contributions? I began to wonder not only about the stories that became an important part of African American history and culture partly through the art of oral telling and retelling, but also about autobiography itself, in which the act of writing a life—one's own life— is an important factor. The beginning questions that led toward my dissertation, *Autobiographies by Black Women Literary Artists,* were forming even then, as I watched the unfolding of "Roots."

That night, after my talk with Treecie, I sat a while longer, facing the sliding window that opened on to the cornfield. I could hear Treecie breathing contently as she slept against my breast, and the sound of corn growing defiantly in the field.

The next day, she told me that the discussion at school had continued, and that she had raised her hand to answer why Kunta Kinte had his foot axed off. Even though she had not seen the episode, she answered, "Because the white people knew he would run away again and that he was a winner and they were the losers!" Obviously she had come to her own branching in the song and was more inclined to "tell ol' pharaoh" rather than "go down" and wait for a more opportune time for rising. Good heavens, I moaned, I didn't have to deal with this stuff until I was thirteen years old at Holy Rosary. This mess keeps recurring. Even for myself, learning the strategies, when and how to "go down" and wait for a prudent time to rise, was harder than any theory proper that I had to master there. I had witnessed more than one fighter refuse to go down, tolerate, or wait whatsoever—which, of course, resulted in the fighter's sudden death. In many quarters outside academia, this kind of death would have been deemed worthy of a martyr's reward. In this case, however, there was a twofold loss: the expulsion of the challenger and the continued debilitation of the academy in its failure to be transformed.

"That's stupid," one of the ringleaders had chided Patrice for her remark, but she had insisted all the more.

"They knew he was a winner, just like Harriet Tubman was a winner."

Her teacher, reportedly ignoring the boy's comment, turned to Treecie and said, "Harriet's not in this story. It's not the same story, Patrice."

Her eyes dropped and her shoulders went limp. "Momma, I didn't know what to say."

"I know, baby, I know . . . Do you know what I think?"

"What, Momma?" she pleaded.

"I think your teacher's mistaken. I'm sure it's the same story. Harriet's in this tale. I'm in this story, too. Everybody is! Why else would they want to make sure you knew about who they *thought* was winning? Everybody is in this here story, baby."

Her smile was radiant again.

"Didn't you tell me yesterday that you didn't want to get caught?"

She nodded her head.

"And didn't I see you duck down behind the bushes, trying to figure out that last little trail to freedom?

"Yeah," she said.

"I thought I saw you down there, your plaits sticking up, checking out the scene," I said. "You can't tell me this ain't your story, then, because didn't you kind of feel it, I mean, just a little bit when you heard them talking about his foot being axed off?"

"Yeah, it must have been pretty bad."

I didn't tell her that they had signaled to him that it was either his foot or his testicles. She was already affected enough.

"And didn't I tell you that he told his daughter, Kizzy, about who he really was, and the real meaning of his name, and that she told her baby when she grew up the story about a man wanting freedom so badly that he made a road leading to it out of his own words?"

165

She looked at me hard, and I whispered to her then the truth as I had come to know it: "Some people, seeing you trying to run to freedom, will just as soon ax off a part of your heart to keep you from getting there. And if you try to tell the story of how badly you want it, they will play you off like you're the one that's crazy just like they did old Kunta Kinte. You've got to look up underneath things to see their true meaning. My grandma told me that a long time before Alex Haley even made his movie."

"Her name was Estella, too, right?" Treecie said.

"Yes. It's part of the same story, baby. Otherwise why tell it? Listen to me, baby. There are the ones who go after freedom, and the ones who help them do it, and the ones determined to do anything to keep folks enslaved. The ones who do that rename folks, call them Toby or call them losers, and try to make the truth a lie. The question is, baby, which part are you going to play?"

"I want to be the one who holds up the baby and says, 'Behold Kunta Kinte!'" she said without hesitation.

"No, baby—it's 'Behold the only thing greater than yourself!' Which Kunta Kinte understood as a declaration of his equality with all created beings and that he should submit to no power less than God."

"Yeah, that's who I want to be, the one who says that," Treecie said.

"Good."

"Which one do you want to be, Momma?"

"I don't know. I'll watch it tonight, then tell you."

"Call Tonie and see if she and Oneida are coming down to watch it." A few others were coming as well. Raleigh Williams, a graduate student in music; Bob and Laura Douglass, my colleagues and friends from Louisville; and a couple of writers from the International Writers Workshop were already on their way. The children, Patrice and Tonie, listened as our discussion extended from the significance of Haley's achievement to the struggle in South Africa and Africans around the world, and they made some connections of their own. The next day Patrice and Tonie told us that two white girls at school had joined their side, deciding they were not going to be the ones to keep folk from getting to freedom. Perhaps, as the series moved toward the contemporary period, the white parents had begun to recognize how their positions outside the film were linked to their support for characters and agendas within the film. Maybe they could see that the nineteenth-century enslaver had metamorphosed into "Bull" Connor.

Later, Treecie asked me again which character I wanted to be, and this time I answered, "The one who writes the story, Patrice."

She sighed, disappointed. "He doesn't have a very big part, Momma. He doesn't even get born till the end."

"But the end is always the beginning, baby," I said with a wink. "Do you want to watch again tonight?"

12

I'M BUILDING ME A HOME

The great day of reckoning had arrived. I had been in this garden wilderness and had taken from its fruits. I had been nourished by teachers and texts, and my vision had expanded. I was propelled by an urgency now, a determination to find a way to take the knowledge that had begun to sprout within me and find relevant expression. I wanted to test it within the community that it was designed to feed. I wanted to come home. The work I started with my dissertation, which included a scholarly analysis of autobiographies by Black women writers, and the writing of my own autobiography needed a cultural, political, spiritual context that would reality-test its spirit and enhance it. The life that I had brought forth in words, like that of my daughter, needed a similar context and rootedness. We would transplant our lives from the controlled environment of African American studies, which was like a culture dish in which my consciousness and vision had germinated, to the open landscape of Black people's lives.

I didn't know exactly what I would do once I got there, but I knew that it was time to come home. Patrice was almost eleven, and we both needed to be part of a thriving Black community again. We needed to smell greens cooking in old family pots, and to be able to just show up at folks' doorsteps without invitation and be welcomed, and to see and feel naturally affirming looks that celebrated our chocolate brown sweetness as sister, friend, neighbor, even stranger, but still kin. I could finish my dissertation right there with good support and seek out the artist group, Montage, that had been forming the last time I visited. I imagined the group had developed into a moving force by now.

The re-entry was wonderful. Gert swept Treecie up in her arms like she was some promised child presented at the temple, and Lu hugged me as if I were Zora herself coming back to the briar patch. It wasn't until I visited sculptor Ed Hamilton at his studio that the glow began fading. I learned that Montage had been dismantled.

"There were only a few of us," Ed said, "the same few. I can't spend all my energy with folk who are not going to get it together." I could almost imagine a new world sun dissipating at its rising. At the African Heritage Weekend, I ran into poet Georgeann Berry, who along with Bob Douglass and Priscilla Hancock had organized the first African Heritage Weekend years before. It had been a class project she had decided to move beyond paper. They had transformed the Belvedere Hotel in the central business district into a cultural festival with traditional flags, African dishes, and various performances. And now, eight years later, it was officially the Mayoral African Heritage Weekend, one in an array of celebrations. The National Mayoral Conference was meeting across from the Belvedere, and Black folk were serving barbecued ribs and offering anything in their booths from rags to wigs, all in the name of culture. At least Umar and Jaja had authentic African fabric. Georgeann sat on the sidelines remembering how it was, how it could have been.

"They'd just as soon call it Negro Weekend or Chitterlings Fest," she said, joining us. "It's out of our control now."

"Some folk don't care what's in the booth so long as they're making a profit. You could've just as well brought back some of that corn from Iowa or some watermelon seeds from the market and sold it to the children as Nubian beans!" Georgeann chuckled.

"Speaking of watermelon," Gloria said, "tell Georgeann your watermelon poem, Estella."

"Actually it's about my re-entry, or maybe our overall condition here. I can't tell."

"Skip the preface, Estella. Let me hear the poem!"

"OK. It's called 'Question: Multiple Choice.' You ready? 'What's red, black, and green and a symbol of black unity?'"

"Goodness. Is nothing sacred?" Georgeann sighed. "Is this what she brings us back from the cornfields?"

"Come on, let me finish. 'The possible answers are (A) the African liberation flag . . .'"

"Here we go."

"'(B) a sun kissed watermelon'—ready?"

"You can do better than that, Estella!"

"'Or (C) a pseudo-Black intellectual who has read all the current definitions of the "Negro problem" and still doesn't understand a damn thing!'—I'm lost."

"No, you're not lost. You're a fool, girl!" she said, hugging me. "I'm glad you're back, Estella."

"Me, too. Maybe we can do something to get this place moving."

"Now that is green, girl. I'm tired. After struggling to get on my feet, raising five daughters and a son, getting my bachelor's and trying to build for years, I am tired. I'm not going to spend my last energy fighting anybody, sweetheart."

"But, Georgeann . . ."

"Naw, girl, you and Gloria go right along. I'm too busy two-timing Arthur Ritis with Mr. Ben Gay."

"Ah, come on."

"And Muse? He's jealous as he can be. I ain't spent a minute with him lately."

"Ah, heck," I said, squaring off. "Muse been out mingling all over town. He was by my house last night trying to get a little play. Couldn't even sustain a decent kiss!"

"Is that right?"

"Yeah. Said he was hungry, hadn't eaten in days."

"Well, there's some baby back ribs on the table, sugar! See do he want some of them!" She laughed. "And when he's finished, tell him I said to bring his behind on home!"

I had not expected this. I thought Georgeann's energy would last forever. "You still my girl, though," she said. "If you and Gloria get something going, let me know."

The situation was more stark the following week at a regional conference that sponsored workshops on career development for artists. Ken Clay, recently appointed minority programs director at the new Kentucky Arts Center, had asked me to do a reading as part of his last project before taking that position. Still, nobody believed that any proposal, however beautifully written, was going to magically persuade funders to back arts projects that unleashed the real expression of Black artists. And nobody thought that the new downtown complex, though it sponsored national groups, was committed to the development of local Black talent.

With all this in mind, when the time came for me to read, I was struck speechless. Many of the artists from Montage were there, as well as some of their children. And even the light in some of their eyes seemed dim. I knew the look. I had watched Treecie's own eyes grow hungry. That was part of the reason I'd come home. What could I say to them and to myself about our condition here? Which poem before me could possibly feed that need? Which could possibly be milk for the children, who when last I left Louisville were being bused out of the community and into white schools amid jeering crowds of protesters, denied any real protection by police? I looked down at my pitcher of water now and fought back the tears. What could I possibly offer?

"A libation," I said suddenly, walking out from behind the podium, "for the Spirit that enlivens us and in remembrance of the brothers and sisters, the mentors and ancestors who have passed from us in this life—that they may join us here in spirit instead of us joining them in their graves."

Alice Walker had gone back recently to resurrect the spirit and get the "laying on" of Zora Neale Hurston. Now I realized even more profoundly than before that it is more than the bodies of our ancestors that are buried in unmarked graves. We bury their spirits, too, when we do not remember them. So I lifted the pitcher high before them and I began calling names and sprinkling the water after each remembrance: "... Larry Neal ... Lorraine Hansberry ... Hoyt Fuller ... Sara Fabio ... Zora Neale Hurston." I looked out at the circle of people who were getting up and gathering around me. Like intermittent lights, they all began pronouncing names of their own cultural mentors: "Bob Thompson ... Bob Marley ... John Coltrane ... Helen Humes ... Paul Robeson ... Langston Hughes ... Roland Kirk." The expression of the one remembering now became charged with the energy of the one being remembered. We were strengthened and eagerly made resolute plans to do great things together.

At the end of the conference, I was asked to come forward again. I repeated the ritual of naming, but this time I looked to the future rather than the past. "For the children," I said boldly, "the bridge and our future. Patrice

Simone Walls!" And everybody took up the torch. Everybody had some-body who embodied their hopes and to whom they owed the legacy.

We had moved to organize for future projects so that arts organiza-tions and funders could not ignore us. And it seemed we were on our way. But after a few meetings, our intentions shifted. Besides not being able to move beyond ego, we just couldn't do it. We were basically a com-munity of exhausted people who, before we could even begin to build anything, needed to rebuild our own energies. My own depletion in a way was characteristic of our group.

I began to feel not only tired but trapped. I tried writing a play, hop-ing to ignite the fuse, to spark some dynamism. I even gathered read-ers to workshop the script, but the reading was only an occasion; it was not a lasting structure. My restlessness grew. I told myself that I was home and that Patrice, thank God, was satisfied. But in time, I had to face the unrelenting fact that nothing I did to sustain myself was satisfying or regen-eration enough. Shaping words of hope over a piece of paper was not regenerating enough. Cutting my first album and singing after the terrible serial killings in Atlanta—"Georgia Moon moans in tones of bleed-ing red—twenty-one black children have been found dead . . ."—was not enough. Working as artist-in-residence in the public schools and see-ing little Black children and little white children trying desperately through their writings to break the spells of ignorance being put upon them by those who have lost their own power to dream was not, have mercy, enough. And certainly, trying, as instructor at the University of Louisville, to cram all the beauty, sorrow, vision, challenge, denial, and triumph of our peo-ple into one single little Black literature course a year was not, and would never be, enough.

One night, while I drove home from Gloria's and thought about leav-ing Louisville, the questions became overwhelming. I no longer won-dered why G. C. Coxe, an elder artist, told Houston years ago to get the hell out of Louisville if he wanted the artist in him to grow. Now I was wondering: what happens to a community when so many serious artists leave for their own survival, or when the ones who stay are either caged, silenced, or starved to the point of turning on each other for the crumbs tossed irreverently their way? And where is the place—not the psychic territory, not the psychological space, but the tangible, concrete-on-ground place—in the community where Black artists can face off and be, when they need to be, each other's grace? Where are our Black institutions? Our nests? Our wombs? Our birthing places? The "I am because we are" thriving Black faces?

I kept on driving instead of going home, heading toward Broadway, looking around. Was it like this in every other town? Liquor stores every five or six blocks, churches every five? A renaissance in Louisville, as some had predicted? No renaissance happens with just one artist or two. The Harlem Renaissance worked because of a whole range of events—migrations to a central location, artists facing off to create a new jazz sound, financial support and commitment from inside and out, a return to Black pride and heritage. It sounded good in Darwin Turner's class, but here in the field, in the wilderness, it was difficult to achieve. I ended up straining in the night. Then the police lights went on behind me along with sirens. My eyes flashed to the speedometer. I couldn't have been going more than five miles over the limit. I stopped and waited for the officer to get out. A beefy man with a John Wayne swagger made his way to my side.

Within moments, I had been arrested and soon found out what it was really like to be caged. For a traffic violation and expired registration that I thought was covered under a thirty-day Iowa grace period, I was fingerprinted, strip-searched, and thrown into a holding cell with eight other women, three of whom were prostitutes, and one of whom had tried to free her boyfriend from jail. It was hot, funky, and noisy, and in that instant I hated all of Louisville. I found out from the others that there would be no early release. We would all be there all night—the nine of us in a nine-by-nine concrete cell with a bench and a toilet and a water fountain on top of the toilet tank.

I had enough time to remember that all of my brothers had already had similar experiences. Houston, on his second day home from Vietnam. "We been waiting for one of you all night" was the reason given. Spivey, on one of two times because the accusing crime victim said, "The nigger was red like you!" And Giles and William, harassed on their way home from a sweaty match of handball. "Oh, Father," one of the cops blurted out after ransacking Giles's identification and discovering that he was a priest, "I was raised Catholic!" I imagine I could have counted myself blessed, as a Black person living in Louisville, that I had made it this far without being hauled off to jail.

The nine of us in the holding cell took turns squatting down and breathing through the tiny air valve on the door or peeping through the window at the top. I quit taking my turn. This was no less wretched than our general condition in this city. Why stay? It wasn't worth it. I could surely do better.

After spending the rest of the summer in courts getting the charges cleared, I called Houston and Shasha in New York and told them I was coming to get a job and an apartment there.

"Stella," Houston said, "I'm not trying to discourage you, but do you know how long it took us to find an apartment? And Shasha had a job when she came."

I didn't care. I doggedly paced the New York streets and filled the wires with job applications. I followed leads and searched for more. If Houston attempted anything like logic, I'd jump him. "What? You don't believe in miracles anymore?"

I walked the streets holding on to Treecie, who at one point pulled against me, begging, "Please don't make me move to the country's city dump!" After moving back to Louisville and feeling the acceptance and security of family and friends, she was not willing to go anywhere. And I, just as emphatically, was not willing to stay in a place where there was hardly any air for a Black person—or a Black artist—to breathe.

"I'll be leaving Christi, Momma. And Buffy. I could never have fun here. Grandma's not here. Gert's not here. And Chickasaw Park and Immaculate Heart School. Why can't you just do your poetry in Louisville?"

Her resistance had caused me for the first time, in any significant way, to look at myself as artist on the one hand and mother on the other. I discovered then that the real division wasn't between me and Treecie. It was inside myself.

The poet and the mother. The last dream I remembered having in recent months featured one of them carrying the other in a bag over her shoulder, taking her who knows where, no doubt to her burial. The one rumbling in the bag was hollering something awful. The struggle to maintain both aspects of self had escalated to crisis level behind the depletion of seven years of single parenting and of struggling to develop my craft. Understanding this now, I felt embarrassed at my one-dimensional "stuff the other in the bag" survival tactic. Surely there was a way for both of them to live. A place where they both could be free. I kissed Patrice and told her I needed to pray. She slept that night more peacefully than I did.

The only thing clear by morning was that I should go back to Louisville with my baby, so that's what I did. Houston called the next day saying that one of the jobs had come through. We both had to laugh.

"Maybe another time," I said. "I got orders to stay."

"And do what?"

"I don't know, Grasshopper! I do know that I got just enough money left to pay Treecie's first month's tuition."

"You been watching too many kung fu movies, Estella. Give Treecie a kiss and tell her she deserves an Academy Award!"

"She really doesn't like New York."

"She made that clear. Some days I could do well without it, too. The trick to New York is timing. When to come and when to get the hell out. You all are good."

"I guess."

"Besides, that's open territory there. There's all kinds of stuff an artist can do in Louisville."

"Don't patronize me."

"Things like checking out the bluegrass."

"Right, Grasshopper."

He could say that while the Alvin Ailey Dance Company was dancing "Revelations" down the road, and the Boys Choir of Harlem was singing "Take the A Train," and the Studio Museum in Harlem, where Shasha was now deputy director, was showing some of the baddest Black artists in the world, and downtown, August Wilson, Ntozake Shange, George Wolfe, and heaven knows who else were charging the stage night after night with new, powerful visions. And jazz musicians were over at Grant's Tomb raising some serious sounds, and crowds of merchants and minglers were streaming Africa Square with three hundred sixty degrees of greener green. And the Schomburg Center for Research in Black Culture was carrying on seminars, and you were liable to see at the next table Woodie King of the New Federal Theater, or Madeline Yoyodole of Women of the Calabash, or Amiri Baraka, or Toni Morrison, or, for that matter, the sister who left Louisville years ago.

"Right" I said to Houston. "There's plenty an artist can do here in Louisville."

"Seriously," he added. "You're the one who told me when you first came back there that 'this is sacred ground I'm standing on.'"

"I know. I know. It still is."

175

"Then take your shoes off," he said.

And I did. I put together a couple of part-time jobs and settled in with the rest of the folk. And soon afterward my dreams began coming again. In one, a woman who looked like a mountain at first sat up and lifted the dark green veil from her long coiling hair, revealing cheekbones full like my mother's and dark crystal eyes like all the women I've ever loved. "Tell them," she said in a deep dusky tone. "Tell them so you'll know."

Tell who what? She veiled herself and merged back into the mountain. I didn't know what she was talking about. Lu didn't. Gloria didn't either, and Treecie was just grateful the mountain woman hadn't said, "Leave Louisville so you'll know." A few nights later, I dreamed that a bearded man was sitting before me. He held an empty book in his right hand and, after speaking, asked what I understood from his story. In relating the story back to him, I found myself even more enlightened and my words appearing readily upon the page. Then, as a teacher well pleased, he leaned forward and whispered, "Ah, symbiosis—the basis of human relationships."

I reached for my pad sitting on the table next to my bed and tried my best to remember the words I had spoken to him. Something about a man and a woman or people joining together on something, something about sustenance? Survival? Wholeness? My babbling was not making any words appear. They faded more rapidly at the exact moment I distinguished—with a kind of suspicion, if not disdain—that the bearded man was, in fact, not Black. "Who are you?" I whispered. "Why didn't you come Black or Native American like the mountain woman did?" Now I couldn't even see him clearly anymore, the purity of our sharing having been violated.

Suddenly, I didn't trust any of it. Here I was trying to figure out a way to feed and to be fed in a starving community, and I'm visited by some privileged, other-cultured, other-world being with plump cheeks glorious with health? The mistrust hung in the air, misting over my recognition. Suspicion had canceled gratitude. I'm being trifling, I admitted. Ashamed, I started over.

The gift of his story had called forth my speech to manifest words on the page. What words? I went hurriedly to the encyclopedia. The entry for "symbiosis" told me that in biology it meant a "close association of two different organisms that benefits both." It went on to say that "the small plant growth known as the lichen is a result of symbiosis." I then flipped to look up "lichen," which I discovered was actually two plants, an algae and a fungus. Unlike a fungus, an algae has neither roots, stems, nor leaves. Nevertheless, an algae is able to make, by photosynthesis, food which it supplies to the fungus, which is unable to make food. Their inter-dependence is completed by the fungus's role in furnishing moisture to the algae from rain and dew that it absorbs. I kept reading until I reached a part that quickened my soul. I saw that "Biblical scholars believe that the manna God fed the Israelites in the desert was a lichen." Manna? Manna? So, through our very relationships with one another, it is possible for us to become manna? To generate food? Through some kind of cooperative system to sustain community?

The metaphor was fascinating. The question was how to make the lichen manifest in our lives. Who were the two people, the two entities, the two forms of life by which this could happen? I kept my eyes open and deter-mined not to look away, no matter how thick the distance of attainment might be. The unreconciled strivings of the mother/poet dream could be resolved. The first glimpse of coexistence suggested by the lichen. The counsel of the mountain woman, "Tell them so you'll know," reinforced the revelation of the reciprocity, the symbiosis involved in sharing and in informing.

In possession of this knowledge, I accepted the charge to name and become my whole poet self. And one day, fully expectant, I saw phys-ically the space in which this would happen. I was driving along Virginia Avenue, the old riot site of the 1960s, and slammed on the brakes before a building for sale in the residential section. Here was my lichen! It was a large duplex with two apartments, two entrances, one that could perform the function of the fungus and the other the function of the algae. Patrice and I could live on one side and the community could cre-atively use the other side for a cultural center. And the courses in dance and poetry, the community building, and other offerings presented by the artists could provide sustenance for them as well as for the house. I jotted down the number and called the real estate agent. "I'm going to get that house," I said. "I'm going to save every dime from my short-term artist-in-residency, set up readings, whatever it takes so we can have ourselves a cultural center!"

I would organize the schedule, bring in teachers, recruit students. Portia White, an accomplished dancer, could teach dance; Gloria, piano. Duffy could teach visual art, and Elder Traynor, who had played on my album, could surely teach guitar. Georgeann would have to bring Muse and teach history classes. And Capri, a local poet friend, could run the poetry workshop. Leadership workshops would help solidify our purpose. Classes would be scheduled every day except Sunday. Saturday would be a full day—dance classes in the back room, piano lessons in the front, art to follow. By two o'clock the children's classes would be over, and Earbie Johnson's percussion ensemble could use the space for practice. I would contact Chuck Cowan, a local karate teacher, about a beginning course for the children on Thursdays, and see if somebody could do African storytelling on Wednesdays.

The first person I told was Patrice. She and Lu were delighted. Then Patrice and I drove to Gloria's to get a commitment and then to our friend Zambia's. We went from point to point, telling folk, getting promises and input. Zambia and Carol Miller agreed to tutor grades one through three. Amy Brown took the middle grades. She had been voted teacher of the year and would be a great resource.

First, of course, I had to get the house. It was owner financed, and I went beyond the real estate broker to talk to the owner himself. I managed to make a financial arrangement I could afford. Two weeks after Treecie and I moved in, we had a thirty-day countdown to get the center ready. We would open on the first day of Black History Month, the birthday of Langston Hughes. Elder Traynor volunteered to help. The first two days we worked just hauling junk away. On the third day, an old friend, Dan Jordan, called offering to take me to dinner. It was nice to hear from him, I said, but we were opening a cultural center and there was no telling when I'd have time for a date. In less than a half hour, he was at the door dressed in bib overalls and brogan boots, holding a bucket of green paint in each hand. I welcomed him in like spring. He and I spent every day working until two or three in the morning, patching the giant holes, steaming off layers of ancient wallpaper, cleaning carpets, and painting. Elder Traynor came with bundles of carpet remnants retrieved from a local department store dumpster. He arranged the pieces to form huge letters "BK" on the back room wall, for Blackaleidoscope. The closer we got to the opening, the harder we worked, the more creative we became. I knew this venture would be on time, unlike my book. The house vibrated with hammer tones, the smell of fresh paint, and boundless hope. Gloria and Zambia helped bring in thirty chairs that the church next door was discarding. As we sat around the table making plans, we watched resources generate before us— children's books and pads, a stereo along with a copy of Nina Simone's "To Be Young, Gifted, and Black," which we played for inspiration whenever we started work, and a chess game, music stands, posters, toilet paper.

After placing about twenty calls a night and hearing everything from joy to jealousy, I was hoarse. I stopped calling one night and wrote up the center's program while Patrice designed the logo. It was ingenious. The letter K from the word "Black" was lowered a little and served for the beginning of the word "Kaleidoscope." I took the program to a printer, but I was running out of money. I would have to get another reading to make enough to pay for them. Walker, Lu, and Mr. and Mrs. Maxwell had agreed to prepare the meal on opening day. Then one night, just when things were beginning to look good, the fuses blew.

"No," I screamed defiantly, and Dan echoed the word after me in the same inflection. I couldn't help but laugh. Obviously, the carpet cleaner and the electric saw together were too much for the circuits. We felt our way to the fuse box, lightly holding on to each other's hands. "Don't try to get no play, Estella, just because we here in the dark together!" Dan said. "I'm a busy man. I've got a cultural center to open!"

"Do you, now?"

"Yes, I do," he said, his laughter trailing to a tender seriousness. We reached the fuse box and turned the lights back on. "When I left California," Dan said while we were still standing there, "I was hoping something would be happening back here in Louisville. But after six months, it was the same old grind. Play tennis, go to work, play tennis, blow my horn. The point is, I kept running into sisters who ain't me, you know? And then somebody says, 'Estella Conwill's back!' And it was kind of redeeming just to hear that. So hey, on the real side, I'm game. Call me committed, too."

"Thank you, Dan," I whispered before we turned to go back upstairs.

The next day, only three days before the opening, Dan and Elder Traynor found me standing with my boots on in freezing water, mopping and crying over the mess caused by burst water pipes. I had turned off the main valve and was wringing out the mop. At first I did not see the package in Traynor's hand. Then I caught sight of the logo.

"Oh, my goodness," I said through my tears. "You got the programs! You two are incredible! Patrice, come down here and see!" She spun down the staircase and Dan held the program like a village caller and began reading our statement.

"Blackaleidoscope is dedicated to the celebration and enrichment of Black Art and Culture." He went on reading the description of the courses offered and of how we had planned to implement our goals.

"Yeah," Treecie said, stretching out her arms. "Sign me up for dance!"

We all embraced and then I stretched the kinks out of my spin. I was ready to start back mopping again when I saw Patrice still standing there.

"The speech, Momma. You promised to help me write the speech. I could do Martin Luther King's 'I Have a Dream,' but I really want to make my own."

"Then let's do it, honey. Let's go." I handed the mop to Dan and zipped down my boots.

On our way upstairs, I asked her, the way I would in time ask over a hundred children who would come through those doors and have to prepare their own presentations, "What things can you remember off the top of your head that impressed you—from anywhere around the world—during the twelve years you've been given? It's your world." She answered, and we began writing and practicing her speech—one whose eloquent delivery would take her beyond the 4-H club, council, and regional level of competition to make her champion of 4-H speech-making in the twelve-year-old category for the entire state of Kentucky.

On the day of the opening, Bale and Tade McKnight of Experience Africa drummed and danced down the aisle, singing a joyous traditional Yoruba welcome. Mrs. Anna Huddleston and Mr. G. C. Coxe, elder artists of the community, lifted their hands over the bowed heads of the teachers, proclaiming to each of us the charge: "May God grant you the ability to create, the will to serve, and the undeniable instinct to love!" Gloria and I then presented the two elders with the first Blackaleidoscope Awards for Artistic Excellence and Nation-Building. Mr. G. C. was totally surprised. "This is the first time," he said, laughing, "that I ever received an award with my name on it. All the other trophies were blank, and I always felt that if I hadn't shown up, they could have just as well given it away to the next fellow. But this one here is mine."

Of course it was. He and Mrs. Huddleston had been performing a laying-on-of-hands ritual in less formal situations for years. We then presented carpenter's trophies to Dan Jordan and Elder Traynor for all the work they had done to this moment. Nancy Ross and Thomas, local dramatists, presented a medley of Langston Hughes's poems, and jazz vocalist Hazel Miller sang, like nobody else could, Al Jarreau's "Can You Believe in a Dream."

The reality had unfolded through us, and we kept it alive, holding classes, festivals, open discussions, and parades. The first year we welcomed Haki Madhubuti for our summer festival, Sandra Govan for our woman's month lecture series, and many participants of the annual Black Family Conference who accepted our open invitation for a community feast. Gloria, Dan, and some other brothers helped to transport them from the downtown hotel, and Priscilla, Zambia, Karen, and Georgeann helped to serve. When word spread that Harlem's Queen Mother Moore, the noted Garveyite and champion of reparations for Black people, had accepted our invitation, people from all over the neighborhood appeared at the door bringing their children to have her bless them.

After Blackaleidoscope's first anniversary, William and Faye and their four-year old son, Giles Burgess Harrison-Conwill, moved back to Louisville and lived at the center. William had completed his doctorate in psychology, and Faye had completed hers in cultural anthropology. They began working at Humana Hospital and the University of Louisville, but also designed new courses for the center. They added new life to the place—Giles by rushing down on Saturday mornings in his dance shoes and motorcycle helmet to take classes.

I marveled especially at the children. There was three-year-old Fulani, who challenged the cut-off age of four for beginning piano, saying, "I know my left hand and my right hand and my ABCs and I can play boogie-woogie chopsticks! So please let me get lessons, too!" And there was Bobby, a disheartened adolescent who was failing in school and would play chess with Patrice and lose every time, his confidence was so low. After six weeks of being tutored by Amy, he and his mother rang the doorbell to show his report. His grades were all As and Bs. When he finished taking in our hugs, he challenged Patrice to a game of chess—and, for the first time, he won!

There was Janeen, whose parents had brought her in for William's Leadership Training Course for Teens because she was having difficulty adjusting to her white suburban school and understanding the friction she encountered. Unlike her peers at the center, she did not live in the Black community and was not likely to pick up much of what they had learned simply by living there. William said that during group discussion, when he made a passing reference to our previous enslavement, she was absolutely shocked. "What do you mean, 'When we were slaves'?" Her parents' attempt to protect her had sheltered her from this vital information, offering her no way of understanding her predicament or constructing strategies for survival. Upon realizing our history, her face grew animated not so much with horror but with relief. The problem was not in her but in society.

And then there was Robin, who studied dance; Capri, her father, had raised her alone from infancy. He brought her by Kaleidoscope frequently, even beyond the classes. She became Patrice's younger sister, and by the end of the second year she asked permission from her father to convert to Catholicism and for me to be her godmother.

The many ways we loved, struggled, and fed each other at Blackaleidoscope demonstrated the full meaning of "Tell them so you'll know." Knowing became not simply a question of recognition but a way of manifesting our human potential: Tell them so you'll grow.

13

STANDING IN THE NEED OF PRAYER

Dan and I had become so much a part of each other's lives during that first year of Kaleidoscope that it was both exhilarating and scary. I knew that if I married him, as he was asking me to do, I would be out of the Catholic Church, and I agonized over this. Four years earlier, I had applied for a church annulment of my marriage, anticipating a time such as this when I would love again. The loneliness I had felt since divorcing Princeton had proved itself not just some bothersome spot that would eventually go away but an ever darkening indigo that was spreading throughout my soul. So I had undergone the three-hour interview for the annulment, opening myself to new probings of my pain, answering questions that I never thought would make it to open air. And afterward I had come home so emotionally drained that I simply crawled into bed.

I was asked by the interviewing priest about my ability at age nineteen to fully comprehend the implications of the marital vows, about my ex-husband's ability to commit himself to the lifetime relationship, about the nature of our sex life, the frequency of our contact, my fidelity, and his moral standing, and if I thought I had subliminally used marriage as a means of getting out of Louisville. I answered him as honestly as could. At the time of the questioning, I did not see the relevance of age to the issue. In my thinking, nineteen was a relative number. I knew at that age what I was committing myself to. Despite the readiness of the interviewer to suggest the possibility of a teenager's lack of preparedness for such a commitment, I struggled to maintain clarity and honesty. Certainly, if I had married at twenty-five or thirty instead of nineteen, I would have been more mature—but the questions themselves had begun to frustrate me. They all seemed to be leading toward a predetermined conclusion. As I saw it, it was my ex-husband who did not understand the implications of the vow—that is, that having forsaken all others, we were each other's best and only choice. I knew at nineteen what this meant, and I was not looking for somebody else to come strutting down the road. I could not simply plead emotional immaturity as the basis for an annulment. Nor was I simply trying to get out of Louisville at the time, or reaching out for comfort while mourning my brother Joseph. I may have been experiencing all of these things, but they were separate from my choice of Princeton. God knew it and I knew it. The thing that needed to be examined by the Chancery was my ex-husband's commitment. He was the one who had broken the vows—or perhaps had never really made them. I realized that the view of my experience that I was revealing did not fit into the predetermined scenarios, but I tried to express myself the best way I could. The interviewing priest at the Chancery office told me then that the process would take about a year perhaps; that they would have to contact my ex-husband, who lived in yet another city now, and interview him, if he was willing; and then the tribunal would deliberate. He made it sound as if I had good grounds for getting the annulment based on all the information I had shared.

However, the process took much longer than expected. Princeton agreed to the interview, but after that the process became more vague and complicated. The first council of the tribunal, it seemed, offered a positive outcome, but the next one was negative and so the case was sent to Rome for final approval. I was put in the position of waiting forever. Over the next four years I would check on the process every time I came home from Iowa—at Christmas, Easter, spring break, and summer. It was my first priority after greeting my family. The answers, or lack thereof, became more frustrating each time. I don't know what Princeton had told them in his interview, but after that, the information on the proceedings seemed like babble to me. At one time, when I had my parish priest check on the status of my case, I found that my papers, which I had waited so anxiously for, had been placed put on hold; they had to be dug out again and reactivated. From age twenty-eight to age thirty-three, this was my obsession, my own private hell. My life was on hold while I waited to hear how my marital status would be regarded by the church. In addition to the anguish I had already suffered in my marriage and divorce, I felt I had no control over my life and future. In the five years that I waited, I had to fight viciously against my growing resentment. Even if they ruled in the end that my marriage was annulled, I would still have a bitter taste in my mouth from the process itself. I felt stripped and invaded. If they ruled that my marriage was not annulled, I would feel invaded for no good reason—that, more important, I had not been heard and the vision of reciprocity or symbiosis between me and the Chancery was still incomplete. I had lived it and knew that it wasn't a marriage. I had brought a wholehearted commitment to the relationship and Princeton had not. Most important of all, if I did not receive the annulment and I ever chose to remarry, I would be barred from receiving communion.

At Christmas time one year, I had even taken my complaint about waiting for my annulment into a confessional.

"How old are you," the priest asked.

"Twenty-nine," I told him.

"And how long did your marriage last?"

"Seven years," I answered.

"Then what are you complaining about? You've had seven good years of sex!"

On hearing that, I got up off of my knees and walked out.

The priest's reaction had re-ignited my disappointment with the Church. At Midnight Mass, I had decided not to take communion even though as a divorced Catholic I was free to do so. I felt ostracized. I was single, alone. I was surrounded, it seemed, by people who were mostly in couples, which only intensified my feelings of disconnectedness. The very things that used to comfort me—the songs, the scriptural readings, the sermon itself—now inspired sorrow. In the midst of the celebration of the birth of my Lord, I felt submerged in the pain of His passion. I sat tearfully in the pew, while the rest of my family and everybody else in the church proceeded to communion unaware of my turmoil. I sat not only because of the impediment of my anger and feelings of rejection, but because I was allowing myself to feel what it would be like never to receive the Holy Eucharist again. The only thing that was stopping me from leaving the Church totally was the Holy Eucharist. This one denial, the single act of not going to the communion rail, was so cata-strophic that later that night I got drunk at the family dinner. Having denied myself the consecrated wine, I drank my own unconsecrated bottle, and ended up creating the conversation I wished I had had with the priest in the confessional that day:

"Are you sorry then for your sins, my child?"

"I am sorry, Father, that the Church is so stupidly insensitive to my situation! That it has never cared about my poor little Black female ass and still has the nerve to call itself the body of Christ, you jerk!"

I sipped some more wine.

"Of course the Church cares for you, my child. It was not the Church who left you. It was you who left the Church. You could have taken com-munion tonight. You just chose not to. You could have stayed on your knees and asked for forgiveness, and I would have granted you absolution."

"Father, you're not getting it. I'm talking about the bread of life. It keeps me alive. It keeps me from dying. And you are telling me that if I choose to get married again, I will have to starve to death? No, no, my dear Father. I don't question God's compassion and power that's been keep-ing me whole till now. It's the Church's compassion that gets me down."

The wine that I kept sipping didn't have the power to enliven me for-ever, but it did take the edge off the pain. A few months after that episode, the results of the tribunal's inquiry come down. My request for an annul-ment by the Catholic Church was denied. In a two-line statement. A cold dismissal. An oppressive obstruction—here again was the jump rope that my brothers had strung across the altar in the basement to keep me from the circle of authority. The obstruction sickened me even more now. Jesus, I sighed, what am I to do?

More than a year passed after my annulment was denied. The more I prayed and threw myself into my dissertation and my cultural work at Blackaleidoscope, the more aware I became of my aloneness—of my need for a relationship. With Dan having so comfortably eased into my life, I began thinking that it was possible for me to be happy again. We spent long evenings talking about our relationship. I spoke to him about my difficulty with the Church, even though I still considered myself Catholic. Though Dan was not a Catholic, he was sympathetic. I knew that the contradictions would not simply go away. And since I had no desire to find another denomination in which to worship, I knew that my conflicting feelings would not just subside.

Dan and I also talked about other aspects of our relationship. We spoke about tensions that might arise because of the disparity in the years of our formal education. I would have a doctorate and he only a high school diploma. But that didn't seem as insurmountable to me as the possibility that if I married him, I would no longer be able to receive the sacraments. In fact, I was beginning to think that Dan was the answer to my prayers. That love was its own kind of law. That what mattered was that a man and a woman love each other and grow together. During our engagement, I could see that we really respected each other's energies and visions. When we were together I didn't just feel connected to him, I felt connected to the community. I felt free. Unlike my first marriage, where I was swept up by love, out of control, this could be a marriage in which my husband and I could design a life together. And I was aware of the ways in which this example was important to Patrice, who was now thirteen years old. The three of us would make a wonderful family. God knows we all could stand some joy in our life.

Dan and I married and began our new relationship together. He moved in with us, and we shared our plans for the future. He said that he would return to pursue his long-deferred studies in industrial engineering. And I said I would definitely finish my dissertation so I could apply for positions in the local area and began training someone to take my post at the center. It felt good to relax a minute, to depend on someone else a minute, to laugh freely. He seemed not to have a care in the world, and I felt I had all the cares in the world. It was like seeking a complement that was not just comfortable, but full.

While I began carrying out my plans, Dan put his dream on hold and began to refurbish our side of the house. At first it was simply replacing a cracked window, stopping a leak, or painting a room. When he blasted the first opening in the kitchen wall to put in a new window, I was delighted by the light that poured like dawn down the stairwell. I was excited to see the potential of the remodeling and of the restructuring of our lives together. I was also excited to see him doing what would make him happy.

But days passed, then weeks with only the frame installed. We swept up dust for months, and then one day, in the midst of mounting tension over time, money, dreams, and life, he blasted an even bigger hole through yet another wall. Our whole side of the building was in a state of disrepair.

One of Dan's classic responses to our problems became "You're the one with the Ph.D. You figure it out!" or "You're the artist, you tell me!" He began to close up on me. He seemed to be only in love with the wife, perhaps, or the mother, or the woman who could envision a cultural center and build it with him—but not with the midnight apprentice, the woman who roamed the forests of literature looking for roots and bitters that could cure blindness or untie the muted tongue. "You know I'm proud of you," he would say, " but I'll be glad when this is over."

"But I'm a writer; even after my dissertation it will never be truly over, Dan. This is also who I am," I'd say, no doubt looking as strangely back at him as he was at me.

Where was the Dan who had showed up that day with his tools and buckets of paint and readiness to create a new possibility in the community with me? The Dan who said he had finally found his dream? He was back wandering the parks again. Sometimes, after my poetry readings, I would see him standing in line with the other audience members to embrace me, seemingly more comfortable in that distant exchange than the closer one we had had. When friends came over and engaged in discussions, he would simply disappear. And at family gatherings, Dan was both attracted and repelled. He was uncomfortable with me, with my family, and with himself. And there was nothing that I could say or do that would make that better for him. The difference in our education levels did indeed matter to him. And by the time I had completed my dissertation and gone back to Iowa to stand before my committee members, I was exhausted not only from the horrendous exercise of defending my scholarly work, but from having to battle my new husband, who did not really understand my quest or those forces in my life that could not be simply buried. When the marriage collapsed after twenty-three months, I was not only disillusioned but pregnant as well. I discovered this the day after we parted.

"You're ten weeks pregnant," the doctor told me, "and you have two weeks to get your abortion." All in the same breath.

"Pregnant?" I whispered. "Abortion?" I could not even say the word aloud. I sat there, stilled beyond trembling and looking down at my womb. I was thirty-five. I knew that it had been fifteen years since I had given birth to Patrice, but the doctor's presumption had jarred me almost as much as the news of my pregnancy.

"You could, I suppose, take an extra few days, but I wouldn't push it too much beyond that," the doctor said. "These things tend to get messy after that."

I didn't even look up to see his uncaring eyes again. "Good Jesus," I whispered after the doctor closed the door, "You're gonna have to help me with this." I went home, barely able to lift my legs, much less to open the center.

"Pregnant," I kept whispering to myself. "Ten weeks pregnant." When exactly did that happen? How?

There indeed had been that one day, hot and full of ether, when I had sat in my room naked after a bath typing some sudden poem about lotuses having their blooming while going to seed. Dan had come home for lunch quite unexpectedly. Patrice was off at summer school. He had pushed the door open with a gentle knock and found me there. I cannot recall that there were any words between us—somehow we were in a space beyond argument, or the possibility of words. We moved purely as if by some unexplainable providence toward each other's fragrant smiles and entered somehow a garden rare. In the midst of that blooming, it must have happened, the creation of this life that I was now carrying. The poem in the typewriter remained unfinished, though it must have in some way paved the way for this. Neither of us ever spoke about that joining afterward. And that had been the last time that we ever truly touched. But that touch, on the cusp of our departing, had spawned a coming forth that now seemed to me almost miraculous. "Two weeks to get your abortion, my Black behind," I said aloud.

In a few days all the symptoms of my other pregnancies returned and I was back being fed through tubes, the doctors having made it clear that I could be endangering my life by continuing to carry my child. The gynecologist wanted to order an amniocentesis to determine whether my baby would have Down's syndrome. I refused. Why go through the examination if abortion was not my choice anyway? I became more guarded and protective. I just wanted to have as little invasion as possible and to not have to carry any more mentally than I was already carrying. After a couple of weeks, I was allowed to go home, under the condition that I would return twice a week for medical attention.

Upon my release from the hospital, I stayed at Lu's house, seeing no one except family, and trying to keep down the spasms. In the room that used to be my own, I tried to initiate my healing, to attempt to look at those things that were so forcefully challenging me. I was unexpectedly pregnant. My marriage had collapsed. The arts center that I had struggled so hard to found was collapsing in my absence. I had finished my Ph.D. but had to give up my first teaching job, and I was separated from my church and not allowed the spiritual comfort that I so badly needed. And if that wasn't enough, I was dreadfully weak and disappointed as hell with Dan.

I had come to the naive but heartfelt belief that our differences would not matter, that we could love and respect one another regardless. But that was not true. He had changed right before me into somebody I hardly knew. And now, at this most difficult moment, I was left alone without his support. And worse, this was not the first time that this had happened to me—that I had gone into a relationship full of love and sincerity and been sadly disappointed. Suddenly I could envision the note William had left for me on the door of Blackaleidoscope: "Closed until further notice." I tried ignoring the spit swelling beneath my tongue. Tried playing off the steady stream of disappointment pumping its way past the memories to my mouth now. I gagged again, then heaved, into a regurgitating fit, then dropped back against the pillow.

"Try not to worry, Estella," Lu said, coming to the room and pushing my frenzied hair from my sweaty face. "Think of beautiful things. Think of God's goodness and mercy. Think of peace." I closed my tired eyes, regulated my breathing as the dietician had taught me. Tried to ignore the nausea. But the ever-present fear of my baby leaving my womb slowly manifested itself in a low leveling growl that forced its way insistently through my lower intestine. I moaned slowly, slowly, until it halted at one of the bends. "Now try and get some rest," Lu said, closing the door behind her.

I pressed my face into the pillow. I knew that the fear was still there. That memories of my last pregnancy were lodged there, too, in the entrails of my being, pushing the fear along. And mixed in with all of it was the pain of this divorce. I forced it back down. There wasn't enough energy to deal with it all.

Lu was cooking in the kitchen, and it was awful. I could hear William in there with her and caught snatches of their conversation. "Processing the pain," he said in his psychologist's voice. "Keep her calm ... she doesn't need to know that right now ..." I was definitely in another wilderness. I realized at this stage in my life that God sometimes calls us into the wilderness in order to speak to our hearts, but at this point all I could hear was the roaring of my stomach. Parts of my frustration began erupting erotically, fusing into my fears for the life of my baby. It all came up along with the very dregs I had forced to the bottom of my soul. Mess I had eaten but could not digest, rot I still had to let go of in order to carry this baby, crud I simply had to face if I was ever going to be healthy again.

Oh, God, I heaved, grabbing on to the vomit bowl, help me to just let go! First came the wrenching disappointment, then the putrefied hurt, and after that all that gall-like guilt for taking Treecie through this! And just when there was surely no breath left in me, something from the lower depths began forcing its way to the surface. This something was me, who I thought I was, not merely the newly spun identity I was as a married woman, but that "in control" self that I thought would always be there no matter what. And then in an awesome final heave, came the stark and bloody fear of losing this baby. It shrieked across my helpless tongue, leaving me seemingly empty at last, seeking now in those first breaths only God's pure will.

I lifted my damp face from the stinking bowl and found myself looking into the dark astonished eyes of Amy Brown, my childhood friend and tutor at the center. She had made it past William and Patrice and was standing there in front of me.

Not knowing, I suppose, what else to do, she extended her hand to take the bowl. I did everything I could to keep her from taking it, but she insisted. After she had emptied it, she came back into the room and just sat quietly beside my bed. Eventually she mentioned something about the children from the center sending their love. I nodded and turned to look at her again. She awkwardly mentioned a few artists who had sent their regards, some of whom were part of a segment that had fissioned off from Blackaleidoscope a few months before all this. That part I had tried not to think about. I looked at her, still exhausted, and shook my head. "The children," I whispered, closing my eyes. I supposed William had told her not to mention Dan. I fell asleep, and when I awakened, she was gone. But she came back again the next day.

"Why come back?" I said in what must have been slow motion, by the look on her face. "It's just vomit. Less of it than before, but still, doesn't it make you sick?"

She shook her head.

"Remember how you let me call you any time of night when I was going through my thing?" she asked. "And you never complained but helped see me through?"

I nodded.

"Then let me do this, OK?"

"But I'm tired."

"Then sleep," she said, taking the bowl again from me. Around the third visit she told me that even though I was sick as a dog, she'd give anything to be in my shoes. She was referring to her hysterectomy and her inability to bear a child. Many times, especially right before the operation, she had called past midnight needing to talk. And we would stay on the phone sometimes one or two hours until she had practically fallen asleep.

"You helped me through that," she said. "I want to stay. I want to help carry a child, and I feel connected to this one."

I handed her the bowl. I decided that day to have her as the godmother.

That night, I thought again about my battles with the Church. Here I was, outside the Church and divorcing again and ironically planning the baptism of my child into that same religion that had caused me so much frustration along the way. And yet I knew that this was also what I wanted to do. In my heart of hearts, I had never left the Church. Sunday after Sunday I had been there. It had never been my desire to find another religion. This was also part of who I was. And it could not be sloughed off in vomit spells or a simple turning away from the altar. The conversion had been made before I was born; for three generations Catholicism had been ritualized in my blood. Not just from my grandmother and through my mother, but God's own blood rituals had made it such. I knew that in God's eyes I too had been invited into the ceremony, had been called and anointed to be whole as a human being. No, this part, Catholicism, stayed with me and I with it, defiantly. I was that part of the Catholic Church that will not go away, the woman of it, and the Black of it, and the divorced of it, and the human of it, that stands open-eyed, signifying and waiting at the jump-rope railings for the veil-rending sounds of Calvary's redemption to reach the ends of the whole earth. In time, I thought of Houston and his marriage to Kinshasha, which was not performed in a Catholic church at all, and the reckoning he must have gone through, especially since I knew of his devotion since childhood and during his years in the monastery. I thought of William, who had been married before for a short time when he first left the seminary, and how he had to come to terms with his own standing in the Church in relation to his family. I thought, too, of Giles, who was an ordained priest working with the National Office of Black Catholics and facing every day the challenges that the Church must still take on in regard to its own transformation in Christ.

I could share some of this with Amy but could not yet face, or even find the courage to name, the more immediate challenge at hand: that is, to banish the thing that was clinging to the darkest part of me, the thing that even through all the vomiting had hid itself and held on tenaciously to my poor soul. I knew its power to justify itself and to destroy me and my relationship with my baby, and I prayed to God to help me. And in time another bearer of grace was let through my family's ring of protection. I lifted my head to the telephone receiver and recognized the voice. It was Haki. Kindred poet. "Our people need you," he said quietly. "What can I do to help?"

I wanted to weep. "God has given me a son to love, and I'm pissed off with all men," I cried out to him.

"I am sorry," he said sympathetically.

"I just found out a while ago that it's a boy. I'm really gonna have to clean myself out and get ready for this," I said, relieved to have my tears flow. "My timing is so off," I said, "so off."

"I care deeply about you, Estella," I heard through the distance. "You're a wonderful, wonderful woman. You can do this," he said tenderly. "You can. I'll call you again tomorrow."

His words of light reminded me that we all had horror stories but that there was a transformative power within me that was calling for bright tomorrows. He sent pictures of opening flowers and budding fruit—of early morning sunrises spreading off the page. He spoke to me of the courageous, forgiving, and transformative moments of our cultural ancestors until I began at last to dispel the wickedness of my anger, and rid myself of its threat.

Although I was relieved of this burden, my stomach continued wringing itself out daily. And I became more aware in the process of my spirit's hunger. My yearning was for something beyond what either of my two grace bearers could possibly bring. I was still confounded, still hurt about not being able to receive communion. Indeed, I think I must have been mourning this loss. And yet I knew that even if I could bring myself to physically prepare to make it to church, or spiritually prepare myself to make it to the altar railing, there would still be the problem of keeping the Host down in my stomach. There would still be the problem of stilling the spasms long enough for my body to consume it. I dismissed the idea, but asked Jesus to allow His spirit to come into me, to be the word that would write straight on these tangled lines I had made of my life, to in His boundless mercy sanctify my body and soul and that of my son, and remove this stupid useless veil that I could no longer deny was between us. I fell asleep, the tears rolling onto my pillow that Sunday morning.

While Lu and Patrice and Gert were at church, I got up and tried to make it to the back door. They would be home in a few minutes, perhaps even with visitors. I thought that if I could make it down the three steps to the chair in the backyard, I could sit by myself, away from the house enough not to have contact with any of them so early. I could spit freely on the ground and not have to worry about the pan or tissues out there. And when I was tired enough to come in, William would surely help me. I sat there, my eyes scanning the trees and the late winter browns. My mind fluttered back to the time I had sit there after the miscarriage. I remembered the glow of the trees that day, the promising brightness of the sun pouring out like grace upon me. It had been as if a little bit of heaven had come down. This day was anything but that, I thought, pressing my feet against the crisp dry leaves.

Then I heard the car coming in the driveway. In my peripheral vision I saw people getting out and moving toward the door. I waved and kept my body positioned to signal I didn't want company, and everybody obliged. Except now I could feel someone coming toward me. In a direct, deliberate manner, stepping upon the leaves. It was Treecie. I smiled into her dark pure eyes. They were so intense that they held me there. Then I looked down into her gathered hands and watched as they unfolded like a flower before me, exposing at the center the Host.

"Body of Christ," she whispered, lifting the Host to my lips. I trembled at the recognition of what was happening. Then closed my eyes and consumed the Holy Eucharist. As it moistened in my abundant saliva, my spirit cried for me to be given the grace to swallow it, to keep it down, blessing my daughter for trying to bring me the only thing she knew that would give me life. I resisted the stirring in my glands, now trying to oversalivate. I held on to the sacred life filling my being like radiant light. My mind resisted anything but the peace of that moment. The spasm relaxed. The saliva I forced to the back of my throat and down again and again, until I realized that it was no longer there. I knew that I was healed. That the vomiting was gone. And that my life was restored again.

After that I went back into my room to meditate and fell asleep. I dreamed that God spoke to me, that He said, "Thy maker is thy husband." I woke up full of the most incredible wonder. What exactly did that mean? "Thy maker is thy husband"? I turned to the Holy Scripture and found the passage in Isaiah: "For your Maker is your husband. The LORD Almighty is His name—The Holy One of Israel is your Redeemer; He is called the God of all the earth. The LORD will call you back as if you were a wife deserted and distressed in spirit—a wife who married young, only to be rejected, says your God." I pressed the sacred living words to my breast, letting them speak to my heart. I understood deeply in that moment that I wasn't alone. That God Almighty would be my husband. He would be my cover. I had the blessed assurance that even though I wasn't properly in the Church, God's grace was sufficient to heal me, protect me, love me, and provide for me and my baby. I knew also that God's grace was bigger, much bigger than any confines of Church doctrine, that it was revealed in His Holy Word.

When the time came for my baby's delivery, Treecie and Faye drove me to the hospital. William went out to inform Dan, and Lu called Amy. Treecie pleaded to go into the delivery room with me.

"No," I said, insisting for the last time. "You'll have your turn soon enough. The next thing you will see is a fine healthy brother." She braced herself to try one more time, but I stopped her. "You've already done more than I could have ever asked," I said, then kissed her wonder-stretched eyes and left Faye with her.

That day, Dominic Jordan was born. He was simply beautiful, not just because he had my eyes, nose, and mouth, but because he truly was.

The first time I nursed him, upon hearing my voice, his eyes opened and stared into mine. I felt a charged mystical energy between us. We took each other in for that powerful exchange like grace. The recognition or transmission verged on the audible. Random light-notes that attune the awakening soul. Then he closed his eyes and rooted more firmly at my yielding breast.

Amy asked me once how it felt to nurse him. She had heard it was quite pleasurable. I laughed and answered her. "Amy, let me put it this way. You can sure tell it's a signature work from God's miracle series. Water from the rock in the desert, milk from the breast, redemption from hard times. I mean, your breasts fill up hard with all this milk, and if you don't let go and give it up, it's really painful. But hey, when you do, then out of all that cramping fullness comes this wonderful, sweet release. Same artist. Same God."

"This is a minor miracle," she laughed, watching Dominic sweat from the forceful gulps.

"Yeah, I say the same thing, each time it happens. He cries and they fill up. He nurses and I'm feeling good."

"No," Amy said, getting me straight. "The miracle is that you finally grew yourself some tiddies!"

"Get out of here," I said, laughing as she reached for Dominic to burp him.

"What's your next step, Estella?" she asked.

"I don't know," I said. "But I do know that in the middle of all this hardship, I'm gonna find some sweet release."

"Yeah," we said together. "Same God. Same artist."

14

TO MAKE THE WOUNDED WHOLE

It was one of those noonday dreams. I was still living at Lu's; I had just finished nursing Dominic and simply couldn't keep my eyes from closing. "After this," the voice exclaimed, "you can go on." Before I could respond, the wall before me opened in the center like elevator doors to show another room, identical to the one in which I was standing, only three times as big, three times as bright. Inside stood an enormous woman, three times my own size. Her back was toward me. Her warrior-like body was naked save for the wrap across her buttocks. And I could see that her bare skin was covered in red oil of some kind. She was an awesome sight. And as I turned to my left to plead my way out of this necessary encounter, the presence of the voice disappeared. I stood alone at the threshold, frightened. I strained to read a medallion strapped to the woman's arm inscribed with numbers—3-1-7-7. Impulsively, I added them up to get eighteen. That's a one and an eight, which equals nine. Nine: The completion? The highest rung? The sure-enough end?

Suddenly the numbers began to fuse and transform from 3-1-7-7 into four similar letters: W-I-L-L. "Will," I whispered. And just as I said this, the woman flexed again, clearly challenging me. There was no time left to figure. In that instant, I accepted all the grace available to me and boldly stepped into her room. To my surprise, she turned toward me—her smiling face some variation of my own.

I had a good idea who she was, and I was in no hurry to confront any personification of that warring band of artists that I had successfully avoided till then—more precisely, that group that had broken off from Blackaleidoscope in its second year to start its own school complete with classes, nation-building awards, and ideas for community development that you would have thought had never been uttered before then. I would interact with them in a guarded manner, and they would do the same with me. It was worse than being in a jungle. It was more like having your garden scattered with weeds or, worse, uprooted during the night—your hard-worked-for seedlings transplanted to the yard down the street.

I could not understand why artists who had committed to build an institution together would go to another part of town and diverge from that commitment. The community was too small and the center still too fragile to sustain such a divide. The pain and confusion I had suffered behind the fission was almost as deep as that of my divorce. I strained to understand what was keeping us from truly connecting. We were supposed to be a community, and yet pride, envy of one another, and desperation at having been excluded from mainstream privileges had interfered with that achievement. Perhaps some had begun to look at Blackaleidoscope's potential as an incorporated institution, at its growing reputation and its media coverage, and seen in this an idea for their own personal attainment. Perhaps I didn't understand well enough the depth of exhaustion, the degree of hunger, or the depth of sacrifice that our communion demanded. After the fission, Blackaleidoscope continued to serve the community. The other school, situated in a recreation center, continued in its own direction and in time underwent further fracturing. No, I was in no hurry to confront the Black artistic faction in Louisville that had torn itself away.

When the need began to rise up in me to creatively engage again, I reached out beyond Louisville to South African poet Amelia Blossom House, who now lived in Elizabethtown with her daughter, Melanie. Our sharing culminated in a poetry performance, "And the Dance Goes On," which included Patrice as dancer and Earbie Johnson as drummer and toured various colleges and theaters throughout Indiana, Ohio, and Kentucky. And when the opportunity to teach at Kentucky State

University came, I gladly accepted, moving from Louisville to live in Frankfort, some sixty miles away. The move gave me the necessary distance from Louisville and still allowed the closeness I needed with Patrice.

She was in her junior year at Presentation Academy in Louisville; she was staying with Gert and had been accepted at the Yale Summer Drama Program. My job would help provide some of the money for that (Presentation had raised most of it) and for her senior year expenses. Teaching at the historically Black college and feeling and inspiring a sense of unity was enough responsibility to take on at this point—taking care of Dominic, Patrice, and my students.

Being away in Frankfort also brought me an unexpected revelation. It gave me more time at the threshold of my dream—time to discern that the numbers on the medallion were, in fact, a date: 3-1-77, March 1, 1977.

What had I been doing on that day? Nothing that stood out readily. I was in Iowa City. I was writing my first paper of the second semester for Survey of African American Literature, on Alex Haley's "Roots." I was waiting, anxiously waiting, for Haley to reach that moment of connection, that point that he had been straining and searching for, in some form, practically all of his life. I was transfixed as he sat in the scorching heat waiting for the griot to get to that one name, Kunta Kinte, and tell the story of a boy who was in the midst of manhood training rites and was off searching in the wilderness for a trunk from which to make a drum. This had been the first time I had so consciously, so viscerally experienced the need for reconnection to an African community. And now here it was again. That moment of waiting, watching, and searching, despite my retrograde motion, for a point of connection. I, who had been inspired by Haley's vision of completion, was now striving toward my own. It struck me that the rupture we had suffered from Mother Africa we were now continuing through our own acts of dismemberment. Thoughts of pairs of visionaries whose visions sometimes conflicted came to mind. Malcolm and Martin, Booker T. and W. E. B., Mary McLeod Bethune and Mary Church Terrell, Langston Hughes and Zora Neale Hurston. I pressed my hand over my mouth. My God. We were doing it again, and again, I thought. This ritual of rupture. Of turning our backs to one another. Of refusing to cross the threshold of reconciliation even after an opening had been made. Of ignoring the prophetic and guiding voices who declare, before their own ascension, that only by overcoming our fear of facing and recognizing self in others can any of us truly go on and engage the path of freedom. I thought of how in the end Malcolm's vision had expanded, how Martin's had, too, and how that picture of them shaking hands and pressing the flesh was a foretelling image after all. I thought of Booker T. and W. E. B. coming to accept the presence of other dreamers and of Langston and Zora coming to terms with their dreams deferred. These were men and women who spent their lives striving and in the end found some vision of wholeness. The search that they undertook is their legacy to us. And since we are connected in spirit to them, and are indeed the beneficiaries of their cultural legacy, when "the will" is rightly read, we do not have to personally go through the same traumas that they did. We do not have to undergo the same deprivations. We can take their offerings as food. We can know their deliberations at the point of their life's completion. We can read their testament and find a point of fulfillment and connection.

I did not fully understand what I was feeling, but I knew that I had to do something that would take me over the threshold toward reconciliation. I knew I had to will it so. It was still too big a risk to come free and openhanded to such a forceful and seemingly disinherited community. What offering of peace could I make? The most I had was writing, through which I could present my vision of wholeness.

I began writing a play called *Purgatory*. In it, the poet is on one side of the stage and a group of ashen gray souls is on the other. The poet is trying to discover a way for the souls to dance their release. It is difficult, because each is ruptured and pained by a blood-red-fire stain that at once draws them toward and repels them away from one another. While they know their salvation is in touching each other's pain, they know as well that the initial connection will be more excruciating than a torturous flame licking up from the lower hell. There are seven in all, each plagued symbolically at a different part of the body. Pride fastens itself upon the forehead of one like a branding iron. Hatred infests the heart of another, a constant hatching of acid eggs. Lust settles upon another's genitals like a giant crab sucking blood from its victim. Greed marks the hands of one like a mass of itching sores. Envy invades the liver of another, tingeing it green with the bile of resentment. Gluttony spreads across the stomach of another, leaving it a giant blister stripped of its skin. And Sloth cripples the legs of the last, leaving it barely able to move.

The poet struggles to come up with a way for the souls to dance their

release, but several attempts fail. They are caught in a limbo and are striving throughout the performance toward that moment of connection,
of reconciliation, toward that eternal moment of being in the presence
of the Divine.

It was difficult. Initially I, of course, didn't know any better than the
poet in my play how it would come together. For weeks I worked through
songs that didn't fit, through scenarios that the souls could act out. In
one, they see a spotlight upon the ground and begin to push each other
out in their effort to gain the center position. You could hear the
growling, groveling, and violence in the dark, and one of the souls even
steals to the center, only to be dragged out. Meanwhile the poet toss-
es crumbs—representing for the community of souls I had in mind the
small change gotten from arts funders—which only intensify the fury.
The circle of light gets smaller and smaller, until, at the size of dime, it
simply disappears. Blackout. The poet even considers renaming the play
Light into Spotlight but decides against it. The souls continue with the
task at hand—how to dance this dance of release.

Patrice was great in helping me make the piece more expressive and
less reflective. Those six weeks at Yale had broadened her perception tremen-
dously. But then, after a weekend together, she would go back to Louisville
or I back to Frankfort, and I would be left to figure it out alone again.
And then one day, late in the night, I had a breakthrough. The poet was
given the revelation that the release of the seven souls was already granted through the seven last utterances of Christ on the cross. Seven
times He spoke, each time releasing one of humanity's seven blockages.
Upon this recognition, the ruptured souls are able to touch into one another's pain and move through the transformative dance into rapture.
Greed, with pock-marked hands, proclaims boldly, "Into Thy hands I com-
mend my spirit!" Hatred begs, "Father, forgive them." Lust sings passionately,
"Woman, behold thy son." Gluttony admits, "I thirst." Envy cries out,
"My God, why have you forsaken me?" and Sloth, "It is finished." On
their own now, and to the poet's surprise, they form a channel inviting
her—with blood-red-fire stain of pride now visible upon her own forehead—to enter. She does so, declaring with the joyful souls, "This day
thou shall be with me in paradise." As they continue singing, joyously
now, "Oh the Word came," the poet returns to her desk to begin to write.

Now I had something to offer. Suddenly the songs that I had struggled so hard to come by would not stop coming. The movements in my

limbs, which were so lethargic at first, would no longer let me sit. I needed a choreographer, dancers, an actor to make the work come alive on
the stage. I needed musicians, singers, and a stage manager. I needed somebody to assess the script other than Dominic—who found it quite tasty
when I could not beat him to the rolled-up balls of paper just short of
my wastebasket. I needed a community of artists, and when I called I
was glad to discover that enough of them needed me, too.

I moved back to Louisville at the end of the semester and began working on the piece as soon as we got settled. I would commute to Frankfort
in the fall. With the help of Janet Rodriguez, I obtained grants from the
Kentucky Arts Council and the Kentucky Foundation for Women to mount
the work. Bee, a local actor, took the script and began practicing the poet's
part. Juju Papaillier, a young musician who was the son of Dr. Hubert Papaillier,
one of my own teachers, and Earbie began work on the synthesizer and
drums. Pat Taylor and Buffy and Camille Weathers, three gifted vocalists
in the community, began harmonizing the songs. Robin Wilson, of
Urban Bush Women in New York, began conceptualizing the choreography. We had a rigorous routine that kept me moving all day long for five
weeks. We met at St. Charles Borromeo Church for practice with the singers
in the morning, the musicians at noon, and the dancers for three and a
half hours at night. When we put it all together, it was incredible. More
needed to be done! Dancers needed more music, the script needed edit-
ing, and the actor who played the poet needed me to stop changing her
lines now, no matter how brilliant my new lines were. The choreographer
needed a stage more elevated for the hell scene. Houston had created magnificent visuals in slides, which would be projected over the head of the
poet continuously throughout the performance; he was now constructing a higher stage in the Kentucky Theater, where the performance was
to be held. We put it together and practiced and practiced, and on opening night I sat in the back row of the full house with Kinshasha and Amelia
and waited. Karen Davis, the stage manager, had absolutely forbidden me
to even come backstage an hour before the performance. From where I
sat, the duality between the poet and the souls was clear, as well the duality between what was happening on the stage and in the lives of those in
the audience, what was happening on the earth and in the not-so-far-off
heavens. When the souls finally got to the point of dancing their transformative release, I felt my own. It was finished. I had made my peace, found
a way to continue to uphold the vision of symbiosis. Now I could go on.

15

DIDN'T MY LORD DELIVER DANIEL?

After producing *Purgatory* and living in Louisville with the community again, I could see more clearly that together we truly were configurations of culture, ever changing and revealing new possibilities. I could see that the commitment of time, energy, and love that I and many others had given to Blackaleidoscope had not been wasted. Its effects would resonate in the community for years to come. Many who had worked at the center were carrying on their work at a more highly charged level than before Blackaleidoscope. They were giving piano lessons in their homes, conducting dance classes at more spacious sites, and naming themselves organizers, storytellers, and more vibrant human beings.

As for me, I continued working at Kentucky State, and at the end of my second year there in 1988, I accepted a job to teach at Hunter College, part of the City University of New York. Dominic was three years old, Patrice was starting her second year at Indiana University, and I felt it was a good time to go. She was happy at school and he was just old enough to move with a little more ease—and too young to protest as Patrice had a few years earlier.

The summer of our departure brought another Blackaleidoscopic turn. Amelia Blossom and Lucy Freibert were taking me to dinner when Lucy suddenly remembered that she had forgotten something at the campus.

We were still laughing and chatting when she opened the door to the auditorium. As soon as the three of us walked in, voices exploded from everywhere. "Surprise!" they shouted "Surprise!" Before me were the bounteous smiles of all the Louisville brothers and sisters I had tried so fiercely and oftentimes awkwardly to love. Overwhelmed, I turned to Lucy and Amelia, and before I could begin to fully embrace them or anybody, I was whisked to my seat and they began an array of performances as their farewell gift to me, with William, sporting a mean porkpie hat, playing the master emcee. Amelia, Karen, Umar, and Georgeann, fellow poets in the community, read original poems dedicated to me. Gloria performed an Anansi folktale on the seven children sharing the sun. Sharon played an original jazz adaptation of "New York State of Mind," followed by Amy, who had always before that moment been a little self-conscious about her weight. She stepped out and started tap-dancing across the stage like her heels and her toes were magic, like her body could be as light or as heavy as she willed it, like the ground underneath her was consorting, too.

I was so moved I figured this must be the culmination, but there was more. Capri read one of my favorite poems of his, as did Leon Driskell, one of my teachers. Bob Douglass, who had come home from Iowa and was now chair of the Pan African Studies Department at the University of Louisville, presented me with a wonderful portrait to commemorate the evening. And Mary Jefferson, Erma Bush, and Howard Owens, friends from the community, roasted me with remembrances of some of my most revealing moments.

Karen Hunter, another friend, dramatized the day, long before I had even thought of going to Hunter College, that I called saying that her name, Hunter, bore some significance to me and that I needed her to help me figure it out. "Now, everybody here knows," Karen said, "that when Estella calls you like that, it's got as much to do with you as it does with her. I didn't want to be going on no voyage with Estella on no Hunter trip. Karen, yes, but Hunter—no way. In fact, that very day I was going to drop my ex's name and go on with my life. So I detoured her through all my nicknames, all my aliases, even telling her my secret name, because that's how Estella is, and when the conversation ended around midnight, after lunch then dinner then tucking the children into bed— we ended up coming right back, you guessed it, to the name 'Hunter.' When my girl got through with her reading on that name, going from seeker—to Atalanta, mythic runner of the race flying beyond the golden apple—to Alberta Hunter singing about leaving her man the day after the marriage and moving to Chicago or New York City, one of them—and on to God Almighty in heaven, playing hunter and hound for the soul Augustine—I mean, I decided I was going to keep my name! Of course, Stella sat there, you know how she is, waiting for me to give her something now, and hey, I ain't got a clue! 'Come on,' Stella's insisting, but it's getting late and she leaves my house, mumbling under her breath, like I done reneged on the deal. But now, Estella, since all this big New York City job has come to light, sister, I can honestly say, I finally figured out what the word 'hunter' means in relation to you!"

Everybody in the place fell out. Lu punched me from behind. "That girl got you down," she said. "She got you down!"

Then Patrice and Robin, my goddaughter, dressed in flowing white garments, performed a going-forth dance that literally made me cry. It was me going forth from Louisville, it was Patrice going forth from me, it was all the faces in the room and through time, moving on and on, in kaleidoscopic continuance.

I went to New York fortified. And upon arrival, we were greeted by Houston and Shasha, who kept the spirit of celebration going for days. I had already gotten a decent apartment in a safe neighborhood—which I discovered was not easy, considering that in New York you could walk down one block and find paradise and turn the corner off into what seemed like hell. Now I had to find a good day care for Dominic. There was a wonderful one run by the Handmaids of Mary. I also had to find a church that took seriously Jesus' words, "I have overcome the world, and if my spirit dwells in you, you will overcome." This undoubtedly proved to be St. Charles Borromeo Church, pastored by the gifted Monsignor Wallace Harris. And last but not least, I definitely had to figure out which side of the subway platform was uptown and which was downtown.

I mastered the last challenge well enough to make it to Hunter in September. This was definitely a new direction for me, with new courses and new colleagues and incredibly new faces in the classroom. It looked like the General Assembly of the United Nations that first day of class. My students were of different races and ethnicities, from all around the world, from uptown, downtown, Chinatown, and Harlem. Many came directly from their jobs through the subway exit at the base of the school straight on into the classroom. Their vibrancy was almost inconceivable.

The train sounds were still in their voices, the rumblings of the crowds still challenging their choices. Some were just out of high school. Others were older students returning to their education after years away. CUNY had educated the people of New York City's poor and working classes and immigrants for several generations. And it cost a small fraction of what private colleges cost.

Here was the place that had nurtured and been nurtured by poet Audre Lorde; Johnnetta Cole, first Black woman president of Spelman College; and Donna Shalala, who would later be appointed to President Bill Clinton's cabinet. Here was the alma mater of Ruby Dee, Martina Arroya, and John Henrik Clark.

I spent a lot of time, that first year, carefully teaching my students and holding off on presenting my own creative works. When finances allowed, I sat in the audiences of other poets and performers. By late fall, the festival-like atmosphere always found around 125th Street, in the heart of Harlem, practically disappeared. The ready connections between everyday folk, bantering at outdoor tables with merchants or exchanging pleasantries at bus stops, were gone, as were the Jazzmobile concerts at Grant's Tomb and the drumming and dancing and picnicking in Central Park that I had so enjoyed with Houston and Sha. Folk scurried from the cold to get where they were going, barely acknowledging one another, even along Africa Square. So to curb my loneliness and hunger for communion, I set out to see performances by various artists—Jayne Cortez and the Fire Spitters at the Studio Museum, Paule Marshall at the 92nd Street Y, and Sekou Sundiata at the Schomburg Center. Their readings were wonderful, but touching into the New York artists' community at large was challenging. The flow among them, as evidenced by the receptions, was difficult for an outsider to enter. And I was definitely an outsider.

At one reception, following a reading by Amiri Baraka, I encountered brothers and sisters who blew air kisses upon each other's cheeks and embraced in a show of kinship through layers of colorful kente shawls and embroidered jackets. My eyes wandered longingly to theirs. Beneath the stylish hats, poised over hair that had been locked or 'froed, braided or boxed, dyed, shaved, or chemically pressed, were eyes humanly complex and strikingly beautiful, some of them quick and searching, others pretentious, others surprisingly vulnerable. Yet my gaze was often met with shuttered glances. Finally, as I balanced hors d'oeuvres and sipped my drink, a brother made his way over to me and smiled.

"Baraka's still got it," he said, and I warmly nodded, glad for the exchange. When I reiterated a humorous line from one of Baraka's poems, the brother's friendly expression dropped. It was my southern accent. He quickly recovered, however, with "Oh, I'm just surprised you remembered that much of it. It was an unpublished piece." He eventually got around to asking where I was from. When I said, "Kentucky," it was clear that he needed more proof of my worthiness to engage him before he moved along to the next connection in the network he was tending. I had always resisted the call to validate my kinship on anything other than my obvious humanity. The expectation was that if you weren't from New York, you needed to earn your way to the circle of kinship, displaying at this point in the conversation your tokens of worth (if you had any), such as my position at Hunter College; my brother's in the art world, my sister's as director at the Studio Museum; my Ph.D. from Iowa; the five Ph.D.s in my family; the poetry book under contract with Third World Press; the album recorded with Grace Gospel; my royal trifling lineage that goes back through queens and conquerors to the great candace herself, Hotep; and, failing any and all that, the carefully crafted articulation of my big city dream "to be somebody" in New York City, have mercy!

I didn't say all this, of course. I simply smiled and tried to touch in with the brother. "Kentucky," I repeated. "Louisville, Kentucky." After a few more unsatisfactory exchanges, he impatiently blurted out, "Well, what brings you to New York City?"

"A teaching job at Hunter."

"Well, why didn't you say so!" he sighed, then drew in furtively as if sharing some wisdom from the Dead Sea Scrolls: "Now, the first thing you got to know in New York City is you got to get pressed."

What was he talking about? Being pressed against the wall or being written about in the press? Surely he wasn't referring to my clothes, which I had steamed well before putting them on? Yes, he was. Who was he supposed to be, Shorty hipping Malcolm X to the zoot suit? I didn't want to do that scene. I fought the rupture for all the reasons and continued to strive for connection. "Brother," I said, coming closer, "surely as sharp as your eyes are, you would've been able to recognize me even without my beads?"

He laughed awkwardly, then continued, "Yeah, absolutely. It's just some of the others, you know. When in Rome . . ."

"Can you imagine that?" I whispered. "This, at a time when our children are killing each other in the streets over a pair of Jordan sneakers?"

I wanted to add: and when tribes in Rwanda, unable to recognize each other, are ritualistically spilling each other's blood into the already overflowing river, and ignoramuses in every fiscal building across this nation are picking their teeth and burping behind drinking the blood of the poor after op-pressing them in inner cities like so many grapes in a vat, and when all I wanted was to touch in to one little soul in this place.

"Absolutely, sister," the brother said. "I totally agree."

Another woman approached us and pressed cheeks with Mr. Interlocutor. "My dear!" she said, sparkling, and we were quickly introduced. "Hunter?" she said approvingly. "Tell Audre I said hello." I smiled. Audre Lorde had been on leave since before I got there. They went on talking. I looked at the card he had given me. Some kind of producer. I sipped my drink, then went home early to save the extra hour on the baby-sitting fee. When I got home, there was a message from Spivey, talking about leaving California and coming to New York to find a job and the good life—if he could stay with me until he got settled.

I called him back and said, "Come on, but the one thing you got to know about New York is, you got to get pressed."

"Oh, yeah," he said confidently, "I'm mainframing for Hewlett Packard out here. I don't mind getting pressed. I just didn't want all my juice to go out for nothing. You know what I mean."

When I told him not to sell his dress suits and to pick up a touch of mud cloth, he laughed. "Oh, it's that kind of party?"

Despite the ongoing struggle to come to terms with the poses dictated by the artistic community, by the beginning of my second year my adjustment in New York was well under way. I would walk more assertively into my classroom, teaching *I Know Why the Caged Bird Sings*. "Maya Angelou claims that 'we live in direct proportion to the dedication of our poets.' Why?" Students would vigorously engage the possibilities, probing the blues aesthetic, the complexities of the cage, and the poet's coming to voice. All too soon class would end, and we'd look forward to the next challenge. "Ms. Gwendolyn Brooks says, 'I—who have gone the gamut—am qualified to enter at least the kindergarten of new consciousness.' What does she mean by that? And how does this single phrase by the poet signify at once the four patterns found in the autobiographies of Black women literary artists: cyclicality, African worldview, the woman/child duality, and multiple selves?" Reviewing the Black women's autobiographies I had studied within this new territory endowed me with a greater capacity to choose my own becoming.

Although I had been hired to teach creative writing, which I loved, I soon found myself designing new African American literature courses. This was welcomed by the department's chair, who had championed a culturally diverse component within the curriculum. With the help of Judylyn Ryan, another Black woman hired in the department my second semester, I designed a course called Images of Black Women in Film and Fiction. Judylyn was fresh out of the University of Wisconsin–Madison and possessed a brilliance and commitment I enjoyed. We discussed literature, legacy, leadership, and life. We basked in the vision of Zora Neale Hurston, the power of Toni Morrison, the saturation of Paule Marshall. The course I subsequently developed investigated Gloria Naylor's *The Women of Brewster Place* and Richard Wright's *Native Son,* Alice Walker's *The Color Purple,* Ernest J. Gaines's *The Autobiography of Miss Jane Pittman,* and several others, together with their film adaptations. In all the works, the community was negotiating survival and regenerating triumphantly from dismemberment. Black women and men and their sons and daughters were confronting the callings and collisions of life. I could not read these texts without knowing more intensely the urgency of my own motherhood and without reaching out more diligently to my students. I was even able to get one of the actors from the film version of *The Women of Brewster Place,* the distinguished veteran stage and screen actor Douglas Turner, to talk with the students.

Often I would set up groups for discussion. The diversity of ethnicities, ages, backgrounds, and expectations of my students made for a creative dynamism, but was not without its tensions. This was to be expected, given the various distances we each had to travel in order to perceive through the eyes of one another. One day the discussion turned to *Native Son*. I began by breaking down the names of the characters in the book and showing that Bigger, according to Wright, came from the term "Big Nigger." I went on to speculate that Dalton signified Daltonism, or color blindness. I explained the ways in which this deficit, blindness to the impact of race, operated within the text to set up the inevitable outcome. I tried to inspire the students to see that in relation to Bigger's predicament, it was not simply Mrs. Dalton, Mary's mother, who was physically blind, but the other characters as well, including Mary, who refused to acknowledge the boundaries of race to the point of embarrassment and brutal infringement upon Bigger; Jan, who, although aware of color or race, was unable to acknowledge the limited paradigm of class analysis; and Mr. Dalton, who has allowed the color of his poor Black tenants to blind him to the full entitlement of their humanity. I wanted my students to see that the rat and its predicament in the first three pages was a "mascon," a saturated symbol, a massive concentration of Black experiential energy—as Stephen Henderson calls it—and microcosm of the whole content of the book, that Bigger was indeed that rat running from hole to hole trying to find liberation—now from the job, then from the preacher, then from the legal system. Bigger stands before every major institution seeking justification, to his utter dismay and defeat. And, just as important, to the utter defeat of all those around him.

I sighed and looked at them. "What is Wright saying about us? It can be a little scary. Break into your groups and talk about 'fear,' the title of the first section of the book. Start with why it was so hard for Bigger to look Dalton in the eye."

The students began from various distances to face off with each other through the lens of the text. At times, the engagement among the students was vibrant, open, and healthy. At other times, the possibility of transformation was reduced because there was more investment in self-concealment. A couple of students, especially one older woman, resisted the challenge to grow under a thin veil of liberalism and feigned admiration; I watched this carefully. Most of the others continued to grow and question. We wrestled, discussed, laughed over discoveries—sometimes, the engagement with students would extend beyond the classroom to the subway, where the closing doors of the train would determine where the conversation ended. They knew that after this class, I had to leave right away to get Dominic.

As the usual handful followed me down the subway ramp at the base of the building, I could still hear Atim challenging Matthew: "No, man, I got one question for you. How much is Dalton making?"

"Surely you aren't suggesting that Bigger's wages should be the same as his employer's?" Matthew scoffed.

"Heck no!" Karen said sarcastically. "Dalton made his million the old-fashioned way. He stole it!"

As the train doors closed I could hear Karen calling out to me, "You still haven't answered why Bessie had to be the sacrificial lamb . . ."

The symbiotic listening during these exchanges primed me for the next class's opening statement, which was intended to inspire students to probe more deeply the analyses they offered. We moved on eventually to Gloria Naylor's *The Women of Brewster Place.* I could feel my own vision becoming more enlightened through each engagement. By the time we got to *The Color Purple,* I was speaking in rainbows, referring to and moving in and out of all the previous texts, and many of the students were breaking out brilliantly in their own hues. We were well on our way to becoming that field of flowers growing radiantly in Celie's back yard.

Then suddenly, unexpectedly, I was called into the department chair's office. He said he had called me in to discuss the concerns of two students who claimed that I was, of all things, hallucinating in the classroom.

I was not yet tenured. I could be forced out at any moment. I knew dozens of Blacks in academia who spent half their professional lives running from one institution to another, being forced out by some foolishness or other on the part of their colleagues.

Suddenly I felt like the rat, incredibly vulnerable before him, as he asked me now how I was feeling—told me that I could get help for such a thing—that surely the students had only mentioned this out of love. Love? I knew what love felt like. I did not know what he was talking about. I went quickly to that part of my soul that I know is sacred ground, and there, as my naked Black woman self and not some transmuted snarling rodent that others would have me be, I pleaded my case. Be still, was the command. And so I was. The chair kept going on. When he finished, I simply looked at him. This was the same person who had fought so diligently for the Black literature concentration in the curriculum, the same one who had taken the die-hard conservatives in the department to task. I asked if the students might have been referring to a difference in interpretation. He said no; they were quite distinct in their description; that I had actually engaged somehow in the classroom with whoever I thought was standing before me.

But we were dealing with the phenomenon of film. We were discussing John Berger's *Ways of Seeing,* for heaven's sakes. I did not have to conjure spirits in the classroom! These writers' works were brilliant enough to make anybody, even the blind, see their vision! I had simply taught the works so that students could see, too.

Then the chair told me that he could indeed suggest help for me; that there might even be a chemical imbalance; that you never know. Before I slammed shut completely behind this diagnosis, I looked over and said as calmly and as strongly and as benignly as I could, "It must have been very difficult for you to bring this to me."

He looked perplexed at this response and began murmuring something about the possibility of this reflecting students' inability to comprehend a different kind of vision or technique; that, my God, he himself was teaching Blake and the mystic poets; that in the future I should be more explicit in introducing a different pedagogical technique.

I didn't know what to make of this. My student evaluations had been among the highest in the department. My peer evaluations were satisfactory as well. I was sure I knew who the two students were, and I had suspected that they at times were bothered by my perspective, but I also believed that they were making efforts to understand the course content. When I left the chair's office I went to my own and cried.

"This is how they are getting rid of me," I thought. "My work is good, my writing is coming along, my engagement with the community is strong, and I'm sold down the river, Fiddler, for hallucinating in the classroom!" I wanted to call Zora into the room and my Grandma and all the great ones!

"They must have gone in separately to make it register as two complaints," I scribbled frantically into my New York journal, barely able to hold the pen. It wasn't enough. I needed to talk with flesh and blood. I called Judylyn, and she came to my office immediately.

"You're kidding," she said.

"No," I insisted.

"Then, my goodness, we are all in trouble!"

"I know."

"How can you even teach this literature Black women are creating without entering it our way?"

"I don't know."

"How in the world can you teach Toni Morrison, who has Beloved, a full-bodied womanchild, emerging straight up out of the water?"

"I don't know."

"And Paule Marshall's visionary elder, Aunt Cuney, who tells the tale of the Igbos walking back to Africa over the ocean?"

"I don't know, I don't know. Take their poetic license away and throw them all under the jail!" I writhed. "Get Zora, too, while you're at it, for hanging out at the crossroads and instructing us to 'tell my horse!' and Langston, too, for declaring, 'I bathed in the Euphrates when dawns were young.' Bad case of hallucination! Everybody knows Langston was born in Missouri! What the heck is he talking about? Take them all back to Africa with their 'visions-hoodoo-holler-here' Larry Neal!"

Judylyn shook her head again at the ridiculousness of it all. The students' reaction should not have been surprising in light of their elders' own shortsightedness. The widespread resistance to a greater inclusiveness was openly displayed by members of the department in their response to the discovery that one of its more perceptive colleagues had offered and taught a course on Toni Morrison's novels under the rubric "One Major Writer." Rather than acknowledge this Black woman's greatness, the department proposed and changed the title to "One Writer."

"I wonder what triggered this off, though," Judylyn said. "Think back, Estella. Did you say or do anything differently in your classroom this week?"

"What do you mean?"

"I mean, did you break from your usual mode of teaching?"

"No," I said, "not really. We were reading *Miss Jane Pittman*. OK, before then we were finishing up Grace Nichols's *I is a long memoried woman*."

"Yes?"

"I held the book, I remember, and told them that for the next class, in order to really began to better understand some of this material, we would have to go back to the slave ship. I asked them to close their eyes, and within seconds we were there in the pit. Darkness was all around and the smell of bile and iron. We stayed there in that nightmare till we could feel Nichols's long memoried woman 'lying there in her own blood, in her own filth bleeding memories in the dark . . .'"

"That's probably what did it."

"What? A little drama into the truth? What would they have preferred to see? Massa dancing on deck?"

"No. Perhaps something that exposed a little less of our pain, though. Or at least something that would have allowed the kind of distance that most are accustomed to. The dramatic engages—invites journeys. And some people don't want to go there."

"I refuse to turn into my undergraduate English professors, Judylyn. This is not a new teaching technique. I was really energized by the transformations that I could see in the faces and hear in the comments of the students who were getting this opportunity for the first time. This was allowing them to deepen their reading of the text. I never imagined this kind of distortion."

We wondered then about Audre Lorde, how she would have handled it. From the time I arrived in New York, she had been on sick leave in St. Croix. How we missed her at that moment. Judylyn reached for my copy of Lorde's *Sister Outsider* and read from "Poetry Is Not a Luxury": "...The white Fathers told us: I think therefore I am. The Black mother within each of us—the Poet—whispers in our dreams: I feel, therefore I can be free."

"Wo-o-t! There it is," I said.

Judylyn went on to teach her afternoon class, agreeing to catch up with me later that evening to help me dream a strategy for dealing with this.

Houston and Shasha said they'd meet us at Sylvia's Restaurant. I was still in a funk. I walked along 125th Street, letting the early spring sound of the Black crowd and boom boxes wash over me: Anita Baker singing, "Giving you the best that I got," and Tina Turner signifying, "What's love got to do with it?" and Queen Latifah letting loose about "having it up to here" in a beat that made you want to raid, too, that made you want to run. And then there was M.C. Hammer—"We got to pray just to make it today." Every two steps the music kept changing, moving in and out of holler range as merchants standing behind street tables offered "mud cloth, my sister?" "Oil for your skin?" "Frankincense to cleanse the air?" "My sister, we have some bad books here. Check it out!"

I picked up Dominic, who was glad to be meeting Uncle Houston, and headed for the restaurant. Surprisingly enough, I ran into Spivey on the corner of 125th before turning on to Malcolm X Boulevard. He had been staying with me for about a month after leaving California and was supposed to be looking for work. He had probably timed his departure from my house so that he left just before I was due home from work.

"I'm just getting out of an interview," he started. "This strange-ass town can't appreciate good help!"

"Spivey," I said, shaking my head, "you know you got another month. Nobody's hounding you about no job. It takes time."

"What's the matter, then?"

"I'm doing the best I can and get called down into the office for hallucinating!"

"Oh, Lord, what you tell them?

"Come on, Spivey."

"Let me get this straight. Those white folk seriously called you down to the office—for what?"

"Hallucinating."

"As in 'I-see something-you-can't-see'?"

"Yeah."

"'—but just give it a minute'?"

"No, nothing like that. As in, I am addressing the entity in the classroom in front of students or something."

"Come on."

"Yeah. They're trying to get rid of me." He didn't know what to say. Neither of us did. So, taking hold of the tool he knew best, he looked down pitifully at Dominic and pretended to weep, "Man, we gon' both be homeless! I done made adjustments in my head for playing Mole Man and surviving if I have to in the crevices of the subway, but what we gonna do about you, man? I just got one superhero cape, little man! How we gonna save the babies?" Dominic fell out laughing and climbed up onto Spivey's chest.

"Spivey, I'm serious."

"I know you are," he said, then followed me into the restaurant.

"This is some crooked crap," I said, telling the story over to the others. "I know who the two students are and there's no way I want to teach them again."

"What are you talking about?" Houston said. "They're enrolled in the class."

"It doesn't matter, I want them out. There's only going to be this back and forth reporting now, from my classroom to the office, from the overseer's field to the big house."

"Did he tell you it was those two people?" Spivey asked.

"He doesn't have to. My 'hallucinatory' vibes tell me. I don't see how I can go back into that classroom and teach like nothing's the matter, like nothing happened."

Houston frowned. "I remember that feeling when I was in the classroom, right before I gave it up," he said. "Academia can be strange."

Shasha started waving her hands. "Wait a second. Hold off on the two students for a moment. This chair who called you in, why would he be offering professional help rather than questioning your teaching techniques or the students' responses anyway? His professionalism is already suspect because he's made a clinical diagnosis on the basis of the students' complaints. If I did that in my position as director at the museum, I would have me out in a heartbeat."

"If that had happened to me," Spivey said, "Jacoby and Meyers would be making sure right this minute that I owned a chunk of Hunter College. I wouldn't have to worry about a job ever!"

"I didn't come here to take the money and run. If that were the case, I would have never come. I came to teach, and I want to continue to teach on my terms. All I'm saying is, I'm going to ask Lu to pray with me to get those two students out of my class."

"Oh, Lord," Spivey signified, "here we go again! Not the Loop de Lu on them!"

"Hush, Spivey," Shasha said cutting her eyes at him before she continued. "There's just a few more weeks to the semester, Stella. Maybe you should pray just to get through them and circumvent anything else that might mess with your tenure."

"I want them out!" I insisted. "I can't do justice to the other students with my hands tied like this. And the way I'm feeling, the issue might slip out while I'm explaining the text that I'm supposed to be teaching. The theme is all the same. One character wants to be herself; somebody else has got other designs on her life—redefinition, misinterpretation, erasure—take your pick."

They all understood that. "I'll tell you what, though," Spivey said, seeing that the food was about to be served. "I'll bet if you go into his office tomorrow and start yelling, 'Get out! get out! I see the whole damn place is gonna blow!' that white man would beat you getting out of that door!" We all had to laugh at this.

When I called them, Lu and Gert said they'd pray I'd get understanding and wisdom from this. But I went back home to Kentucky the very next day for spring break and looked Lu and Gert dead in the face. "I got myself some understanding. That ain't the problem. It's a different world up there than what you think. You think that the fight is to get to Hunter College, Wall Street, City Hall, or wherever. But the real fight is to remain healthy, Momma, and creative, while withstanding the blasted assaults that just keep coming at you in more subtle, more insidious forms from both enemies and allies alike! I need some more power in on this. I'm telling you. I need some space, Lu."

They agreed to pray with me. We all prayed. And by the time I went back to New York, I was refreshed on my first day back to school. I went into my office before class and found a letter in my stack, my first with-drawal from one of the women. There was sickness, she said, and the doc-tor had sent her to the desert to deal with her problem of breathing. By doctor's orders she was lessening her course load.

"Thank you, Jesus," I whispered, slipping the note back into the enve-lope. "Do take care of her, but please, Lord, I asked you for two. I want both of them out of my class in the name of my sweet overcoming Jesus."

I went onto my classroom and there was the other student, head bowed, not as empowered now that she was alone. I stuck to the text, for the meantime pursuing only a few of the avenues open for inquiry. At the end of the class, just as I was ready to sigh and leave the room, I saw her standing outside the door.

"Yes?" I said, leaning forward to hear the news. And she told me that she was dropping my course, that she had been messing around with her life too long and was going, yes, even at this late point in the semester, to stop wasting her parents' money and take control of her life.

I certainly could understand that.

"Do well," I told her as she walked away. Then I danced right up to Judylyn's office and we practically did the ringshout right on out of the building.

"I think God wanted me to know that with grace I could handle this," I said, moving down Park Avenue. "That's why the second one came for one more class. God wanted me to know that with grace, I can teach even the hell-raisers!"

"Well."

"I know she ain't the last of them."

"That's the truth."

"But I also know now I can handle it. I've got at least that little bit of wisdom now," I said, smiling.

But then, later that night an uneasiness about the thing set in. Had I really taught the hell-raisers or had I simply taught in the presence of one of them for another day? What transformation had really taken place? It seemed that I had simply prayed to have my mountain moved and had enjoyed a full measure of satisfaction at seeing it leap from before my sight.

When I called Lu to tell her about the students dropping out, I was reluctant to reveal my tension, but she picked it up anyway.

"What happens to them now?" she asked.

"I don't know," I said. "I almost don't care."

"Almost?"

"Yeah," I said, then explained as well as I could my mixed reactions.

Lu responded, "Well, Estella. This is what I was trying to tell you before. It's not always about running those students who are oppositional back out into the wild blue yonder. It's about taking on the challenge, figuring out the most appropriate demeanor or manner that will allow you to accomplish your goal."

I didn't say anything.

"Hello?" Lu said.

"I'm still here."

"You're a teacher. I'm sure you see differently than most of your students. Help them to see."

"See what?" I said to her suggestion.

"It's not 'what,'" she said. "It's 'how.'"

16

TELL ALL GOD'S CHILDREN

I was writing a poem in my sleep. The first two lines were surprisingly new and childlike; the second two grew in complexity; and the third two bore tiny lenses in the vowels through which an incredible landscape of marvelous writings emerged. I struggled to wake up and capture it.

> Come here hoping
> and full of trust—
> Come here seeking
> blood gone to dust—
> Lend your soul to the songline
> and become its gust!

In the morning, I found the piece scribbled on Dominic's Teenage Mutant Ninja Turtles coloring book. Come where? I wondered. Seeking what? Did "lending my soul" mean generating more grace for my children? My students? Reaching out more to my elders—Lu, who was approaching seventy and living alone; Gert, who was coping with physical changes in her life—or did blood gone to dust refer to the AIDS crisis devastating the community? Or did the words make bare again my unkept promise to Houston to make a pilgrimage through the five cities charted in his Cakewalk Cosmogram, a floor design made in the tradition of African ceremonial ground markings? Before I could delve any further, Dominic jumped onto the bed.

"Let's go somewhere! It's Saturday."

"Where?" I teased "To the grocery store?"

"Uh-uh," he said. "Some place fun."

"OK, baby. How's Uncle Houston's studio sound?"

"Cowabunga, dude!" he shouted, then ran ahead of me into the kitchen. When I got there, I saw that Spivey was already sitting at the table.

"How you doing?" I asked. He didn't answer. "We gonna give Houston a call at his studio in a while. You want to come?"

"No. Y'all go on without me. Look," he said clearing his throat. "You think you could let me hold a few dollars till payday?"

"You never paid me from last time."

"Yeah, well, the big city adjustment is more costly than anticipated. Come on, sister."

I looked in my purse. I only had a five. "I'll get ten out of the machine for you on the way home."

"How long will that be?"

"Around noon, I guess."

"That's cool," he said, staring out of the window.

"You OK?"

"Yeah, I will be," he said rather defensively. "Go, go. I'm fine."

I left him and went on to get ready. On the way out of the apartment, I grabbed the coloring book page on which I had written the poem.

"Yeah, Momma, take it," Dominic said. "Uncle Houston has lots of crayons. But he thinks Medanardo is a artist." He pointed to the picture of his favorite Ninja Turtle.

"Leonardo, baby."

"And Raphael, too," he confided.

"I know," I whispered. "There really were two artists with those very same names, Leonardo and Raphael."

"Oh."

"Sometimes a name can mean many different things."

"Oh."

He stared curiously before settling it in his mind, then, leaning in closer, he said, "Spivey thinks Raphael is a angel."

"Come on, honey," I chuckled. "We can talk on the way over."
When we arrived at Houston's, he lifted Dominic into his arms. "What's
happening, Estella? You sounded up."

"Look," I said, handing him the image. "I think it has something to
do with the pilgrimage."

"What? This purple Ninja Turtle?"

"No," I said, pointing to the script. "It's the poem there in the corner."

He read it aloud. "'Come here hoping / and full of trust— / come here
seeking / blood gone to dust— / lend your soul to the songline / and
become its gust'? So you're going?"

"Yeah, if gone to dust means trudging across the territory."

"What do you mean, 'if'? What did you mean when you wrote it?"

"I'm not sure. I dreamed it and inside all the vowels in the last two
lines were these tiny lenses where you could look and see another whole
dimension of words."

"Really?"

"Yeah, each lens bore another set. You peek into the 'o' and there it
is. You look through the 'e' and there's another revelation."

"What did it say?"

"I don't know."

"Estella?"

"I can't remember."

"You mean you peeked into the journey and can't tell about it?"

"Oh, hush. You didn't make sense for months after coming back from
Rome. Besides, I didn't really go. I still have to see inside the words."

He pressed the poem up to his eyeballs. "Like this, Master Splinter?"

"Oh, let me see!" Dominic insisted.

"He's not really seeing, baby. Uncle Houston is teasing."

"Yeah, just kidding, dude," Houston said, handing the picture to Dominic.
Then he turned seriously to me. "I hope 'blood gone to dust' means you've
come to give some new life to the work. I've put so much into it but
know I've just scratched the surface. It's getting so complex I'm not sure
where it's going anymore."

In stockinged feet I stepped onto the cosmogram—a thirty-foot, sandblasted, glass floor design meant to be walked on and engaged. It traced
the struggle for civil rights through five cardinal cities of the American
South. Houston had told me many times that it was a metaphorical journey through life and death to rebirth and resurrection. An original ver-

sion had been presented a few years ago in New York, accompanied by a performance by Ron Alexander, Shasha, and other professional dancers; and another had been shown at the High Museum in Atlanta over a year ago.

Two intersecting arrows quartering the cosmogram circle were the King and Malcolm Lines: the King Line passed though Atlanta, King's birthplace, and Memphis, where he was assassinated; the Malcolm Line passed though New Orleans and Louisville and continued through Detroit. They intersected at the geographic center in Tuscumbia, Alabama.

I stood on New Orleans, which Houston had designated City of Grace, place of the Mardi Gras, Congo Square, and jazz funerary marches, then followed the spiraling line onto Louisville, City of Vision, recalling the Kentucky Derby, Muhammad Ali, and artists like Sam Gilliam, who challenged our way of seeing. Proceeding to Atlanta, City of Speech, I remembered the King Center, and the Black Arts Festival. Turning toward Memphis, City of Balance, I thought of the blues, Bessie Smith, and B.B. King, and the fact that Martin Luther King had last marched in that city.

"Here," Houston said, "is where the dancer experiences symbolic death, a death necessary for new birth."

"What exactly does that mean?" I asked. And before he could respond, Dominic answered by falling dramatically across my feet. "Like this, Momma!" he said, holding his heart and making his eyes roll back in his head.

"We're gonna take him downtown and make some money," I said. "They're holding auditions for four-year-old hams in the morning." I stepped to the center, the culminating point of the spiral, designated the Mount of Joy. I had no idea what breathed there, but I definitely wanted to know.

"I'm going," I said. "This time I'm sure."

"Good," Houston responded, joining me at point of intersection. We stood staring down at it as if trying to see what lived in the name, Tuscumbia. A place originally called Ococoposo by Native Americans, meaning "cold water."

"Oh," Houston said, moving from that creative stillness, "before I forget, give this to Spivey for me. He's a little short."

I took the twenty and stuck it in my purse. "What's he doing with his money, eating it? It's not like he's paying rent."

Houston smiled and said, "You know New York is a monster."

"Houston," I said, feeling the weight of the words on my tongue even as I formed them. "You don't suppose 'blood gone to dust' has anything to do with Spivey, do you?"

"What do you mean?"

"I mean his mood swings. He borrows all the time. I hope he's not—"

"What? Doing drugs? He's not that stupid! The chance of our blood going to dust that way is as likely as me waking up and not wanting to be an artist anymore."

"But you don't have to be stupid to do drugs. Look at Richard Pryor, Billie Holiday."

"I'd bet my left arm on it," Houston said. Maybe the idea was too painful for him. Or maybe I was mistaken. "Stick to the pilgrimage reading," he said.

When I handed Spivey the extra twenty, he held it like it was gold. "You two are super. Now I can get around town on my off time and get my comedy act going. I met a couple of people yesterday. It's all about connections. I might be able to get that jump start now."

"Good," I said, "good—" And before we could go any further, he grabbed his hat and made for the door.

"What's the matter?"

"Later," he mumbled without even looking back. He stayed out all that night. When he did come back, he was practically singing his monologue.

"Dig this," he said, pouncing dramatically into his prize-fighter act, "I beat Joe Frazier, I beat Mike Tyson, I beat Muhammad Ali! Wait a minute, I am Muhammad Ali! Seriously though, you know who I saw on the train?"

He kept on, line after line, until I pressed him. "Spivey, I was worried about you."

"Why? I'm cool. I got a woman and life is fine. I'm talking T-K-O. You ain't forgotten what that means, have you?"

"Houston wants you to call him," I laughed a little, "and mind your mouth around Dominic."

"Ah, naw, you ain't dragged him and Shasha in on this?"

"I was worried. I thought you would call, for heaven's sakes."

"You have forgotten what it's like," he laughed. "'Oh, excuse me, baby, hold it right there. I gots to get up and call my sister!'"

"OK," I said, just as the phone rang. "Keep on playing." He jived with Houston a while and then handed the phone back to me.

"He's fine," Houston said. "The way he's sounding. He just might get his New York act together before we do this pilgrimage."

I let it go and began focusing on my own direction.

To prepare for the journey, I designed a system of rites for cultural renewal in five letters to Houston entitled "Libation." I gave him the first one during Christmas break after my grades were turned in and Spivey had not only found his own place but successfully performed his first comedy act. "See," Houston assured me, "the pilgrimage reading was right." The last letter I shared with him a few weeks before the pilgrimage. The letters included "The Creed," "The Choreography of the New Cakewalk Ritual Dance," "The Libation Litany," and a tracing of a Black Male Genealogy and a Black Female Genealogy. In the genealogies, I expanded Houston's original naming from Malcolm X and Martin Luther King, Jr., to include David Walker, Frederick Douglass, Booker T. Washington, King Oliver, Marcus Garvey, and W. E. B. Du Bois; and I forwarded eight black females as their counterparts: Phillis Wheatley, Sojourner Truth, Harriet Tubman, Ida B. Wells, Bessie Smith, Mary McLeod Bethune, Josephine Baker, and Zora Neale Hurston.

"This can help blow the cosmogram wide open," Houston said, reading the genealogy letter in amazement. I had been up working on it all night and was looking forward to going out to dinner, but already he was pulling books from the shelf: King's *Why We Can't Wait,* Malcolm's speeches, W. E. B Du Bois's *The Souls of Black Folk,* Joseph Campbell's *The Power of Myth,* and Robert Farris Thompson's *Flash of the Spirit.*

"We're hungry," Shasha and Spivey protested, stacking the books back again.

"I am, too," Houston defended, pulling them right back down.

"Yeah," Shasha insisted, "but we want some greens and chicken!"

"OK, baby, OK," he said, then winked at me and quoted from Du Bois: "'I sit with Shakespeare and he winces not,' and neither does he demand a break for dinner!"

Shasha punched him. "'I move arm in arm with Balzac and Dumas'— but they always take time for a repast."

After dinner we walked for ice cream and promised not to even mention the "C word." But simply because we said that, everything began signifying on the thing—billboards advertising trips to the Holy City, folk asking for directions to the Wynton Marsalis concert, and even the ice cream cone spiraling to a peak resembling the summit at the center of the cosmogram.

"Look," Dominic said, making the connection, "I'm biting off the Mount of Joy!"

"I give up!" Shasha said, kissing ice cream over his grinning face. Only after I had tucked him into bed that night did I realize that the two genealogies traced in the letter could well be the fulfillment of the first two lines of my dream poem.

The fulfillment of the next two came in the letters from the field. I took Dominic home to Louisville to spend a few weeks with his father and a couple of days later Amelia Blossom House and I began the pilgrimage. We went through each city, performing libation ceremonies and collecting oral histories of the communities that received us. I drafted Houston letters from each site. Unlike the contemplative pre-journey letters, which anticipated discovery, these journey letters recounted the entry into the territory and traversing of flesh and blood, my ancestors' and my own—and like the middle lines of the poem, they had grown in complexity.

Returning to New York, I discovered the pilgrimage did demand a new language. I had speculated on the importance of constructing one, but the journey confirmed its necessity and gave clear direction on how it might be done. I accepted this new language, Tongue of Fire, as the third couplet of my dream vision. Like the lenses embedded in the vowels of my poem, it provided a new way of seeing.

Houston and I decided that the writings should be shared, and in a short time we presented them as part of an exhibition entitled "The New Cakewalk: A Cultural Libation" at New York's Museum of Modern Art. It featured the New Cakewalk Cosmogram along with quotations by African Americans sandblasted onto a large glass window facing onto the museum's garden. Mounted before the window, on the altar-like glass table, were a container holding stones collected from the pilgrimage cities and a cruet of water taken from Tuscumbia's cold water spring.

The book, *Libation: A Pilgrimage Through the African American Soul,* was stationed in the middle of the table. It was signed Estella Conwill Májozo, the new name I had taken from the female genealogy in honor of Mary McLeod Bethune, teacher and founder of Bethune Cookman College; Josephine Baker, dancer and mother of "The Rainbow Tribe"; and Zora Neale Hurston, writer and anthropologist. Selected participants from the New York community, including several Hunter students as well as friends Eve Leoff and Carmencita Romerez, performed daily readings from the book. I felt surely then, when the exhibition was performed, that the dream vision had been accomplished.

This project, however, proved only a beginning. The work that the three of us —Houston as sculptor; Joseph DePace, whom Houston had met in Rome, as architect; and me as poet—would do together over the next seven years as a collaborating team of artists creating permanent site-specific monuments around the nation blossomed beyond our imaginings. The team took on challenge after challenge, from New York to California. And each work, like the New Cakewalk Cosmogram, could in some way be experienced as a rite of passage. And I came to see all of them as the fulfillment of the last two lines of the poem, lenses making the journey of our souls more visible.

The team would meet regularly, uncovering histories of each city, challenging each other's visions, and then, along with the communities, determining the form of the work. We were similar to several other teams working in the new public art genre, but we were also unique in several ways. We were sculptor, architect, and poet; we were brother and sister, Black and white, male and female; we were friends mostly, but sometimes formidable foes. We shared what came to be clearly defined objectives, but our creating was not without conflict.

I was challenged as a woman working with two men; as a Black person working with a white person; and as a poet collaborating with visual artists, whose work was to mine what rhythmic breath and sound was to terrazzo and brass. No doubt, the greatest challenge for me was accepting the mandate to design multicultural offerings, especially when I knew how much our own people needed and how committed I was to that cause. I had no idea—and I'm not sure Houston did, either—that when he said my inclusion of the female genealogy "blows the thing wide open," that it really was the beginning of an even greater, ever-expanding inclusion.

I bore some resistance to participating in the creation of a multicultural offering, however. Historically, opening up a cultural realm to greater white participation had always endangered the very Black people for whom the work is life-sustaining. As Zora Neale Hurston wrote, "The Negro is very reluctant to disclose that which the soul lives by." I appreciated the fact that Joe brought to the collaboration a different multicultural interaction, but I remained concerned about the dangers of engaging in work that was not created primarily by—and for—the Black community. I knew that the risks of opening up our cultural world to whites included the possibility of having our creative efforts stolen, twisted, exoticized, and demeaned—a pattern that had begun long ago with the sixty million creative beings who were stolen from Africa for the babies they could create, the songs and sculpture and wealth they could generate. And it continued into the twentieth century in ever new and debilitating ways. I expected a willingness on Joe's part to make this artwork available to nourish many others. I was unprepared, however, for my brother Houston's seemingly sudden stance on the issue. We fought vehemently over our official statement of purpose and the growing number of symbols of inclusion. During his Prix de Rome tenure in Italy, he may have experienced some degree of inclusion in a broader human community outside of America that helped him embrace this worldview, or perhaps he had fallen off some ass on the way to Damascus by way of Vietnam or Korea. But I had no such conversion or conviction.

What I experienced and remembered from my life's journey were scenes in the South of Blacks and whites pitted against one another. I remembered the expressions of white friends at Rosary who had chosen the side of least resistance, and the frustration of Vietnam veterans, would-be freedom fighters in Nashville, who had given up the struggle. I remembered the voices of our white neighbors in Missouri, cursing through walls over our common bond and twisted fate; and the cries from hundreds of books in Iowa, wailing tales of our strivings. I remembered my own daughter's efforts to hold on to her burgeoning dignity and the rock-hard promise I made at Kaleidoscope and how I had to let it go. I remembered the poems scratched out during a thousand midnights as I tried to chart new trails to hope and freedom, and the dark, hungry faces around Harlem, where I now lived and moved and had my being. Houston surely must have gotten some kind of amnesia, I swore. Something must have cleared my brother's memory banks.

When he called on the phone after one of the team's weekly meetings to categorize my views as conservative, I quoted Shasha, who had had the same thing put upon her by some journalist interviewing her at the Studio Museum. "Conservative, you'd better believe it. We're a rich and vital people and have a lot to conserve!"

"The conservation that Sha's talking about has nothing to do with your attitude!" Houston insisted. "You're just reluctant to—"

"To what?" I continued. "'To disclose that which the soul lives by'?"

"This ain't about Zora, Estella!"

"Yes, it is. It's about Zora, Sojourner, Malcolm, Patrice, Dominic, and Grandma, for that matter!"

"And since that's true," he rejoined, "then it's got to also in some way represent Helen Keller, Josiah Tryon, John Brown, and Andrew Goodman."

Ironically, I remembered my argument with Amelia on the pilgrimage over her not wanting to visit Helen Keller's birthplace, Ivy Green. Now I was being challenged from the other side. "If people want to make those connections, fine," I said, "but art's not supposed to be a road map for the blind!" Before Houston could even gather energies for a comeback, I continued, "You tell me how folk can let their children nurse at your breast and still deny your humanity. Let 'em make their own milk. Our brothers and sisters are dying in the streets!" I insisted.

"Precisely," Houston said.

"Yeah, precisely," I repeated.

In my quiet times, I became more self-reflective. What were these feelings rising so in me? Defensiveness? Fear? What was I afraid of? I caught momentary sight of Dominic falling to my feet, pretending to die. No, not that, I whispered. Death doesn't feel like this exactly. Growing pains? Perhaps, but not simply. These pains were more akin to the pre-sucking sensation of breasts responding to cries of hunger, of breasts that have been filled up completely with milk but still have not yet yielded their offering. My soul had to feel just that way. But I resisted this revelation. I could not, as a Black woman and artist, accept what I deemed to be the stereotypical, culturally assigned role of wet nurse for the world, feeding from my substance whatever viper voiced a loud or greedy enough demand for food. In my prayers for discernment, I asked God to look down upon the dismembering mockery we have made of the sacred mystery of becoming food for one another, to see the confusion that this mockery had set up in my own soul. Look at the vulnerability I feel for myself and my people over this and the tensions it has brought between me and my brother. I don't want to resist your call to feed, Lord. I just want you to teach us, Lord of the wilderness, how to make of our art an offering like manna, invulnerable to the greed of those who would hoard it for themselves and control the supply and try to resell it to the needy. I just want you, dear Jesus, to show us how to make art that truly serves the hungry.

After this, my fear of giving dissolved, my willingness to feed strengthened through each subsequent project that the team created. And create them we were blessed to do. The team brought forth works across the American landscape from California to Niagara Falls—all of them public art monuments where our children, and our children's children, and all peoples from around the world can come and celebrate and be inspired by the African American struggle toward justice and freedom. They included "Stations," an installation by the Castellani Art Museum on the Niagara River honoring the Underground Railroad Freedom Movement; "The New Charleston" at the Avery Center in South Carolina as part of the Spoleto Festival USA; "The New Calypso" in Miami, Florida; "The Freedom Ring" at the Community College at Philadelphia, formerly the United States Mint; "DuSable's Journey," a tribute to the Honorable Harold Washington, Chicago's first African American mayor, and Haitian American explorer Jean Baptiste DuSable, in the rotunda at the New Harold Washington Library in Chicago; "The New Ringshout," a tribute to the thousands buried at the African Burial Ground in New York City, a National Historical Landmark in the core of New York's civic center area; "Rivers," a permanent installation at the Schomburg Center for Research in Black Culture in honor of poet Langston Hughes and bibliophile Arthur Schomburg (for which Mayor Dinkins awarded the team the the Award for Excellence in Design from the Art Commission of the City of New York); and "Revelations," a Martin Luther King, Jr., peace memorial commissioned by the San Francisco Redevelopment Agency and the Martin Luther King, Jr., Civic Committee in Yerba Buena Gardens (for which Houston was presented the certificate of special Congressional Recognition in Art).

In creating one of the earlier temporary installations, "The New Merengue," for the Brooklyn Museum, we discovered that through the very arrangement of the triptych we designed, the terms of cross-cultural entry could be established. Reflected in the sixteen-foot Middle Passage mirror map, behind the viewer was a large free-standing photograph of the anonymous "Weeksville Lady," reproduced from a tintype found in a 1969 archaeological excavation of Weeksville, the first African American settlement in Brooklyn. Not only could I, Estella Májozo, stand before the mirror and get a view of myself under the guardianship of this foremother who symbolized all Black women ancestors, but anyone seeking a new vision could stand there and see him- or herself in the arms of this New World Blues Madonna. Those who had previously entered as masters and conquerors would have to review themselves, by reflection, as having been nurtured, mothered, and sustained by, and therefore indebted, to this cultural matrix.

"Well, team?" Houston said as he, Joe, and I stood in front of the mirror on the day before the opening. "I think we're moving on something here."

Our eyes traced the huge magnificent mirrored trail of our uproot-edness in Africa, our great passage across the Atlantic Ocean, our dis-persion beyond the Caribbean Sea, and our survival at New York Harbor. We looked at the fourteen signposts marking African American historical sites throughout this city and the critical voicings of fourteen male and female cultural prophets etched upon the map, and were charged with the prospect of witnessing hundreds of people the following night catching that vision anew. Several young artists and students would join us in leading the welcome. Papa Aly Ndaw and Mark Salisbury would drum and trumpet the opening. Ingrid Schofield and Anna Salisbury would join with the team in dance and pouring the liba-tion, acknowledging ceremoniously in a ring-231

shout ritual the legacy and words of those cultural prophets whose names were etched upon the mirror, culminating in everybody in the end joining in the spirited dance of remembrance.

I wished in my heart that Patrice could just see this. The next day, as we were getting ready to go to the opening, she called to say she wished us well but that hearing about the success of the project only stirred her up again over her decision to get a graduate degree in theater at Indiana University. "Maybe I should just jump out there and get my own feet wet," she said. "Maybe researching the history is a waste of time. I'm twenty-three years old. There are people out there in major roles at twen-ty-three. It's the practice of the craft that I need, Momma, but this is excit-ing, too. I don't know. Maybe I'm just hiding out."

As I pulled Dominic closer and brushed his hair, I told Patrice that being able to sustain a vision of oneself within one's context couldn't hurt. "Besides there's nothing worse than seeing one of your students get an opportunity and stand there in the spotlight speaking non-sense. You look at TV and there they are, not only an embarrassment to themselves but to the rest of us as well."

"Who, me, Momma?" Dominic asked.

"No, honey, not you. You're a sweetie. Being able to stand in your own way before the mirrored passages made by others who came before you can be liberating. New York will be here, baby.

"I hear you."

"I think this blood gone to dust thing I've told you about has a lot to do with acknowledging the trail. You might need to know the actors who were here before you when you come. It helps sometimes to know there's a reason to be full of trust."

"Do I need a master's degree, for that though?"

"No, of course not, but, off the record, you might want to get it in case the fighting gets dirty and you have to slap somebody across the face with it once or twice!"

"Oh, Momma," she said.

"OK, then," I said, "take it higher. You might think about getting it to enhance yourself and the field, and be in a better position to serve humanity! How's that?"

"Better," she said. "I love you."

"I love you, too, Treecie."

After this project, I came to know just how demanding going to dust— or, as Treecie put it, "hiding out"— could be. During the team's research for conducting workshops on "Stations," a tribute to the Underground Railroad movement in the Niagara Falls region, I entered one of the actual hiding places of the runaways. Houston, who had been there before, had made arrangements for us to come. It was a root cellar that had held the very bulb of survival at one time in history. Small, windowless, and airless. A dark cistern of damp remembering musk. My eyes searched the narrow cement walls as if seeking some redeeming hieroglyphics. From one corner to the other they trailed, until they met Joe's eyes. This was the space of the enslaved—the recognition or identification drew a profound sadness to his eyes. Turning from him, I looked inside and saw as never before my own passion to survive. I bent down, blessing the ground of that place that inspired the creation of seven copper-sheathed, human-sized structures in the shape of buildings whose cellars and attics bore the names of seven families in the region who had provided shelter. Houston was right. Naming the sculptures could inspire the coming forth of new world abolitionists. Ones who hopefully would not only be committed to liberating the oppressed but would take on the more difficult task of liberating the oppressors as well from their anti-human consciousness.

And I could see now that just as the excavated tintype found new meaning in the "New Merengue" exhibition, and just as Langston Hughes's ashes, yielded by George Bass, became a new symbol of ancestral return when buried beneath the "Rivers" cosmogram, the abolitionists' names recovered in the "Stations" project—Chase, Shephard, Fox—affirmed the earth call to regenerate the truth of our triumph over adversity. The names affirmed that freedom was being written across our entire historical landscape by a hand most vast and wondrous. The poet in me, who before that moment had pondered spending the night there in the cellar, was eclipsed by the ancestral spirit who would not suffer another night in that past. I climbed out of the hole and left, nodding my head now with more reverence to Houston and thanking the people in the house who had allowed our entry.

The ancestral vibrations would not leave us. As we sat at dinner that afternoon, Houston tried to loosen the hold, reminding me that Alex Haley had stayed the night in the hollow of a slave ship long enough to hear the ancestral voices tell him, "Write! Go on, write! You must tell our story!"

"They didn't say that to me," I told him in a whisper.

"No?" he asked, leaning closer now to hear.

"Uh-uh," I said, setting up royally. "They told me to tell your brother to stop flashing that camera in our faces."

The strain melted from his countenance and we fell out, all of us, laughing—grateful, utterly grateful to have our souls released again. A few days after we got back to New York, I noticed billboards in Harlem showing drugs as the new slavery. "Deep," I said to myself, "too deep." Of course, I thought of Spivey, who was "switching jobs" as he called it, breaking dinner dates, and disappearing for several nights in a row, according to his lady friend. I approached him headlong on the issue, and he denied it.

Houston took him on, as did Shasha—all to no avail. The drug had begun to overtake his life so much that we decided as a group to confront him at his house and tell him just how we saw what was happening.

"Spivey," Houston said, "we're here because we see how you're destroying your life and we won't just stand by and watch you do it."

"What do you mean by that?" Spivey asked. It had become his favorite phrase.

"I mean the drug has got you, man. It's over. We see you."

"What do you mean by that? I'm fine."

"No, you're not," I said. And we watched his eyes draw back into his skull.

"Y'all can't come up in here in my house and front me off," he challenged.

"We're here," Shasha said.

"For what? Y'all don't even know what's going on. Y'all don't care about me. Y'all don't even know me. I ain't shit. Leave me alone!"

"Naw, Spivey," Houston said. "We do know you, and Estella's got something to say."

I unfolded the letter I had been holding all day in my pocket. "To Spivey,"

I said, and began tracing in words the watershed events of his life as far back as I could remember. Spivey's losses; his disappointments; the once defiant hope now forgotten. I named his fears of failure; his endurance of the family's demands; the damming of his most potent dreams in the midst of their flow. I was barely able to read on through my tears but I was determined to finish. When I did, Spivey broke down crying, finally admitting to his problem. Then we all called aloud on our God to bind and heal his wounds, to use us in any way that would allow that to happen. We told Spivey we were there for him, that we loved him. Houston acknowledged how difficult it was to accept the mission of being a Black man in the world that the white man is bent on claiming as his. Shasha acknowledged how hard it was to lose, even as she had recently, so many of the people one loved, and I admitted how hard it was to feel so utterly disconnected at times and still claim a share in wholeness. We remembered our brother Joe and Spivey's friend Guy, and his other running partners in California, and Daddy, our daddy, all of them gone so early. Jesus, we wanted Spivey back. We didn't want to lose another brother. Lord, not this way. He wept, swearing he'd beat this.

And he would. We went through group sessions with him and sat listening to the tales of the other addicts, all of them struggling souls in the songline that would symbiotically help make Spivey stronger. After a while he gained new momentum. He switched friends and avoided places that would bring him down. He kept his focus, thank God, on what he had to do.

Soon enough, our lives began to have some semblance of normalcy. I continued challenging my students in the classroom. Houston continued making new connections in the field for our next project. Shasha continued with heightened awareness her work at the museum. She herself was in the throes of several projects: "Five Contemporary Artists," an award-winning entry in the Venice Biennale; and the groundbreaking exhibition, "The Decade Show: Frameworks of Identity in the 1980s." She was also preparing for the opening of the new expanded storefront museum shop. The team went on to collaborate with Castellani Art Museum director Sandra Olson and Relena Jones in locating permanent sites in which to place the "Stations" sculptures previously exhibited in the Niagara woods as signposts for the Underground Railroad journey. The community responded further, by forming the Underground Railroad Committee, which in the summer of 1993, under the direction of Kevin Cottrell, organized the "Trek a Mile in My Shoes" Freedom March through fourteen cities along the Harriet Tubman trail.

Tired from the semester's end and my recent tenure review at Hunter College, I had to renew my commitment to travel the fourteen days by van. A multicultural group of twelve started out in Atlanta and headed toward Canada—among us, Betty Brown, great-grandniece of Harriet Tubman; Denise Easterling Mlee, a member of the committee; and Lu, who at seventy-three brought a much needed perspective to the journey.

By the time we got to New York, the tenth city, it was wonderful to see Shasha and Judylyn on the steps of City Hall and to hail Sunni Malik, Jo-Ann Morgan, and Glenda Self, strong links in my New York support system. It was clear by then that the people throughout the cities witnessing our arrival were inspired to reflect upon many things, even as we were. Most salient was the ambivalence of the gift of shelter at the site of oppression: if this site was the site of an Underground Railroad station, it was also, inevitably, the site of enslavement.

I looked out in the distance from the stairs of City Hall and there was Spivey moving in with his camcorder. When he lowered the lens, I could see, beyond his ready smile, the glaze in his eyes. We were back in the cellar again, hiding, and desperate, miles away from freedom. This was worse than seeing the shackles in Rochester that Frederick Douglass wrote about in his narrative, or visiting the plantation from which Harriet escaped in Bucktown, Maryland, or feeling the antebellum book from Charles Blockson's collection at Temple University in Philadelphia, which was bound in a Black man's skin. I was seeing my own blood brother being dragged back into slavery, the pain and desperation in his eyes even more fierce than before. By the time I returned to New York from crossing Canada's Rainbow Bridge, I knew that Harriet's words were serious, and that they applied to Spivey: "Go on or die!"

Houston, Shasha, Spivey's lady, and I went with him as he checked himself into a residential facility provided for by insurance from his job, which was hanging now by a gray hair. The people in this circle were black, red, brown, and white, all struggling to get free. We learned new terms like "co-dependency," "enabling," and "denial."

It was my fourth year in New York. I was forty-two years old. By the time I returned to the classroom, there was no way I could ever teach *The Narrative of Frederick Douglass* the same way again—nor any of the literature or writing courses, really. I was set afire by the cumulative effects of the changes in my life, my new awareness of slavery and my awareness of new forms of slavery that were ensnaring my whole family, and an urgency regarding my life's purpose. And that fire spread and reflected back to me in the faces of my students. I became more and more aware that "gone to dust" was a call for me to give, to die to self, and, for the betterment of my family and my students, to align myself with all those great ancestors who had given so much in order that we might live. Before long, I was spending more time with students in the office than I was in the classroom. At first, there would be the usual one or two waiting to see me during office hours, then more edged into my lunch break and the fifteen minutes I had between afternoon classes. The students began to recognize and resonate with the issues in the various texts in a most powerful way. They were seeing in the text the possibility of gaining control over and transforming their own situations. The first sign of that transformation was the breaking of silence. The freedom to name their particular crisis. While one student found the mirror of her situation in the words of Maya Angelou, another wanted to linger critically in the tenth chapter of Frederick Douglass, where he fights Covey and the spirit in him rises, never to be enslaved again. Another wanted simply the words in the opening passage of Paule Marshall's *Praisesong for the Widow*: "with a strength born of the decision that had just come to her in the middle of the night, Avey Johnson forced the suitcase shut." And still another formed and inserted her own interpretation of Toni Morrison's whole sermon in the clearing from Beloved before she decided to give up on her planned suicide. As she explained it, she came to see the will to destroy self as an externally imposed death wish. Clearly these texts were also among the crooked lines upon which God is able to write straight the truth of our lives.

And in that instant I thought of my grandmother, of her own silent knowing that at times had scared me.

"Grace," she would say, explaining the mystery to me, "grace is what allows me to know certain things."

"Then there are eight gifts of the Spirit? Grandma, you said there were seven."

"Child," she whispered joyously, "there are thousands."

Now I remembered the vision I'd had through the lenses in the vowels of my dream-poem and I began to wonder if the writings inside the lenses also bore lenses in their vowels—if the discoveries and connections of our being were likewise infinite. I had begun to realize through my students that the literary works themselves could be the lenses through which whoever entered with hope could see and experience a wondrous field of grace, enlightening and healing.

I tried whenever possible to steer students with severe problems to counselors. But often their first touchstone was me as teacher, and many were reluctant to go any further. I felt the challenges of my role. The call to be compassionate and to extend oneself into the lives of others as a human being, mentor, and role model to whoever is before you—and especially to young people who do not see themselves reflected often in the faces they meet—can at once inspire and deplete one's physical and spiritual energies. Being a Black woman in such a position carried added responsibilities that were not written up in the job description. I definitely had to learn to strike a balance.

Patrice must have needed a similar balancing, because a few weeks later she showed up at the door unannounced.

"I just took some time, Momma. I been working so much assisting Dr. Fletcher and doing my research that I couldn't see the letters from the words."

"You don't have to explain to me. It's always good to see you," I said, laughing and hugging her again.

"I'm reading stuff, but it's not performance. I need time in the field, too. There's a period film showing downtown. I figured I'd see you all," she said, grabbing hold of Dominic's smile, "and we could catch the film, too."

"Good," I said. "But I've a meeting at Dominic's school tonight. You know he's preparing for first communion."

"Maybe I'll just hang out with you two, then."

"No," I insisted. "Catch the film. I can see you when you get back."

"It's not that important." Then she smiled. "Well, actually it's got a lot of the earlier dancers and routines that fed into the 'Swing Mikado,' the piece I'm working on."

"Great."

"I really need to visualize some of this. It's just so long that you can theorize about dance. The reality is breaking down for me."

"I know," I said, "I know. You'll reconcile it, though."

"Maybe Shasha would want to go," she said. "Or Spivey."

I told her what had happened, as much as I could in front of Dominic—that Spivey was having a hard time of it and was back getting care.

"Oh, Momma," she said, "I'm so sorry. I've been going on about my stuff. I didn't know. How is he? How are you?"

"Fine, honey. We're just walking through this a step at a time. Shasha's going up tonight to be with him. Houston's gone to San Francisco."

"What can I do?" she asked.

"Catch the film," I told her.

Patrice found the theater and sat in the audience. Writing through one of the scenes, she suddenly became conscious of the voices around her.

"It was not your usual audience, Momma," she told me later. "They were punching each other and jiving and cracking and signifying."

"Yeah, you must have been mad that day to roll over like that," one of them said.

Another sang out, "Yeah, baby, but watch my somersault!" The whole place was snapping.

"Wait till you see the next part. Look over there in the corner, yeah. There I am, child, pregnant and did not even know it."

"Stop lying. You was as big as a house. Like to have had the baby on the floor!"

"These people in the audience were the folk in the film!" Patrice laughed. "They were all around me, in front of me, behind me."

Mr. Joe Randolph, a gentleman next to her, asked what on earth she was doing. "Sounds like chicken scratching over there!"

"Writing," Patrice said. "I'm working on my master's thesis. It's in dance theater."

"Well, why didn't you say so?" The lights went up, and the people from the audience started onto the stage. One, Patrice said, even got up and gave the same agile movements she had done in the scene years ago, ending with a leap and landing in a split.

"Momma, she was Lu's age," she said in disbelief.

"Don't ever underestimate your grandmother," I said. "She was kicking on that pilgrimage when some of the young folk were giving up. I got pictures of her in Richmond stepping into the box modeled after the one they mailed William "Box" Brown in to freedom!"

"I hear you," she laughed. "Mr. Randolph told me, 'Come Monday night to the club and I'll introduce you around. I'm not a hoofer,' he told me, 'but I've known them for years. We go there every Monday. It's musician's night and the Harlem Renaissance Band plays.'"

She went, and they opened their lives to her. She met many of the people who, before then, had only been faces in photographs. She was also able to get one of the last interviews with Honi Coles. When I went with her at a later time, it was clear that this group shared something special and were able to share that something with Patrice. I was proud that she was able to dust some of the truth and that their telling had enabled her to enter the songline.

She went back to her studies ready to stir up new revelations. Shortly afterward, Spivey was released from his rehabilitation program. He was clean. He looked good. He spoke with new dignity and pride. He went back to work and even got a promotion. When we came back from Kentucky after the holidays, however, we found him talking off again. I was pissed now. My patience had worn out. He was standing there at my door needing stupid shelter! By then I was armed with words like "co-dependency" and "tough love" and "who the hell do I look like, Harriet Tubman?"

I walked into the kitchen and fixed some goldenseal tea. "Why in the hell didn't you stay in the group? Why did you quit?"

Nothing.

"The damn shelters here in New York have strains of tuberculosis in them that nobody can cure!"

Nothing.

"It's on you, Spivey. I can't do it for you. You have to do it. Every time I see one of those brothers out in the street going down all raggedy and smelly, I see you. I don't want you like that. But you're doing it to yourself."

"Bitch."

"OK. Let's go."

"I wasn't talking to you, ball-headed off-talking bitch! I was talking about that other one."

"I'm not listening to this."

"She's so fucking high and mighty now."

"Oh, boy."

"What's that supposed to mean?"

"It means, you gonna have to leave here and deal with yourself."

"I ain't fucking going nowhere! And don't bother to call Houston. He knows I'm getting it together. He just ain't got no money right now to give me."

I went and opened the door.

"Leave."

He turned and flipped through my Bible.

"You got it the last time you were here," I said. His eyes darted as if caught in the act.

"I didn't take your money. I don't steal."

"Leave."

He went to Dominic's coin bank. "Yeah, this'll work. Tell him I borrowed it." And then he broke out past me and left.

We didn't hear from him for three days. I was so worried that I started a fast. "My Lord," I cried, "how many times does he have to wash himself in this pool before this thing is done? I don't want to see him chopped away like Kunta Kinte's foot. And I know they talking about tough love, but they been defining love so many ways since I been here in New York and through history that it ain't easy to know exactly what to do anymore. The system's got some of our finest men being tough-loved to death! Our leaders sucking on bones in soup lines. Our healers laying up themselves among the sick. Lord, Spivey was our medicine, our cheerful heart when nothing else made sense. He could always grab hold of that wretched laughter coming at us from everywhere out of the dark and make us own it. It was as if to say, 'I got it right here, this screaming demon, and now you can tell it to go to hell if you want to!' And then we'd laugh. Oh, we'd laugh. He was our cheerful heart, Lord. But only you know his own heart's bitterness, Lord, and how tough it is for him to keep on loving—not just us, but Jesus, loving himself. Give your angels charge over him, Lord. Protect him, please, and lead him back to your healing in Jesus' name."

On the third day, I walked down Malcolm X Boulevard searching, and there in the flow of Black faces just after 125th Street I caught sight of him. I followed him at a distance. He walked, his shoulders no longer able to defy the slump that bore them down. He looked in and out of store windows, then stopped suddenly and turned back toward me as if forgetting something. He walked right past me without even seeing. "Lord, have mercy," I whispered, and stepped slowly behind him. He walked about a block more, then stopped again, looking as if something had called him. I came upon him and touched his shoulder.

"I was just thinking about you," he said.

"Where did you sleep?"

"In a little dank ten-dollar place, about so big," he said, measuring with his hands.

His eyes were pitiful, dark like somebody just getting out of a dungeon.

"I hear you."

"With a bed full of chinches and other niggers' nightmares caught in the fucking mattress and coming all loud through the walls on the other side making you feel like you fucking want to die." There was this awesome silence between us. "I don't want to ever go back," he said, turning to me.

"I believe you," I said. Then we walked a bit, the cold wind harsh against our faces.

"If I said anything the other day to hurt your feelings, hey, I'm sorry."

"OK," I said. And we turned another corner. "You know, Spivey, what that guy was saying in the circle the first time we went—'No one, with the exception of no one, gets out of this the very first time.'"

"Yeah," Spivey said, shaking his head and taking on the voice of the man. "'You're clean, and a false security says you don't have a problem anymore. You go and listen after you think you hit rock bottom to all those who've been there before you, but inside you think you're better than the other losers. Then you slip.' Boom," he said, switching over now to his own voice. "Then you start feeling like the sludge of the earth. You no damn good again. You're mad that you did it. You're mad that you have it and nobody else does. Then you say fuck it, it's not so bad. The endorphins in your brain are so screwed up they keep signaling that the shit is pleasure. And the shit gets into your blood," he said, his feet coming to a sudden halt, "and all the while it's turning your ass to dust." He looked somewhere beyond the people hurrying along their way, and began addressing some unseen circle of listeners. "You know you've got to get rid of it, man, but it's hard. You love it. It's like your friend. It's what makes you feel alive. Yeah, it's definitely love. But you got to get rid of it, you've got to. And the sooner you kill it, mourn it, and bury it damn good, the sooner you can go on with your life." Then he turned straight-forward to me. "I'm back in the circle forever, Estella. I swear, my ass is back."

A year later we celebrated his first year anniversary of freedom. Twenty months after that, he was standing with the rest of the family in San Francisco, celebrating the opening of "Revelations," the team's Martin Luther King, Jr., peace memorial at Yerba Buena Gardens. At the fountain's lookout, the team stood looking down at the crowd, ready to perform our part of the day-long celebration. Inside the grottolike sacred space at the heart of the fountain, we created a long wall of twelve glass tablets bearing twelve powerful quotations by Dr. King, in English at the top and beneath in the twelve languages from around the world spoken by San Francisco's sister cities. Commissioned by the San Francisco Redevelopment Agency, it proliferated in a kind of Pentecostal release the utterances of a single soul, calling whomsoever will to witness the truth of a people's deliverance. It testified even as a circle of voices freedom's holy intent.

Geraldine Johnson of the Martin Luther King, Jr., Civic Committee, who had worked more than ten years raising funds for the monument, had timed the final pouring of my libation and chant to coincide with the first gush of the fountain's water. ". . . Make a wailing wall of water from the words of our king. Make it womb and way and wisdom, that we may be born again!" As the last waters flowed from my pitcher, those from the fountain came slipping, turning, gushing over the great gray boulders, a perpetual libation honoring the prophecy that justice will roll down and "righteousness like a mighty stream."

At this, I could see hundreds of people gathering to pass joyously behind the veil of water. I could see Dominic and Patrice and Jim Lowe, her fiancé, reaching out to touch the mist; I could see William embracing old California friends and taking pictures for his sons, Giles, Mondlane, and Justin. And I could see Spivey, beside him, this side of freedom, rolling his camcorder to share the event with his sons, Maurice and Little J. I could see Lu and Shasha and Joan DePace, Joe's mother, dancing behind the falls, and my brother, Giles, who was teaching at Morehouse, King's alma mater, standing, nodding proudly; and Martin Luther King's children, Yolanda and Martin III, greeting Father Jim Goode, Ms. Rosa Crumes, Danny Glover, Mayor Frank Jordan, and hundreds of others. And through the pale blue rising mist my spirit embraced them all, and all those other souls in life whom I have known and loved and read and learned from and given to and lost and now found again. I blessed them there along with the countless others through the years with whom we would come again to dance in the roar of the rushing waters.

I realized, in time, that my dream vision was about more than merely writing *Libation,* or helping to create monuments with the collaborative team, or nurturing my students at Hunter College or even my children at home. The dream was about all of our souls being called to life, that we might all magnify the meaning and enliven the dust through field after field of grace.

DISCOVER THE BEST WOMEN WRITING

AFRICAN AMERICAN FICTION FROM THE FEMINIST PRESS

Brown Girl, Brownstones by Paule Marshall. $10.95 paper.

Daddy Was a Number Runner by Louise Meriwether. $10.95 paper.

*I Love Myself When I Am Laughing . . . and Then Again When I Am Looking
Mean and Impressive: A Zora Neale Hurston Reader*, edited by Alice Walker.
$14.95 paper.

The Living is Easy by Dorothy West. $14.95 paper.

Reena and Other Stories by Paule Marshall. $11.95 paper.

This Child's Gonna Live by Sarah E. Wright. $10.95 paper.

MEMOIR AND AUTOBIOGRAPHY FROM THE FEMINIST PRESS

Across Boundaries: The Journey of a South African Woman Leader by Mamphela
Ramphele. $19.95 cloth.

Always from Somewhere Else: A Memoir of My Chilean Jewish Father by
Marjorie Agosín. $18.95 cloth.

Among the White Moon Faces: An Asian-American Memoir of Homelands by
Shirley Geok-lin Lim. $12.95 paper, $22.95 cloth.

Cast Me Out If You Will: Stories and Memoir by Lalithambika Antherjanam.
$11.95 paper.

A Cross and a Star: Memoirs of a Jewish Girl in Chile by Marjorie Agosín.
$13.95 paper.

Fault Lines by Meena Alexander. $12.95 paper.

Juggling: A Memoir of Work, Family, and Feminism by Jane S. Gould.
$17.95 paper.

I Dwell in Possibility by Toni A.H. McNaron. $12.95 paper.

Songs My Mother Taught Me: Stories, Plays, and Memoir by Wakako Yamauchi.
$14.95 paper.

Streets: A Memoir of the Lower East Side by Bella Spewack. $10.95 paper.
$19.95 cloth.

To receive a free catalog of The Feminist Press's 180 titles, call or write The
Feminist Press at The City University of New York, Customer Service Department,
Wingate Hall/City College, New York, NY 10031; phone: (212) 650-8966; fax: (212)
650-8893; email: sstovin@broadway.gc.cuny.edu. Feminist Press books are available
at bookstores, or can be ordered directly. Send check or money order (in U.S. dollars drawn on a U.S. bank) payable to The Feminist Press. Please add $4.00 shipping
and handling for the first book and $1.00 for each additional book (outside the U.S.,
add $7.00 for the first book and $2.00 for each additional). New York residents must
add sales tax. VISA, Mastercard, and American Express are accepted for telephone,
fax, and email orders. Prices are subject to change.